Mother Emily Power, O.P.

MOTHER EMILY
OF SINSINAWA
American Pioneer

By MARY SYNON

THE BRUCE PUBLISHING COMPANY
MILWAUKEE

Nihil obstat:
JOHN A. SCHULIEN, S.T.D.
Censor librorum

Imprimatur:
✠ ALBERT G. MEYER
Archiepiscopus Milwauchiensis

Die 27a Septembris, 1954

Foreword

THE late Bishop Francis J. Haas, who was to have written this foreword, once said — and only half in jest — that a book on Mother Mary Emily Power should be titled "On, Wisconsin!" She had represented, he declared, the best of the spirit of his native State: pioneering vision, rare courage, and high idealism expressed in practical progress.

Mother Emily had been part of Wisconsin history for more than fifty years. She had learned in her girlhood the economic philosophy of Father Samuel Mazzuchelli, that amazing Dominican missionary who was chaplain of Wisconsin's constitutional convention. It was a philosophy nearly a century ahead of its time, embracing in essence the social doctrine of the Catholic Church, and a philosophy that arose at intervals in Wisconsin political leadership. She had transmitted this social philosophy to her teaching Sisters so that they, too, went forward under banners of justice and charity, setting in American Catholic education the spirit of traditional Catholic thought which later found fulfillment in the great social Encyclicals of Leo XIII and Pius XI.

In any period Mother Emily would have been a heroic figure. Small, quiet of manner until circumstances demanded speech, she had so many facets that those who remember her choose — with one exception — different elements of her personality for emphasis: her scholarship, her executive ability, her wide friendliness, her deep human understanding. The exception, observed and felt by all, was her powerful spiritual magnetism. "It met you like an electric current, lifting you to a power you never knew you had," is their memory.

Coming to the United States from Ireland when she was only eight years old, she found the American frontier both a promise and a challenge. Her father died on the way, and her mother bravely continued the family journey to the Wisconsin lead mines. There they met Father Mazzuchelli, and the child's destiny became the destiny of thousands of others who would follow her.

She went to Father Mazzuchelli's school in Benton, one of the mining towns of the frontier. She joined the Dominican community which the missionary had established. She became its Superior when she was only twenty-three years old and assumed authority over her own two elder sisters. She moved the convent from Benton to Sinsinawa, a valiant undertaking. She continued the Mazzuchelli school, making it one of the outstanding educational institutions of the Middle West. Time and again she instituted educational reforms which set Saint Clara in the front rank of academies; meanwhile she was setting up mission schools throughout the United States.

Not chance but Mother Emily's concern for social justice brought about the opening of schools in districts where this justice was most needed and its teaching most appreciated. She sent her Sisters to Spring Valley, Illinois, in the year of the lock-out which caused John Mitchell to start the United Mine Workers; and the Sisters were the welfare group of the stricken town. She sent Sisters to Anaconda, Montana, in a year when another lock-out almost paralyzed the town. She provided for schools in the Stock Yards neighborhood of Chicago, schools which attained distinguished records of national and civic service. She started at Sinsinawa the college which has become Rosary College.

Most of all, she built her community into a widespread but entirely unified organization. She sought no loyalty for herself, but she aroused in her Sisters a loyalty to God which carried them through trials and tribulations to the victorious consummation of their high purposes. For forty-two years she captained her company with love and with wisdom.

The late Archbishop McNicholas, who read the first draft of this book in manuscript, set down something of his own impression of her. He was the last of the great men of the Church in the United States — Ireland, Spalding, Keane — who had known her well and who appreciated her high worth. She belonged to a magnificent era, a splendid scene, a glorious apostolate. On the high Sinsinawa hill she set a beacon of faith which still shines.

It was a great privilege to have known Mother Emily, a greater privilege to have been trusted by her, and, greatest privilege of all, to have been taught in childhood by Mother Emily's Sisters. To their memory and hers this book is dedicated.

MARY SYNON

Preface

A HUNDRED years ago an innocent, attractive child of eight years — Ellen Power — arrived in America from Tramore, Waterford County, Ireland, where she was born, January 12, 1844. Her half-brother, Thomas Power, who seven years later was ordained a priest of the Dominican Order, was here to welcome her.

The Power family, including Ellen and her four sisters, lived for a short time in St. Louis. When death claimed the father, Mrs. Power with her daughters providentially moved to Wisconsin and settled on a farm near Sinsinawa Mound. The widowed mother sent her daughters to the school at Benton, Wisconsin, which was founded by Father Samuel Mazzuchelli, O.P. This school was conducted by the Dominican Sisters, whose founder was also the intrepid, peerless, and saintly Italian priest of the Northwest. Four of Mrs. Power's five daughters became religious of the Sinsinawa foundation.

At the early age of seventeen, Ellen Power was received into the community of the Dominican Sisters of Sinsinawa and given the name Sister Mary Emily. But a few years passed and this young religious was chosen Superior of the new community, at the age of twenty-three. It might be assumed that her youth and inexperience would disqualify her for the pioneer task of guiding the destinies of a new community; but her strong, persevering faith, her tender love of our Lord, her deep and abiding affection for her associates, her adamant conviction that the work of her community was God's work, her native prudence and her Celtic resourcefulness, her unbounded charity toward all, her humility and self-effacement to enhance the value of her Institute, her superior gifts of mind, her fixed purpose to have her community discharge its duties and carry on its mission in the best possible way, and the trust that she reposed in those who labored with her, inspired confidence in the members of her Congregation and communicated to them a zeal for the House of God that was contagious. These qualities of Mother Emily built up a community spirit that has never been surpassed in our country.

When Mother Emily entered the infant Congregation of Sinsinawa there were only a score of Sisters. When she assumed the responsibility of government in 1867, the number was thirty. Succeeding groups of religious, until they numbered about seven hundred at her death, continued to have unquestioning confidence in their Superior; first of all as a spiritual mother, then as a leader of sterling qualities and as a valiant woman, whose keen intellect, fertile imagination, studious habits, humble gentleness, captivating approachableness, common sense judgment, and rare wisdom won and maintained for her the respect and love of her spiritual daughters.

Mother Emily was an extraordinary executive and a pioneer builder who welcomed difficulties, when surmounting them indicated an advantage for the Church. In all her executive work she had a happy sense of humor. Her sunny disposition, her marvelous ability to compose difficulties and to settle matters in a constructive spirit of harmony made her the prudent and trusted superior, who was held captive for more than forty years by her religious as their interpreter, leader, and superior.

The progress of her community in scholarship and in spiritual formation during Mother Emily's term of office was phenomenal. As the Superior General she was the inspiration of all. She had a keen appreciation of the fine arts, music, and painting. Her long years of administrative duties did not permit her to dedicate herself personally in an exclusive manner to sanctified scholarship; but she was resolute in giving to her Sisters the opportunities which administration denied to her. Her rare gifts of mind and heart, her artistic temperament, her utter unselfishness, her humble spirit, her knowledge and love of the traditions of scholarship in the Order of which she was a member, made her glory in the achievements of her Congregation, which gave to the

Church of America scholarly and saintly religious Sisters of the Dominican Order.

Mother Emily was a pioneer in sending Sisters to Europe for study. By word and by letter she taught love of Dominican scholarship and of the traditions of learning in the Order of Preachers. Mother Emily's vision took in the whole Church. She loved her Institute more than her life; yet she saw clearly that her Congregation occupied but a small part in the universal grouping of the Church throughout the world. Mother Emily did not work for the *gloriuncula* of her Congregation, but for the service it could render the Church and souls. *Holiness* and *learning* were the watchwords for the Sisters of her Institute.

I may be permitted to say a personal word about Mother Emily's deep appreciation of the interior life. In the spring of 1909, she asked me to give the annual retreat to her Sisters at Sinsinawa during the summer months. I gave the retreat. The ever-present solicitude of Mother Emily, as I learned, was to have holy, learned religious in her Congregation. She wished no taint of pride or vanity in the judgment of her Sisters. She wanted humility as the foundation of their intellectual and spiritual life. Before I left St. Clara's Convent, Mother Emily asked me to give again the annual retreat to the Sinsinawa Community in 1910. That retreat stands out in my memory. Mother Emily did not attend the retreat for which she had made arrangements. She had been called away — to eternity — on October 16 of the previous year.

When Mother Emily visited Italy, she asked to be received as a guest-religious in the Enclosed Community of the Dominican Monastery of Holy Rosary at Marino, a few miles south of Rome. On many occasions when I visited this Monastery, the Sisters who had known Mother Emily spoke of her in a spirit of deep reverence and genuine affection. It was so like Mother Emily to spend a short time in a cloistered monastery, in order that she might gain a better appreciation of the interior life.

In the funeral eulogy preached over Mother Emily, on October 20, 1909, in the community chapel of Sinsinawa Convent, Archbishop Ireland said:

Mother Emily was one of the noblest types of the Christian woman and the consecrated daughter of the Church that I have ever known. . . . She was the humble, gentle, retiring nun. Bold in action, she was, when back to herself, the child, the timid girl of other days, anxious to be unnoticed, to be the servant rather than the mistress, to be all things to others while nothing to herself. But her humility of heart never betrayed itself into weakness of soul where trials were to be borne, or obstacles to be overcome. Duty bidding her to be firm, she was the immovable rock, against which wavelets of opposition broke in vain. . . . In response to duty, Mother Emily knew neither fear nor faltering. And cheerful she always was, and solicitous that others be cheerful. . . . On her couch of death, her words to her Sisters were: "Be cheerful; be trustful in God."

May the centenary of Mother Emily's coming to America, and the inspiration that she and her spiritual daughters have given to countless souls, and may the solid foundations of a truly wonderful religious institute which she laid — prayerfully and resourcefully and on which an enduring superstructure has been wisely built — bring not hundreds, but thousands, of vocations to her Congregation!

✠ JOHN T. McNICHOLAS
Archbishop of Cincinnati

March 29, 1949

Contents

MOTHER EMILY OF SINSINAWA

CHAPTER ONE

Sinsinawa: The Mound
1952

SINSINAWA is not a city, not a town, not even a village. The name itself is either the Sac and Fox word meaning "clear water," or the Siouan word for "home of the young eagle." Against a massive, wooded mound in the southwestern corner of Wisconsin, in sight of Illinois and Iowa, a long line of mellow red brick and mellower white limestone buildings rises high above farm lands that terrace from the mighty Mississippi. There is no airport near, no railroad within six miles, no direct bus service to Dubuque or Galena, the nearest cities. Only a tiny post-office building asserts association with the outside world; but, for all that, Sinsinawa stands on a world highroad of its own.

For Sinsinawa is more than a place. It is the institution founded more than a hundred years ago by that valiant, farsighted, young Italian, the Dominican missionary, Samuel Charles Mazzuchelli, and maintained by the community he also founded, the Dominican Sisters of the Congregation of the Most Holy Rosary. A landmark of the brave pioneering of the Middle Border, it is a living force in the nation it once outposted. Even beyond the continental United States the name of Sinsinawa stands for Christian educational leadership and for building the kind of good American citizenship which has made the upper Mississippi valley a stronghold of American democracy.

Every day — but most often on summer Saturdays and Sundays — there extends over the Illinois and the Wisconsin roads a long line of vehicles. In shining station wagons and shabby sedans, in

1

limousines and in jeeps, in taxicabs from the railroads, and in the rural mail truck, visitors make their way up the hills. Their ranks number pilgrims who are seldom strangers: Sisters coming from the missions to make their yearly retreats; former graduates bringing their husbands, their children, and sometimes their grandchildren; relatives of Sisters who joined the Congregation last year or sixty years ago; friends of Sisters home on retirement from mission duties; young women hoping to enter the community; nuns from other communities; bishops and priests asking for teaching Sisters for their schools; educators examining subjects and methods of teaching; parents inquiring about the registration of their children.

They do not come as to a shrine. Except for an occasional alumna and for the young women seeking entrance to the community, their errands are usually practical. They talk with the Mother General and her Sisters about the thousand and one affairs that crisscross the running of a great establishment: courses of study and tuition rates at St. Clara Academy; situations at Bethlehem Academy in Faribault and Edgewood College in Madison; developments at Rosary College in the archdiocese of Chicago; supplies for the missions, the parochial schools scattered across the land; overseas shipments for the colleges in Fribourg and Florence. They bring estimates on supplies for St. Dominic's Villa, the community infirmary on the heights of Dubuque. They offer prices on new cars, on deep freezers and lockers, on dairy machinery. They observe approved scientific methods of farming on the wide acres the Sisters operate. They enter into plans for the extension of the teaching of Gregorian chant. They discuss modern educational methods, sometimes in the highly technical language of graduate schools of philosophy and pedagogy, sometimes in the simpler language of old teachers who know students even better than they know books. They bring and take away inspiration for music, art, and literature.

Sinsinawa has three aspects of activity: the Academy, the first institution of its kind given a charter by the legislature of the state of Wisconsin; the Convent, home of nearly seventeen hundred

Sisters of the Third Order of St. Dominic; and the mission headquarters for more than a hundred schools, elementary, secondary,
and collegiate, in the United States, Switzerland, and Italy. All
of these activities are related; and yet each one has a distinct
structure.

The Academy, the oldest in the upper Mississippi Valley, is a
secondary school modern in equipment and outlook, but traditional in basic educational, as well as theological, doctrine. Its
use of advanced and imaginative motion picture technique for
the presentation of its symbolic panorama, *Centennial Song,* gives
evidence of the success of the associative method. For almost a
hundred years its students have been coming from solid Middle
Western homes, some urban, some rural, most of them Catholic.
Here, at St. Clara, these students have acquired a cultural and a
social education which has given them ability in both leadership
and fellowship. The school has returned them to their homes,
young women equipped to take their place in the life of their
choice, whether it be in the home, in the professional or business
life, or in a religious vocation. The attitude of the alumnae toward
the academy is shown by the number of fifth-generation students
now in attendance. There are some years when most of the girls
are the grandchildren of women who were graduated from the
school.

Every day Sinsinawa welcomes the guests whose interests are
somehow concerned with the lives of the nearly seventeen hundred Sisters of the community and of the tens of thousands of
children whom they teach. There is one day in the year, however,
when the inpouring of visitors grows to greater size and greater
significance. That is the fourth of August, the feast day of St.
Dominic.

On that day, year after year, there takes place in the high-
roofed, rose-windowed chapel a ceremony thrilling with beauty
and awesome with holiness. It is the ceremony of reception when
the young women, who have for a year been postulants in preparation for their entrance into the community, are taken into the
Congregation.

For their coming the chapel blooms in the loveliness of golden candlelight and great clusters of flowers. The bishop comes from Madison, monsignori from Dubuque, Milwaukee, and Chicago, priests from all over the United States and sometimes from Rome. They march, after the cross-bearer and the white-haired Dominican chaplain, to the sanctuary where they await the beginning of the ancient Dominican Ceremonial of Reception.

Slowly, from the cloister side of the chapel, comes the procession: often more than two-score girls, most of them in their early twenties, garbed in black save for their rounded white linen collars and the little festoons of bridal white flowers fastened to the short postilion capes. Two by two, they walk up the middle aisle, between the people kneeling in the pews — their own people, fathers and mothers, brothers and sisters.

The general aspect of the families gives insight into the backgrounds of the slowly moving young women. For all the individual dissimilarities of style there is in them the likeness of their Americanism. Whether they have come from Maine or Minnesota, California or Connecticut, they are the kind of people that have made and preserved the United States a democratic nation. They have come from stock of many lands, English, Irish, German, French, Polish, Norse, Negroes — St. Clara's was one of the first American sisterhoods to admit Negro members. They have come from farms, from villages, from towns, from cities. War has, sooner or later, touched all their homes. Struggle has been their lot, although no one of them has ever known the crushing poverty of older places. They are the solid backbone of America, farmers, merchants, mechanics, doctors, lawyers, newspaper editors, men and women giving of themselves in their everyday lives that their children and their children's children may have opportunities a little higher, a little wider than their own.

These, their daughters or their sisters, are girls who might have chosen to marry, to work as artists or musicians, clerks or stenographers, to enter the profession of law or medicine, to take up the work of nursing or of teaching. Some of them are girls just out of high school. Others have already tried out these lines of endeavor. A year ago one of them was teaching at Cornell University, and another nursing at the Mayo Clinic in Rochester. One was an artist in Washington, another a newspaper reporter in Wisconsin. One was winning her master's degree in home economics, another was studying music at the Juilliard in New York. Six of them were seniors in a famous college. With lovely slimness and glinting curls, there are those among them who might have tried for the precarious careers of Hollywood. They have chosen, answering the inner call of their vocation, to give their lives to Christ, in prayer and in service to others. Their choice tells even more than their volition. It tells of the spirit of their families who have made their own sacrifices in order that these girls may move onward to the altar of God.

They go up the aisle slowly, apparently oblivious to the crowd in the chapel: but one girl, as she passes, puts her hand upon the shoulder of a kneeling woman. It is a little gesture, eloquent of a comforting affection, not a farewell, but a promise of future nearness; and, after a moment of tears, the woman smiles as her eyes follow the moving procession.

Quietly, when the solemn high Mass is over, the girls ascend to the altar rail. There the Bishop of Madison, himself an alumnus of a parochial school taught by these Dominican Sisters, reads the service of Reception. He says the words of investiture while black-veiled sponsoring Sisters remove the little capes and filmy veils and place on the girls the white habit, the white scapular, the black rosary, the black mantle, symbol of their garb until death, and the white veil which they will wear for their year as novices of the Third Order of St. Dominic.

If the ceremony is breath-takingly solemn, it is not sad. These girls are renouncing the world and its pomps, but before them stretches a lifetime made joyously happy in the service of God. No one can look at them, as they come down from the altar rail, without the realization of the radiating goodness of those lives in their chosen work of teaching boys and girls to know, to love, and to serve God. The *Te Deum,* triumphantly chanted in the sweet, pure voices of other novices, who a year ago donned the white veil and who will tomorrow exchange it for the black veil of Profession, rings out with solemn meaning. Upon the labors of women like these rests the future of their land and ours.

Looking like new angels in their white raiment, they surge from the chapel to join their families for a day that will be memorable for them all. They meet, too, their pastors who give them a blessing. Until the evening bell rings from the high tower little groups cluster under the trees. Then, in the firefly-studded darkness, the families go and the novices turn to the convent.

Tomorrow they will begin their new lives as members of the Congregation. They will remain at Sinsinawa in preparation for the well-ordered religious practices and duties of the community. "There are various means," says the Constitutions of the Congregation, "by which persons may prepare themselves to work for the salvation of souls: regular life, monastic observances, and the choral recitation of the Office." Prayer, penance, and obedience reinforce these aids. The study of theology, sacred scripture, liturgy, and Church history widens both cultural knowledge and religious comprehension. Their religious training is also based upon the study of the Rule and Constitutions of the Congregation, the vows they will take for full membership, and the lives of the many Dominican saints. Through intensive study they will come to understand better the boons and graces of their lives, particularly the unusual privilege enjoyed by these Sisters of the Third Order of St. Dominic in having daily Exposition of the Blessed Sacrament.

Each Sister is launched upon a course to which her talent best adapts her, a talent that will be cherished and developed so that she may give of her best, not only to her own community, but to the betterment of parish and neighborhood, nation and world.

With the ending of the novitiate comes the taking of the vow of Profession and the donning of the black veil. This is a simpler but more awesome ceremony, when the novice gives her three-year vow of service — the final vows come after this period — to the Mother General. Sisters now, they join the working ranks of a Sisterhood whose dominant characteristic is an active happiness that permeates every corner of the long line of buildings, old and new, that make St. Clara.

They will go out to teach at the missions in Montana, Wyoming, Oklahoma, in crowded sections back of the Yards in Chicago, in uptown and downtown New York, in Alabama's Tuskegee, in little towns and growing cities all over the West and the Middle West. They will be teaching not only Catechism but the most scientifically developed courses of study, interpreted in the light of Christian doctrine and imbued with the consciousness of Christian justice to all men. They will be taking with them, as thousands of other Sisters have taken for a span of a century, the feeling of democracy which is so essentially part of the Sinsinawa tradition.

That tradition is the outgrowth of the tenets of their founder. In the Congregation Annals for December, 1860, that fateful month which split apart the American nation for long years of Civil War, there appears the following remarkable paragraph:

> Father Mazzuchelli predicts, from the signs of the times, one of which is the rapid growth of large fortunes held by the few at the expense of and injustices to the many, that eventually there will be great disturbances, probably anarchy and bloodshed. In his talks with the Community he has often spoken of these serious and threatening questions. He says religious teachers should understand them well, if they are to do justice to the pupils entrusted to them.

More than thirty years before the issuance of the *Rerum Novarum* of Pope Leo XIII, and more than seventy-five years before the letter of Pope Pius XI to the Catholic University of America advocating the establishment of a system of social education to combat the evils of modern society, this teacher-training in religious responsibility for the solution of social problems was set within the community's educational program.

Father Mazzuchelli's social consciousness, while it seemed isolated in the time and place of his enunciation, was not entirely fortuitous. His creed was the age-old creed of Christianity. Christ spoke it upon the hillsides of Galilee, lived it in the streets of

Jerusalem. St. Paul trumpeted it in Ephesus, Corinth and Athens; St. Peter preached it in Rome. Men and women practiced it in the Catacombs and died for it in the Colosseum. For centuries the Church of Christ taught His new Commandment. It brought tribes out of barbarism, built nations, established cultures. Then, driven by inexorable forces of change — Lutheranism, Calvinism, the coming of the Machine Age, the loss of authority of the Church — this rule of social justice submerged. But, like an underground river, it flowed onward, finally to flash out into the sunlight.

In the year 1848, the year when Father Mazzuchelli established the nucleus of the Congregation, Europe seethed with revolution. Paris was in turmoil, riots broke out in German cities, the *Communist Manifesto* was published in London. Against this tide of social protest, young Wilhelm Emmanuel von Ketteler, then a member of the German Diet, and afterward Bishop of Mainz, flung up for a dike a plan of social reform. Let men live in justice, he proclaimed. Let them practice Christian love of neighbor in their relations with one another. Give the worker a wage sufficient for himself and his family. Make religion the base of social as well as of individual life.

Albert de Mun, French prisoner of war in Mainz during the Franco-Prussian War, took Von Ketteler's doctrine back to France and founded a school of economic thought based on its philosophy. In England, Cardinal Manning put the doctrine of Christian social justice into operation when he championed the striking London dock workers. In the United States, Cardinal Gibbons proclaimed the creed of social justice when he espoused the cause of the Knights of Labor. Then, in Italy, Pope Leo XIII issued that Magna Charta of labor, the *Rerum Novarum*.

The application of the doctrine to American social life came sharply into focus with the publication, in 1919, of the Bishop's Program, largely the work of Bishop Peter J. Muldoon of Rockford and Father John A. Ryan of the Catholic University of America, and approved by the archbishops and bishops of the American Catholic hierarchy. A bombshell in 1919, the program became a high point in controversy, only to be gradually adopted by the nation in less than twenty years. Largely because of its success, Pope Pius XI, in 1938, requested the Catholic University to work out a program of social education at all grade levels. For this purpose the Commission on American Citizenship, established as a department of the university, has been at work upon the building and integration into the Catholic schools of a program for the teaching of Christian social living.

Laboring on a frontier remote from Europe, Father Mazzuchelli moved far in advance of other Catholic social theorists. His own example of citizenship was notable. He built not only churches but two courthouses, a college, an academy, a market hall. First chaplain of the first session of the Wisconsin legislature, he interested himself in civic improvements, the advancement of just legislation, the promotion of neighborliness and colonization efforts. He deeply prized his American citizenship and accepted its responsibilities. He impressed on the first Sisters of the community his own admiration of the principles of justice and equality as embodied in the American Constitution. He explained their rights under it, their duties as citizens. By word and deed he emphasized Christian social living.

The Sisters were therefore ready when they met the problems directly and dramatically: in the Spring Valley lockout which aroused young John Mitchell to organize the United Mine Workers; in the Anaconda lockout when copper capital and labor grappled in death struggle; in the great Chicago Stock Yards strike that revealed working conditions which shocked the nation; in other situations not so well known but none the less vital to the interests of the workers. From their mission experience the Sisters of Sinsinawa have known the problems of modern society. From their traditional teaching they have known the solution of these problems.

This teacher-training in religious responsibility for the solution of social problems remained in the community's consciousness, and grew there as a result not only of formal pedagogy but also of the actual democracy of the place.

Here there is no distinction of class or casts. The Sister washing dishes or working in the laundry is as important, as revered as the researcher in science or the lecturer on the theology of labor relations. In fact, the Sister who specialized in Canon Law may sometimes be found, in summer, working in field or orchard or at the kitchen sink, and thoroughly enjoying her employment. The server at the guest table may have taken a doctor's degree at the Catholic University or labored over old English literature at Oxford. All such toil is voluntary but, like that of the state of Wisconsin, the motto of Sinsinawa is service; and its way of working out that service is by actual and active participation in a unit of Christian democracy. For how could they teach that democracy unless they practiced it?

Here, then, is an institution as American as the tall corn in the Iowa fields beyond the river, as American as its own traditional Fourth of July picnic celebration. Every day, after Benediction, the hundreds of Sisters filling the chapel join in the *Prayer for America*. Even when foreign wars are happily over, the great war for the souls of the nation goes on. Why, one wonders, is this convent upon a Wisconsin hillside so impressively aware of the spirit and of the problems of our United States? Why is it so essentially characteristic of the region, so cognizant of the needs and riches of America?

The answer lies in its history.

Sinsinawa owes its existence, its standards, its ideals to two Americans, both of them foreign-born: to the man who founded it more than a century ago when the Wisconsin country was the American frontier, and to the woman who carried on his purpose in spite of poverty, disasters, and discouragements; to the Italian-born Father Samuel Charles Mazzuchelli and to the Irish-born Mother Mary Emily Power.

Father Mazzuchelli was the bringer of the light that shines over and beyond the Great Valley from the Mound of Sinsinawa.

Mother Mary Emily Power was the keeper of that light through long, hard years.

This is her story.

CHAPTER TWO

Ireland
1844–1852

ELLEN POWER was born on January 12, 1844, on a farm at Barrettstown near the town of Tramore in County Waterford, Ireland.

To those who know the history of Ireland during the following seven years — the terrible Famine Years — that simple statement is no time-worn opening line of biography but a bell ringing a tragic knell. For those seven years marked a time when the South of Ireland was a place stalked by the most terrible want, the most intense suffering, the most corrosive injustice that Europe knew in the nineteenth century. Any child — even a child of the privileged landlord class — growing up in those years of misery bore through life in his memory the mark of what he saw and what he heard. Ellen Power was no mere observer. She was one of the millions of sufferers from a governmental policy of oppression of industry and suppression of population. The English government was destroying Ireland by decree; the men and women, boys and girls who huddled, homeless, on the roads, or crouched, starving, beside cold hearthstones testified to the extent of that ordered destruction.

David Power was a small farmer at Barrettstown, working a tenant-right which had been in his family for generations. He knew that, in Munster, this right, although based on the same national custom, had not the standing in law of the Ulster rights which assured their possessor not only security of tenure, but value in cash if he wished to transfer his tenancy. He knew, too,

11

that Daniel O'Connell's failure to win Repeal of the hateful Act of Union, which put Ireland at the complete mercy of England, would have dire consequences for the Irish tenant-farmer. Victory for Catholic Emancipation would be a Trojan horse if the British plan of closing Irish industries and devastating Irish farms resulted in the decimation of the Irish people. Whether the policy was based on the commercial desire of British manufacturers to cut off their Irish competitors, or on the political wish of British statesmen to whittle down the legions that rose at O'Connell's cries, the result was the same.

In 1844, the Devon Committee, composed entirely of alien land-holders, recommended for Ireland disallowance of all tenant-rights, consolidation of small farms, and encouragement of emigration. One million people were to be removed from the land which they and their fathers had cultivated. They were to be set out on the highways where, as John Mitchel said, their choice would be America, the poorhouse, or the grave.

By 1847 the pursuance of these recommendations had caused the Great Famine. Even the help given by some few kindly land-lords and by the overworked clergy — who often gave up their own meager suppers so that their flock might have food — could not stem the tide of death. In 1847 the agricultural product of Ireland amounted, according to British governmental authority, to more than 224 millions of dollars, an amount which would have fed double the population had it been left instead of being exported to England. Yet in that year more than a half-million people died of famine and fever. By 1851, over a million and a half people had died and another million had emigrated to the United States.

Evictions blackened the roads. Year after year, no day went by when families were not driven out of their homes, either on the pretext of unpaid rent or by the more honest statement that the landlord wanted the land for more profitable grazing. Any Irish child of those years knew the sound of the battering ram on his own or his neighbor's door, knew the cries of the dispossessed, knew the sight, even if he did not know the feeling, of gaunt hunger.

David Power, holding to his little farm among the pleasant green hills of Waterford, within sight of the ocean, knew that his own order of eviction would one day come. He grieved to leave the land of his forefathers. Here, in spite of the troubled times, he had kept together his family. He had married twice: first, Mary Power, then Bridget Kelly. There were four children of the first marriage, Thomas, David, Michael, and Mary. The children of the second marriage were Richard, Catherine, Anastasia, Ellen, Alice, and Margaret. All of them had been born in the farm house. Then, in 1851, came the dreaded notice. The landlord needed increased acreage. The Powers — all of them who were still in their birthplace — must go.

Some of them were already gone. Thomas, the eldest of the first family, had studied navigation in Waterford with an idea of becoming a ship officer. He had shipped thrice to Quebec, then decided to try westward exploration with the younger Mrs. David Power's brother. They found their way to Wisconsin, coming into the lead mining region in the southwest corner of the territory, and going to work for a farmer. There one Sunday morning on his fourteen-mile walk to Mass — as Thomas wrote to his father — he met a priest riding horseback.

The priest, an Italian, one Father Samuel Mazzuchelli, had taken the young Irishman to a college he had established at a beautiful place called Sinsinawa Mound. There Father Mazzuchelli was teaching young men in college work the same kind of studies they would have in older universities. He wanted Thomas to come to the college. "You will be a priest of God," he told him. "I'm not worthy of that, but I'll come as a lay brother," young Power promised. "You will come to study for the priesthood," Father Mazzuchelli insisted. "Then I'll come," said Thomas, "when I've helped my family a bit." He found work in the neighborhood. Out of his earnings he sent over two hundred dollars to Barrettstown. "We'll put that away," said his father. "We'll need it yet."

Meanwhile, the younger David and his wife, reading the letters from his brother and her brother, made up their minds to leave

Ireland. They set out to the Territory of Iowa, even beyond Wisconsin. "You'll be following us soon, Father," David said. His father shook his head. "I'm not a young man, David," he said, "and I've six girls and two boys to look after." But in a few years, the doomed knock of the evictor sounded on the farmhouse door. David and Bridget Power and their children, with Michael of the first family — Mary had decided to stay with her mother's people in Tramore — went forth from the home they loved. By dint of God knows what privations they had saved passage money to America. With pitifully few possessions and rations for the long voyage, they set out to the port of Waterford where they would take a ship westward.

Years afterward, Mother Mary Emily Power — who had been the seven-year-old Ellen — went back to the place of her childhood. There was no house where she remembered it. The green fields of a grazing pasture covered even its ruins. Sadly, she looked across them to the misty blue line of the hills. "They took everything but our souls," she said, "but, after all, what else does anyone need?"

CHAPTER THREE

Journey: West by North
1851–1852

1

NOTHING but the providence of God, asserted a British parliamentary committee that belatedly investigated conditions on the immigrant ships of the early 1850's, had kept the vessels afloat and the immigrants alive.

Overcrowded, undermanned, the immigrant ships from Ireland to America were risks few underwriters would care to take. The immigrants, however, pushed out by a government anxious to erase from the face of Ireland evidence of its own mistakes and lured by the promise of a land of freedom, were willing to take the risks. Early in 1852, with hundreds of others, David Power and his family crowded upon the *Asia*, a leaky, unseaworthy vessel bound from Southampton by way of Queenstown and Waterford to New Orleans. Thomas Power, with his knowledge of navigation, would never have let his father take passage upon such a ship; but Thomas was now Brother Louis at the Dominican house of St. Rose in the state of Kentucky, studying there for the priesthood at the advice of Father Mazzuchelli of whom he had so often written his family. Without his guidance, the Powers boarded the ship with a hopefulness that soon turned into misery.

They brought, as all immigrants did, their own provisions and bedding. The ship was to furnish them only the space in which to cook and sleep, and fresh water for drinking. But danger of fire prevented use of the stove in the galley, even had the place been big enough to accommodate the women who crowded around it.

The barreled fresh water ran out so that, for weeks, men, women, and children suffered agonies of thirst. Food began to give out. Those who had any, shared it with those who had none; but there was never enough for all. People fell ill. A man died while David Power recited the Prayers for the Dying. The body was buried at sea, wrapped in a weighted winding sheet. Afterward his widow weepingly told Bridget that the twenty pounds which had been in a belt on her husband's body had been taken. "Now we have nothing and no one," she said. Through the rest of the long voyage Ellen saw her weeping; and the child held her father close as if to ward off from him the fate of the dead man.

Weeks late, they saw the American shore as the ship turned into the Gulf of Mexico. After days of storm, when the ship rocked in mighty waves, they came near to Belize, that port of pirate and buccaneer, and saw ahead of them New Orleans, the town of their entry. Kneeling upon the worn and rotting planks of the ship, they said the *Te Deum,* and as the sunset gilded the spires of the city, that was already old in a world they called new, they sang that hymn of the Blessed Virgin, "Gentle Star of Ocean," even little Margaret joining in its supplication:

> Still as on we journey,
> Help our weak endeavor;
> Till with thee and Jesus
> We rejoice forever.

"Thanks be to God," said David Power, "we are here, at last."

2

That most literary of all the chanteurs of New Orleans, Lafcadio Hearn, once wrote that his city brewed magic in her marches. (Like Rome, the town always merits the feminine pronoun from her panegyrists.) Low, flat, dirty, crowded, the port could not have seemed any too prepossessing, however, to weary adults and tired children just disembarking from weeks of turmoiled travel in a risky vessel. The levee was a confused mass of strange races, brought to it by ships from Genoa and Glasgow, Leghorn, Liverpool and London, Antwerp and Antigua, and a score of other places whose names the geography books in Waterford had never taught. Dark men with gold earrings swung through the streets, jostling fair men in heavy northern woolens. French, Spanish, Portuguese, and a dozen stranger tongues sounded above the measured work songs of the toiling Negroes. It was all strange and almost terrifying; but in a little while, thanks to an Irish sailor, the Powers found themselves in a boarding house in St. Patrick's parish, a *maison* operated by a landlady who welcomed them in the mellifluous accents of Kerry.

Perhaps the elder Powers never found the glamor which lurks in sudden glimpses of Spanish magnificence and French elegance through gates of courtyards flowering in azaleas and oleanders. To children, that finding was inevitable. Through long lifetimes the three girls old enough to go through the New Orleans streets would hold in their hearts the memory of Lafayette Square and St. Mary's Market, the old Cathedral of St. Louis and the Convent of the Ursulines. If New Orleans offered them promises of a civilization that the up-country did not fulfill, it none the less gave them the welcome of its charm and showed them how the New World might graft upon its soil some of the beauties and glories of the Old.

As the eldest of the three, Catherine should have monitored them; but Anastasia, probably because she had a sharper sense of adventure than her elder sister, led the expeditions. She marshaled Catherine and Ellen to the Cathedral where they said a prayer of thanksgiving before the statue of the saint who had not returned from his last Crusade. She showed them the iron bars of the Cabildo and the walled Convent of the Ursulines. Girls, big and little, were coming out of its gate, day students going home under the careful chaperonage of Negro women servants. "They say," Anastasia told her sisters, "that this was the first school in this whole country. The Sisters came from France long ago to bring education to this place when it was nothing but a wilderness."

"Did they have as hard a crossing as we had?" Catherine asked.

"Worse, far worse," said Anastasia, though knowing nothing whatever of the narrative of Madeleine de Hacheres.

"But we are going farther," said Ellen.

"We aren't nuns."

"Perhaps some day we shall be," Ellen said.

"If God calls us," Catherine amended.

They drifted away from the thought as they looked into an auction room where a raucous-voiced man was shouting the sale of furniture and boots, oil and cheese, bales of cotton and sacks of coffee. They gazed at a window on Camp Street where little pictures called daguerreotypes were on display. They halted before the show windows of P. and E. Reilly, at Canal and Royal Streets, to look upon French calicoes, cashmeres, embroideries and muslins, kid gloves and fans, parasols and mantillas. They even looked into a candy shop, its counters gay with such delights as they had never before seen, bonbons and marrons of pink and green, white and yellow, and deep chocolate brown. "This is a rich country," said Catherine.

Ellen was to see another side of its life when she went out one day with Michael. They wandered around the market, staring wide-eyed at the great piles of food: shrimps, and lobsters, pompano, crabs, and oysters; multicolored vegetables and fruits whose names they did not even know; big cakes topped with sugar decorations, and little cookies bulging with fruits and nuts and dark with spices. Then, suddenly, they were in a square of crowding men. In their desire to get out of it they only came closer to the cause of the crowd, a low platform where a white man, booted and wide-hatted, stood beside a burly Negro. Sharply Ellen Power heard the man's voice, calling out the working qualities of the black man just as the auctioneer had cried out the values of the bales of cotton. "Why, he's selling him!" She clutched tightly on Michael's hand. "Michael, he's selling him!"

"They do that here," Michael said. "It is the law."

"But it is wrong. They're God's children just as we're His children. Father O'Malley told us that when he came from

Buttevant to speak to us on the missions in Africa where he'd
spent long years." Closely Ellen watched the gloomy face of the
slave on the platform. "Can't someone do something about it,
Michael?"

"Not that I know." How was he to know that in another decade
a man who had once gazed on a scene like this was to issue an
Emancipation Proclamation, setting free the slaves?

She turned away with him; but she was to think long and
often, as the years rolled up the clouds of civil conflict over the
issue, of the black man in the Slave Market. Little as she knew
of the politics of a strange land, Ellen Power knew that all the
children of God should be free men.

In the boarding house in St. Patrick's parish there was constant
talk of opportunities open to immigrants. "Stay here," one man
advised David Power. "This is a rich city. It will soon be a richer
one. You can open a little store. In a little while you'll be able
to buy a house, and there are five Irish pastors here already."
"Come with us to Texas," said another. "Land is cheap there. A
man with two sons can make a fine living for his family." "We're
going to California," a third man said. "There's more gold in
the mountains there, and we'll be near the sea, as we were
in Ireland."

"We are going to Wisconsin," David Power told them all. "My
son Thomas, the half-brother of these children, will be there.
He's a Dominican brother now — Brother Louis they call him —
studying for the priesthood at the Dominican college near Spring-
field in Kentucky. But he's going back to Sinsinawa soon."

"What will you do there?" men asked David Power.

"Work in the lead mines," he told them, "until I've money to
buy a farm."

"But it is so far," one objected.

"Nothing is far from God," Bridget Power put in.

As their elders waited for a letter from Brother Louis giving
them more definite directions about the last stages of their
journey, the Power children came into deeper knowledge of the
city. Somehow, in the way of children, they came to know how

the Catholics of New Orleans cared for the sick, the orphaned, the old, the school children. They stood outside the doors of the Charity Hospital where the Sisters of Charity had nursed yellow fever patients in the dreadful plagues which sometimes over-whelmed the city. They saw the Female Orphanage on Camp Street, and learned that the Mother Superior of the Sisters there was called the Sister Servant. They glimpsed the sad old women in the Widows' Asylum for whom the Ladies of Providence cared. They watched white children going to the free schools of the Ursulines for girls and of the Christian Brothers for boys.

"Will Wisconsin be like this?" Ellen asked her sisters.

"We'll be on a farm," said Anastasia.

"I'll be glad," said Catherine.

"And I'll be glad," Ellen echoed her; but always New Orleans stayed in her memory, a gateway city in a bright new world but in itself strangely darkened by shadows of old wrongs and coming troubles.

3

The Mississippi River packet, *Uncle Sam*, Robert Smith, Master, seemed to offer palatial accommodation to its passengers as it dodged the shoals and found the channels of the great river up from New Orleans. The luxury, however, was confined to the hurricane-deck around the pilot house and to the saloon-deck just below. Here were the ladies' lounge, the dining room, the bar, the officers' quarters and the cabins for first-class passengers. Here were the excitements of river travel which made famous the Mississippi steamboats. Below was the boiler-deck, more than half of it taken up with engines, cargo, and cook's galley, the rest left for the use of second-class travelers.

The boiler-deck had, however, compensations of its own, and the Power children found them long before the boat came to Natchez. Seated against coils of rope, they looked out over gray waters upon constantly shifting traffic. They passed flatboats on which solitary men poled against the current and shanty boats on which families lived as if on shore. They went by swamps and bayous and wide plantations where gray moss hung on high trees. They saw great flocks of birds, wild geese and ducks, sometimes swans and strange birds on floating snags. They whirled by high-stacked sugar boats going upriver, and cotton boats going down. They passed little landings where black men waved to them. For them the river was a thrilling spectacle by day, a mysterious passage by night, when shore lights and boat lights twinkled around them.

To them the journey was a carnival, as different from the immigrant ship as day from night. After the wide stretches of the gloomy Atlantic, the passage up the Mississippi seemed almost like land travel, with shores and trees and houses visible, and landings every little while. Activity and gaiety ran high on the low boiler-deck, so high at times that passengers came down from the upper deck.

Almost at once the Power children caught that feeling of America which they were never to lose. Here, in this new land, was freedom. Here was hope. Here was opportunity, not only for the making of a livelihood, but for the practice of their beloved, cherished, and too often buffeted, faith. Here was a largeness of life which both comforted and inspired them. "It is grand," they told one another; but the meaning went far deeper than the words.

The view was a shifting kaleidoscope of land and water. The landings were backdrops for excited scenes where passengers left or boarded the boat, where Negro stevedores sang low rhythmic songs as they swung bales and crates, where little Negro boys danced for pennies thrown them by men at the rail. The plantation houses, sometimes gleaming white above the banks, gave glimpses of the luxury to which New Orleans had been the gateway. Then the scene changed from these leisurely vistas to cruder pictures: little gray cabins, hard-baked fields, rickety docks. Then came higher banks, larger towns, more bustle of excitement at the landings. Through it all ran the easy cheerfulness of the frontier, punctuated only once in a while by hot words that presaged the coming conflict. To the Irish children their fellow travelers showed a kind friendliness, accompanied usually by some curiosity. Where were they going? And why? Did they like the

United States? With varying degrees of shyness they answered that they were going to Wisconsin, that they were going because their father would work there, and that, yes, they liked the United States.

They sighted at last the old French towns of Ste. Genevieve and Kaskaskia, and were told that they were nearing St. Louis. Again they knew the thrill of arrival. St. Louis was the last city of their journey. They would be there only a little while. Then — ho, for Wisconsin and their new home! They did not know, as they saw the spire of the old cathedral in the Missouri city, how much they would endure before they arrived at their chosen destination. With the other passengers from the *Uncle Sam*, the Powers crowded to the rail and waved greeting to the city.

4

The dock at St. Louis lacked the picturesqueness of the New Orleans levee, but boiled in an excitement foreign to the indolent Louisiana wharves. Here South met East and North, and with them pushed onward to make the West. The day of the waterways was going, the day of the railroads beginning; but the line from Chicago to St. Louis would not be finished until the end of 1853, and in this year of 1852 the Mississippi was still the route of the immigrant, whether he came by way of the Ohio from Cincinnati or up from New Orleans. From St. Louis the road ran southwestward to Independence; and from Independence the wagon trains lumbered to the Cimarron and the Rio Grande, Fort Laramie and the Sundown Slope.

For nearly ten years the town had been the corridor of the western immigrant. From the lands of Western Europe, but particularly from Ireland, families came to it in the magnificent but unfounded hope that somehow they needed only to reach its streets to be assured of further passage. The helpless lot of many of them had moved Brian Mullanphy, mayor of St. Louis, follower of Frederic Ozanam, and founder of the American branch of the Society of St. Vincent de Paul, to use some of the great Mullanphy fortune as a fund that, after long litigation, became the base of the Travelers' Aid. The Powers, fortunately for themselves, had no need of the Mullanphy charity, although it was here that they were to meet dire misfortune.

Someone — probably a steamship agent in New Orleans — had advised them to go to Wisconsin by way of a steamer from St. Louis up the Mississippi and into the Fever River to Galena. At St. Louis they learned that the ice on the Fever River had not yet broken. They would have to wait a little while in the city. Finding another Irish-kept boardinghouse, in the Jesuit parish of St. Francis Xavier, they waited in reasonable contentment.

David Power went about the markets, looking over American farm machinery and farm products and comparing prices with those in Ireland. In the shops, Bridget found cottons cheap enough to buy for dresses for the girls. The older children, as they had done in New Orleans, looked over the town, marveling a little at its already established evidences of Catholicity, the Cathedral by the river, the Jesuit University, the orphan asylums for both boys and girls, the hospital, the academies of Ursulines and Visitandines, of the Sisters of St. Joseph and Ladies of the Sacred Heart. There were the free schools also — these had been established in the Catholic settlements of America long before Horace Mann lifted his voice in Massachusetts — conducted by the same sisterhoods who taught in the academies.

"Do they teach the free scholars the same as the others?" Ellen wanted to know from Michael.

"How else?" asked Michael. "They're the same Sisters, aren't they? How could they teach one thing to the pay scholars and another thing to the free scholars?"

"Will there be a school in Fairplay, Michael?"

"There are schools in every place in America," Michael assured her with a confidence as great as his ignorance of the subject.

There came rumors that cholera, that dread disease of the frontier, had struck at Jefferson Barracks, the army post outside the city. "I wish we were gone," Bridget Power said. "It is not likely to find us," David told her reassuringly. But find them it did. It was no widespread and terrible epidemic like earlier and later outbreaks, but within a fortnight David Power was stricken.

No one of the children was ever to forget those days and nights when their father tossed in misery, when their mother bent over him unceasingly, and when, at her direction, they prayed on the stairs of the boardinghouse. Most of all they were to remember the night when she bade them kneel while the priest from the Jesuit Church came to the sick room. "The Last Sacraments," Michael said, and had to stifle his sobs. When the priest had gone, hurrying off to another victim, Bridget Power came out and gave Michael his father's prayer book. "Say the Prayers for the Dying," she bade him. "Let the rest of you follow him."

In the dim light of a candle the boy read the old, majestic prayers with which the Church has ever convoyed the souls of her departing children. "Depart, O Christian soul, out of this world in the name of God, the Father Almighty, who created thee. . . . Let the splendid company of angels meet thy soul at its departure; let the court of the Apostles receive thee; let the triumphant army of glorious martyrs conduct thee; let the crowds of joyful confessors encompass thee; and let a happy rest be thy portion in the company of the patriarchs; let Christ Jesus appear to thee with a mild and cheerful countenance, and give thee a place among those who are to be in His presence forever."

They came to the end. "Lord, have mercy on us," Michael entreated.

"Christ, have mercy on us," the children responded.

Bridget Power arose from her knees and came out to them. "He has gone," she said. Even then she did not weep. Nor did she weep when she led the sad little procession to the church and then to the strange cemetery. "If only he'd died in Ireland!" Richard mourned. "What does it matter," his mother said, "from where God has taken him?" Dry-eyed she spoke to them all. "We shall go on to do what your father planned to do," she told them.

Not even when Brother Louis came from St. Rose's to help them did she change her determination. "You are to go on with God's work," she told her stepson when he offered to give up his novitiate in order that he might earn enough to help in the family's support. "Michael is old enough to find work in the mines. Richard will be old enough in a little while. The girls will find work if they do not marry young. I'm strong. We'll find a way. God never yet shut one door that He did not open another."

If Brother Louis' coming made no change in the material plans of the family, it made a change in the attitude of his frightened young half-sisters. Catherine and Anastasia and Ellen had huddled, night after night, in fear they dared not show by day before their mother. Even Michael's boyish bravado was no comfort to them. Their father, the pillar of their house, was gone. What would they do without him in this strange land of crowding perils? Why had this happened to them, they asked one another, and found no answer. Then their elder brother — they were never to look on him as one of a different family — saw their terror as well as their sorrow. Quietly, as he did all things, he set out to comfort and cheer them. He told them tales of the Wisconsin region to which they were bound, of mining settlements, of wide farms, of the college beside the Mound, of the priests and Sisters already there, and, most of all, of Father Samuel Mazzuchelli.

"He has made over the settlements," Brother Louis said. "Everywhere he goes he builds churches and schools and in some places even market halls and state houses. More than that, he has made over the hearts and souls of many people. When you meet him, you will understand what I mean."

He could stay with them for only a little while; but in that time he put into their courage the iron of faith. He taught them to say, "God's will be done," with their souls as well as with their lips. Less by word than by example, he led them into the exercise of that valiant spirit of fortitude which was to make them leaders in their generation and which was now to bear them over a river of sorrow wider than the Mississippi. They told him good-by with tears in their eyes but hope in their hearts.

They were going to Wisconsin, as their father had planned, and life in Wisconsin would be as brave and bright as David Power had promised.

5

Northward from St. Louis the Great River narrows. The current seems to run more swiftly. The banks rise higher. The cities on either side front one another more closely. In these middle years of the twentieth century, the upper Mississippi is a main-traveled thoroughfare as definite, as well charted as any numbered road on a tourist's map. In the middle years of the nineteenth century, the upper river, like the lower, was still a luring stream with glinting promise of adventure; and the Power children, setting forth upon it with the hopefulness of brave youth which transcends even the sorrow of loss, found it a happy highway into a land that was to be their own as long as they lived.

The river boat to Galena was smaller, less ornate, less glamorous than the New Orleans packet. Because of the difficulties of navigation in the narrow tributary to the Galena docks, the Galena boats had a peculiar, sawed-off structure with a high smokestack. "Like a candle in a cup," Ellen Power told her sisters. They had plenty of deck space, however, and on the deck the children, wide-eyed in wonder of this strange, new land, met for the first time the democracy of the Middle Border.

Young as they were, they recognized its difference from the exciting, glamorous society they had glimpsed on the *Uncle Sam.* The people on this clumsy carrier lacked the sense of established social cohesion that glued the groups on the lower river into a close, though inharmonious whole. The men on the Galena boat were frontiersmen, with all the individualism of the frontier. Fur traders, lumberjacks, miners, land speculators, soldiers of fortune, drawn from diverse stocks and backgrounds, they held in common a firm belief in the future of the region they traversed. In an accent sharper than the slow drawl of the lower river, they vociferated that belief. In a little while the upper valley of the Mississippi would be the heart of the nation. Tomorrow, tomorrow, tomorrow ran the theme of their talk.

The hope of that tomorrow colored their judgments of the day at hand. They were seeing the river towns, not as they were, small settlements of hardship and struggle, but as spreading cities of vast promise. Quincy, Burlington, Davenport, Rock Island, Dubuque, Galena. The names rolled off their tongues to set signposts of the future. And, as they talked, Ellen Power heard again tales of the man whom Brother Louis had praised: Father Samuel Mazzuchelli.

Few of his historians on the river boat could achieve the difficult Italian pronunciation of his name. Some referred to him as "Father Matthew Kelly." Most of them compromised with "Father Samuel," perhaps because the intimacy of the term gave them a sense of closer association with the missionary. All of them, talking with one another or with Mrs. Power, had something to tell of the amazing exploits of the little Italian priest. Few of his panegyrists were Catholic; but all of them voiced such friendly admiration for him that Ellen Power came to see the upper valley as Father Samuel's Parish. She would continue to regard it so for more than fifty years.

Story by story, as the boat chugged up the river, the girl heard the epic which was to influence her life and, through her, the lives of thousands of others. From fur traders she heard tales of Indian missions. From lead miners she garnered stories of Galena, of Benton, and New Diggings. From timber cruisers she learned sagas of the Wisconsin woods. From a Dubuque doctor she had the tale of a city's foundation. From an Illinois land surveyor who was a political scout for Stephen A. Douglas she heard accounts of town building. A Wisconsin lawyer described his state's constitutional convention. An Iowa builder spoke of Iowa's state capital building and the town in which it was set. Rivermen told stories of heroic adventure. Women narrated kindnesses to the sick, the orphaned, the poor. In all their tales Father Samuel was there, a spiritual Paul Bunyan who performed these wondrous deeds of daring, of church and town building, of human kindliness, having a splendid citizenship broad enough to include all men, high enough to lead them to God.

"The builder of the Northwest," the people of the steamboat called him proudly.

Set upon Brother Louis' briefer reference, the epic piled into
a huge monument to a living man. Not then, but in later years,
Ellen Power was to realize the magnitude of Father Mazzuchelli's
mission. Then it would determine her own part in its continuance.
Now she thought of him only as a priest of almost gargantuan
strength, beloved by his many and strangely assorted friends in
his vast parish of this wide American frontier.

The French fur trader from La Crosse had known Father Samuel
for many years. "Since long ago," he said, "at the Straits of
Mackinac." The trader's cousin, Madame Laframboise — and what
a great woman she had been! — had been the first to tell him
of the young Italian missionary. Here was the story as he
remembered it.

Samuel Charles Mazzuchelli was the sixteenth of the seventeen
children of a Milanese merchant whose business included banking.
At the age of seventeen he had entered the Dominican Order at
Faenza in Lombardy, and at nineteen, the Dominican Studium of
Santa Sabina in Rome. Three years later, in 1828, he was a sub-
deacon when a priest from Cincinnati, delegated by the Dominican
Bishop Fenwick, spoke to the young men at Santa Sabina, asking
them to come to the American wilderness. He told them what
they would suffer: blazing suns and beating storms, canoeing over
unmapped lakes and down churning, rapid-rushing rivers, dwelling
in Indian villages or in brawling wilderness settlements. They
would be poor. They would be hungry. They would be in danger.
They would win no reward but the satisfaction of knowing that
they had preached the Word of Christ to men who needed to
hear that Word. Of all the students only young Samuel Mazzuchelli volunteered.

He came to the United States in that same year, 1828. Without
knowledge of English, he traveled by stagecoach from New York
to Philadelphia, to Baltimore, then to Pittsburgh and by river
steamer to Cincinnati. He had difficulty, but strangers helped him.
In Cincinnati Bishop Fenwick welcomed him joyously. Immediately the young Italian resumed his ecclesiastical training and took
up the study of English. Two years later he was ordained in the

Cincinnati cathedral. Within a few weeks he set out for his mission of Michillimackinac.

Father Mazzuchelli was not the first priest to go to the Island, the Frenchman said. Many missionaries had followed the good Pere Marquette who had first taught the wild Ottawa the glory of the Redemption. But wars had crossed the Straits so often that the Fathers had been forced out. The Island had become a wild settlement of Indians, French, English, and Americans. The Indians were distrustful of all white men. The hunters and trappers and traders, most of them French-Indians, coming to the Island after their dangerous work of the winters, ignored the precepts of the Faith they professed. Nearly all the Catholics were careless. The Protestants were bigoted. The church building was a wreck. The town was a place of ill-will, of wild brawls.

Father Mazzuchelli changed all that. He worked on the church with his own hands. He preached incessantly in both French and English. He addressed the Indians through interpreters and set about learning their language. He called public conferences to which he invited the Presbyterians in order that he might answer their challenges and correct their mistakes. Amazingly, they came; and if some of them still held out against friendliness, most of them liked the young missionary so well that they began to help him in his rebuilding of the church. Together, Protestants and Catholics began to work to make the Island a better place. In that work Madame Laframboise gave the greatest help. And why not? asked her cousin. Was she not the *grande dame* of the North, a rich and pious widow who carried on her husband's business and had prayed, year after year, that a priest might come to Michillimackinac to save the souls of the people.

Father Mazzuchelli rebuilt the mission on the Island, then set forth on farther trailways. Northward to Sault Sainte Marie, southward to Arbre Croche and westward to Point Saint Ignace and Green Bay, he went in Indian canoes or in the bateaux of the fur traders. At Green Bay he built Wisconsin's first Catholic church, St. John's, and opened Wisconsin's first Catholic school for Indian and white children.

"The people loved him," the trader said, "but he was not with them long."

On into the Wisconsin wilderness he went: to Kaukauna, then to Fort Winnebago, first at the command of Bishop Fenwick and later that of Bishop Resé, who had been the missionary he had heard at Santa Sabina and who was now, as Bishop of Detroit, shepherd of souls in the vast Michigan Territory. In the wilderness Father Mazzuchelli wrote a Winnebago catechism which was printed in Detroit and an Ottawa almanac which was printed in Green Bay. The latter work was the first printed text in any of the dialects of the Sioux tribes. In five years he baptized 1500 "children of the forest," as he called them. Then, suddenly, the circumstances of his missionary labors tossed him into the politics of the American frontier.

One of the timber cruisers, a tall, lank American, set the next spoke in the wheel of the story. "I knew Father Matthew Kelly in Prairie du Chien," he said. "That was nearly twenty years ago."

The Prairie du Chien of the 1830's was, as he described it, a wild town, a bad town. Like Michillimackinac and Green Bay, it was a combined trading center and Army post. Before, during, and after the Black Hawk War, Indian troubles boiled in and around it, most of them created by the stupidity and greed of the traders. At nearby Fort Crawford, desertions were common, disorders frequent. Drunkenness, the bane of the frontier, was both cause and result of the chaos of the place; but the white men blamed the Indians for all ills, and the Indians, with more reason, blamed the white men.

Father Mazzuchelli came on horseback and by canoe across the wilderness of Wisconsin — then part of the Michigan territory — to reach the town on the Mississippi. He had found there nearly six hundred Catholics "dying," as he said, "of hunger of the soul." He could not stay then but he made up his mind to return. In 1833 he tried to get a school for the Indians.

Old Chief Whirling Thunder of the Winnebagoes had petitioned the government through John H. Kinzie, the subagent at Fort Winnebago, for such a school. Kinzie approved the petition, and Father Mazzuchelli took it to Governor Porter of Michigan. It was understood that this was to be, as the Indians desired, a Catholic school east of the Mississippi River; but when the priest came back, he found that the new Indian agent, Street, had chosen as superintendent a Presbyterian minister. Street had also set the school across the Mississippi where the Indians, although they would go there eventually according to their treaty with the government, were not yet ready to send their children. The priest, seeing the situation on his return to Prairie du Chien, started there a school for the Indian children.

His efforts to better conditions brought him in contact with two men, one already famous, the other to be known far beyond the Wisconsin frontier. In 1835 he wrote a letter to President Andrew Jackson in behalf of the Winnebago school. Jackson, evidently impressed by the letter, referred the matter to his Secretary of War who asked the Governor of Illinois, Joseph Duncan, to conduct an investigation. The investigation was neatly whitewashed by Colonel Zachary Taylor, then commandant at Fort Crawford who raised the point that the complainant was "a foreigner, an Italian Catholic priest," whereas the Presbyterian superintendent was "a native American." The native American was held in office but the school failed.

The missionary kept on working for the Winnebagoes, however, not only in the ordinary subjects of school training, but also in agriculture and mechanical arts. It was a losing battle, for the tribe was already doomed by the westward push of the frontier. "He had good ideas for the Indians," said the timber cruiser, "but just about all he could do was fight for justice toward them and teach them religion. And that was more than anyone else was doing for the Winnebagoes."

The doctor from Dubuque had met Father Mazzuchelli when the missionary had stopped in the town — then within Michigan Territory — on his way to St. Louis from Prairie du Chien. He was going back to the Dominican Provincial House at Somerset in Ohio for clearance of the difficulties caused by the changes in diocesan jurisdiction. He had started his work in the diocese of

Cincinnati, had seen his territory transferred to the diocese of Detroit, and now he had come into a region which should logically be part of the diocese of St. Louis. He sought clarification of his own situation on this changing frontier, a situation caused by conflicts with the diocesan jurisdiction under which he had worked: his order needed priests in Ohio and Kentucky; his Bishop was retaining him in the North. In the conference at Somerset, Father Mazzuchelli's graphic account of the spiritual desolation of settlers in the lead mining region won the day. He went back to Dubuque delighted.

"Meanwhile," the doctor went on, "the Catholics of Dubuque had sent a petition to the Master General in Rome asking that he be left to them. The people in Ohio and Kentucky had priests enough, they wrote him; whereas they had none but Father Mazzuchelli. They didn't think they could carry on if their pastor was taken from them. They wrote," the doctor chuckled, "that they did not expect to see a church built soon in Dubuque if someone did not listen to their petition. Well, someone listened. The Master General wrote back that he would arrange to have Father Mazzuchelli stay with his people 'for the good of their souls.' He had a sense of humor, that man, as well as a sense of justice.

"Father Mazzuchelli stayed and built the church that's now the cathedral. He helped to build the State of Iowa. He led the first civic meeting in Dubuque on July 4 in 1836. He built churches in Garryowen, in Bloomington, in Davenport, in Burlington, and in Iowa City. The first legislature of Iowa met in his unfinished church in Burlington. I hear that he did the actual planning of Davenport and of Iowa City; and I know that he made the plan of the Iowa Territorial statehouse there. He was the only man in this part of the world who could combine engineering principles and practical methods for such a building. He has many and great talents, and he has used them all for the benefit of the many communities he has served."

The Illinois politician cut in. "Father Mazzuchelli has certainly been the moving spirit of the lead mining country. Of course, he built St. Michael's Church in Galena but he did much more than that. He traveled the frontier, helping Protestants as well as Catholics to see their way to a better way of life in this world as well as in the next. I heard him preach at the laying of the cornerstone of his church in Galena — there were more of us Protestants there than there were Catholics — and I've never heard a better sermon. I remember how he said that religion should serve as the solid foundation of all human societies by sanctifying the laws upon which they rest. Why, he knew far more of the works of Thomas Jefferson than I do and I'm a Jeffersonian democrat. And what do you suppose he had carved on the cornerstone of St. Michael's? He set down the name of the Pope — Gregory XVI, I think he was — and of Bishop Rosati of St. Louis, and of Andrew Jackson — he was President of the United States then — and of Joe Duncan, the governor of Illinois. Some of us thought that Old Hickory and Old Joe would be surprised to find themselves in such holy company; but, after all, it was a good idea to show that the Church and the State could work together for the glory of God."

The Wisconsin lawyer was an old man who had known his state when it had been almost entirely frontier "Indian country," but he had never known it, he said, as Father Samuel had known it. "He was the one priest for hundreds of miles. He walked, rode, paddled in canoes to get to his people. He nursed them through epidemics. He helped them build schools and homes. He laid out towns for them and their fellow citizens. He knew every trail, every wagonpath, every waterway in southern Wisconsin. His first care was for his own people but he got along with everyone. He never went into politics but he did insist upon the right of religious freedom guaranteed by the Constitution and told men that they should exercise their political rights for the general good.

"I was one of the thirty-nine members of the first assembly of Wisconsin. There were only two Catholics in that body; but we voted to name Father Mazzuchelli chaplain of the first Territorial Legislature at Belmont — that was in October, 1836 — and we asked him to make the opening address of its first session. And that was right because he's really been one of our foremost citizens."

"Yours?" challenged the doctor from Dubuque. "He made application for his citizenship papers before Judge Charles Mason in the United States District Court at Burlington on November 29, 1842."

"That was before it was Iowa," said the lawyer.

"He belongs to Illinois," said the man from Galena.

"Does he not belong to us all?" asked the French fur trader.

Belong he did — to them and to all the people of the region that had been his vast parish. Missionary-Apostolic to a territory which ranged from Lake Huron to beyond the Mississippi and from Illinois to Lake Superior, he had lived among savage Iroquois, Menominee, Sacs, Foxes, and Winnebagoes, sharing their shelters and their food as he sought to better their conditions, educate their children, and save their souls. Architect, log lifter, stone setter, and fund raiser for almost twenty parish churches in the struggling white settlements of the swirling frontier, he had helped his fellow Americans in the erection of public structures, in the laying out of towns, and in the more important building of moral integrity and good will. Planner of schools — as Brother Louis had pictured him — he had started uncounted informal groups, using any place and any teacher at hand to carry on his instruction. He had set up a Dominican provincial house, a college for boys, and a Dominican Sisterhood. His most lasting achievement, the training of that Sisterhood in high standards of Christian social education, had just begun and was being carried out in the little mining town of Benton just over the Illinois state line in Wisconsin.

The child who was to conserve and extend Father Mazzuchelli's ideals listened wonderingly to these tall tales of a priest's trail blazing. Although her amazing memory stored these scattered facts of his wanderings, she could not yet envision him as a personality. To her youthful mind he seemed less a human being than a gigantic force, moving with incredible speed, setting up churches and halls and capitols, teaching, preaching to Indians and whites, talking and praying in the halls of government. She may have thought him a veritable giant, able to reach into clouds and stride over hills in seven-league boots. She was to live for fifty-seven more years under the orbit of his influence; and she was to say, almost at the end of those years, that Father Samuel had covered a range so wide that she had never quite caught up with him.

In time she was to come into wider and more intimate knowledge of the area Father Mazzuchelli had served, men and women he had helped, and children he had taught. She was to become one of the great forces of its development. She was to make it, in a sense, her own bailiwick. She never signed herself anything but "Sister Emily"; but to tens of thousands of citizens of the Mississippi Valley she would be "Mother Emily." Always, she was to think of that valley as she saw it from the deck of the slow-moving river boat: a wide expanse of fertile land, big as all Ireland, where free men of all creeds were living as neighbors at peace in the unity of their freedom and in their common love of God. She only knew then that she had come into her father's land of promise. Only the rolling years would show her what she would do to keep it Father Samuel's parish.

CHAPTER FOUR

Fairplay: An American Village
1852–1857

THE boom years of the lead mining region were over when Bridget Power and her fatherless children came up the Mississippi and the Fever River to land at the Galena docks. Most of the good lodes had been worked out in thirty years of furnaces and smelters. Adventurers who might have continued to come had been diverted by the greater promise of quick wealth in the California gold rush. The bustling town of miners and traders, land sellers and land buyers was gone with the prairie schooner. Long lines of wagons no longer crowded the low streets near the river while their drivers waited turns to pile on queer, top-heavy boats the heavy bars of lead for St. Louis. Even the belated victory won by Stephen A. Douglas in 1850, making possible the railroad southward from Galena through Illinois, had failed to bring back the roaring days of the thirties and the forties.

Twenty-five years earlier, the region had become the frontier of the nation. The wealth of minerals in the valley had been known to the early French explorers. Radisson and Grossilliers heard of lead mines among the Boeuf Sioux, probably in the neighborhood of what was to be Dubuque. Hennepin's map of 1687 shows a lead mine located at the present site of Galena. Nicholas Perrot tried to mine south of the Wisconsin River but found the lead requiring a blasting he could not undertake. The riches of the Missouri lead mines, which had their market first at Ste. Genevieve and later at St. Louis, seem to have made needless the French research along the upper river.

Under the Spanish rule, the mining and sale of lead became one of the most profitable employments of the valley. Miners, working by themselves, sometimes took out thirty dollars worth of metal in a day. The traders made large profits and the search for new mines went farther afield.

Julien Dubuque, *la petite Nuit* to his companions, a French prospector on Spanish-governed land, obtained from a full council of the Sac and Fox Indians in 1788 a formal permit to work lead mines "tranquilly and without any prejudice to his labors." His prospectors, mostly Indians, roved about as they pleased, finding other lodes on the Illinois side, all the way from Elizabeth on the Apple River to Galena on the Fever River. French-Canadians and half-breeds followed them. Julien Dubuque grew rich in the industry, and his Indians and their successors kept off other men until the 1820's brought a general movement of American prospectors upon the region.

Ignoring Congressional enactments about mineral land leases, a horde of squatters and prospectors flocked by boat from Missouri, Kentucky, and Tennessee, with others from southern Illinois coming up the old Indian trail from Peoria. Galena, given a name and zooming into a town, became the center of the boom, although the city Dubuque retained advantages for greater commercial growth.

By the mid-thirties the "suckers," those miners who came from southern Illinois in the spring and returned there in the fall, and the "badgers," the group who lived near the diggings throughout the winter, had settled into fairly permanent communities. The fame of the mines had gone even to Cornwall, and brought a considerable number of "Cousin Jacks" to the region. Besides the earlier French, there were a few Spaniards and Germans, a few Negroes, and a growing population of Irish, couriers of the great Irish immigration which followed the famine.

The Catholic Church had already — thanks to a little Italian-born Dominican — established a lasting foundation. The Father Samuel Mazzuchelli of whom Brother Louis had spoken so eloquently, had pioneered the region, building churches and schools and, at Sinsinawa, even a college, seminary, and Sisters' convent.

The long shadow of his greatness fell upon Ellen Power as she looked up from the docks and saw the springtime sunshine gleaming upon the spire of the church the priest had built upon the hill above the river and on the towered courthouse he had created in Galena for Jo Daviess County.

In that time of 1852, the Illinois town, with its impressive houses on the high bluff, was supposed to have a generally southern aspect, legacy of the pioneers from the Missouri lead mines. To the child whose idea of American life came from what she had seen in two southern cities, the place seemed not markedly like either. It possessed a combination of traits which she was to learn in time were named by points of the compass. Galena, even more than Dubuque, the capital of the mining area, had correlated characteristics of East, North, and South to make a Western town. It was to that westerness, which extended out into the farm lands of northern Illinois and southern Wisconsin that Ellen Power responded with Irish appreciativeness of true freedom.

The country around Galena was already breaking into farms. On the slopes might still be seen the towers and derricks of the mines but men no longer looked to them for entire means of livelihood. It was true that there would be work in them for Michael, her half-brother, and her own brother, Richard; but that very work would shift them only too soon to the far West. It had been her father's intention to take up land in this new country and farm it as he had farmed the land in Waterford. His death had changed that plan but it had not deflected her mother's desire to continue to the neighborhood which they had chosen. They had set out from Ireland, bound to a strange place with the strange name of Sinsinawa Mound, and, come epidemics or come floods, to Sinsinawa Mound they were going. You need only look at a photograph of Bridget Power, taken in her old age, to know that she was a woman of determination. Doubtless a widow with six young children of her own had to be grimly determined if she and they were to survive.

Luckily for them all, she had humor. She saw the joke of trying to put themselves and their possessions into the little mail stage which ran from Galena to Sinsinawa Mound and Fairplay on its way to Potosi. She marshaled her flock into divisions, leaving Michael in charge of Catherine and Anastasia while she went off with Richard and the younger girls.

Tucked among the mail sacks for Snake Hollow and Van Buren, Ellen gazed out upon the panorama of hills and prairie which was to be the arena of more than fifty years of her lifework. Under the high, blue sky of the Great Valley, the hills rose wider and longer than the hills of her Waterford. There was no glimpse of the sea but there was an ocean of prairie flowers, white, blue, yellow, stretching away from either side of the narrow road. There were no rose-wreathed cottages with fragrant peat smoke drifting above their turf roofs; but from little gray cabins people waved them welcome. Over the wide scene danced that spirit of gay hope with which the West has always beckoned to youth. As the horses climbed uphill steadily, the massive Mound of Sinsinawa rose in dim, blue beauty, lifting from the lower landscape like a great backdrop for a vast drama. "'Tis beautiful," the child said, almost to herself, and knew, with a strange happiness that surged over her homesickness for Ireland, that she had come into her own country.

The stage circled the Mound to come to Fairplay where the Dominican Fathers of the college had, at Brother Louis' request, found a house for his people. The find was half of a fairly large house, set a little back from the road within three acres of ground. For the Powers, reunited with the arrival of the next mail stage, the most fortunate circumstance of their residence was the fact that the house was divided into two sections and that the other section sheltered the Heffrons. With a hospitality both Irish and Western, the Heffrons shared with their new neighbors anything which the Powers needed and the Heffrons possessed, blankets, food, candlelight, and advice. The double house must have looked like the domicile of the Old Woman of the Shoe when the children of the two families overflowed its rooms. For all of them it was to be a happy place for many years.

Fairplay, a one-street village in the hollow of the hills, was, in

1852, a microcosm of the wide American frontier. Tiny as it was, it housed a far more mixed population than Vinegar Hill or Garryowen, recognizable by their names as settlements of liberty-loving Irish, or Maquoketa, which was then Irish in spite of its name. English, Scottish, French, German, and Swiss made their homes in or near the village. Some of the English, coming by way of generations in New England and upper New York State, brought with them an opposition to the institution of slavery which was bitterly resented by the English who had come by way of generations of slaveholders in the Southern States. The Germans, fugitive from the defeat of their liberalism of 1848, cast their political lot with the Northern element. The French, accustomed to personal administration of interracial justice in the New World, kept out of the storm area. So, in the early fifties, did the Irish to whom the freedom of America was still too vast to permit sight of its differentiations. Although the clouds of conflict already hung on the horizon, Fairplay, like most American communities of the time, went about its daily living with slight concern for the threatening future.

To the Power children the life, though different in setting from that of Waterford, still had many points of resemblance. The Heffrons led them into rapid acquaintanceship with their neighbors. The yard near the road resounded with the shouts of their comradeship. Day after day, London Bridge went falling down, and the farmer took a wife. Little girls chose their east, and chose their west. In the twilights they sang "Oh, Susannah!" and "The Prairie Flower" which their new compatriots had taught them, and they in turn, taught the others "Down to Black Rock," and "The Rose of Tralee." Some aspects of the Wisconsin countryside they learned for themselves. There had been no fireflies in Ireland. Through the summer nights in the great Valley hundreds of the darting insects flashed before the astonished eyes of the children from Waterford. "What do you think those lights are?" Ellen asked Catherine who, at a loss for explanation, devised her own. "The fairy tinkers," she said, "going out at night to seek iron to mend the pots of the fairy folk." The fancy held them in pleasant appreciation until Anastasia, either by report from the Heffrons or by scientific exploration of her own, learned the truth. "They're bugs," she asserted.

"Oh, Annie," Catherine grieved, "you've taken out all the wonder!"

"She has not," said Ellen. "Isn't it just as wonderful that God made such bugs?"

The snow and ice of winter was a never ceasing delight to them, although the work of getting wood and water was doubled. The Heffrons had a homemade sled on which they all took turns in coasting down the longest hill of the village. The boys had to dig paths through the high-piled snowbanks to clear ways to school and post office. Sometimes they built snow fortifications modeled after the old blockhouses which still stood in the neighborhood, and pelted one another with snowballs.

In winter, too, came long evenings when Bridget Power — before they knelt to say their nightly Rosary — told her children tales of the land they had left: tales of St. Patrick, who had brought the Faith to Ireland; of St. Bridget, who had taught it in her wonderful school of Kildare; of St. Columbkill and the other great missionaries who had taken back the light to a Continent of Europe darkened by long wars. She told them, too, of Brian Boru and Clontarf, of Malachi who wore the collar of gold, of the grievous persecutions under Elizabeth of England and of the terrible devastations under the army of Cromwell. She recalled the Flight of the Earls, and the broken Treaty of Limerick — she had once seen the Treaty Stone — and the valor of Sarsfield, and the going of the Wild Geese, nevermore to return to their native land. She told them tales of Robert Emmet and Wolfe Tone and the Irish Rapparees; of Daniel O'Connell and Catholic Emancipation; of the men who had awakened the West, the Young Irelanders who had failed in their venture but who were still carrying on — some of them here in America — the struggle for Irish freedom. "Pray God," she would say to her children, "that you may live to see Ireland free."

Always, for all her love of Ireland, she drilled into them their debt of gratitude to this new land. "She held open her doors to us," she said. "She shelters us, and feeds us, and gives us our chance to live good, honest, upright lives. We must love her, and prove our love for her. She is our country. What is that song you've learned at the school? Sing it now."

With high, clear, childish voices they sang it,

"My country, 'tis of thee,
Sweet land of liberty."

If they had little idea of why it was the land of the Pilgrims' pride, they had a clear idea of what they meant when they chanted,

"From every mountainside
Let freedom ring!"

Bridget Power and the new state of Wisconsin were making a group of good American citizens.

The future success of that effort lay in the Irishwoman's determination that all the children should know their religion. She taught them the questions and answers of the Catechism, often when she was so weary with work that she could hardly see the worn pages of the one book. More than that, she told them, over and over again, the story of Christ's birth, and passion and death. She read the words of the Gospels, going back, time and again, to the Sermon on the Mount and the Good Samaritan. "Let you live as Christ lived," was her admonition. She knew no theology; but she made her commands, "Be a good boy," or "Be a good girl," eloquent with the truth that all theology must have to be a living force. Good herself, she made goodness both means and end for the two boys and five girls to whom she was the fulcrum of life.

Winter or summer, the village had few diversions. There was a tavern, operated by Mrs. Huldah Allen and advertised in the Miner's Express at Galena as "able to entertain travelers in the most agreeable manner, with prices moderate, as is best suited to these hard money times." There the stage paused on its way to and from Galena, but, except for the arrival of the mail, the place held no lure for childhood. The bakery, started in her home by an enterprising German housewife, had its attractions, but the Powers did their own baking and had no money to spare for the luxury of "sweeties."

Home was the beginning and end of social life. Every morning Bridget Power and the children said together their brief morning prayers before they sat down to the simple breakfast she had made ready. At noon they said the Angelus even though no church bell sounded it for them. At night they recited the Rosary, and prayers for the soul of David Power. They studied, and they read — although books were few, and they treasured the big, many-pictured volume, Butler's *Lives of the Saints,* which Brother Louis had given them. And, over and over at first but with daily decreasing loneliness, they talked of Ireland. Swiftly the life of the village and the region and the nation became their life, although they were never to move far away from the sturdy base of their foundation. There was no church in the village, the Catholics attending Mass at the Sinsinawa Church of St. Dominic which the amazing Father Mazzuchelli, who had built it in the valley at St. Augustine's, had renamed and moved to the upper slope of the Mound. "Salvation," said Michael Power, "came high in Wisconsin but was worth every step of the steep climb."

The church, by this time presided over by the Dominican Fathers from St. Rose's in Kentucky, to whom this same Father Mazzuchelli had transferred the Mound property with all its buildings and equipment, was a center for the religious life of the neighborhood. To it every Sunday came men, women, and children from farms and from little settlements to hear the Word of God. Because of the many German farmers in the parish, instructions were given in that language as well as in English. The Powers heeded the latter, delighting to realize that six thousand miles could make no difference in the teaching of the Church; but they drowsed through the German lessons, listening to the birds in the oaks in summer and watching the snow on the pines in winter.

In spite of the fact that Brother Louis Power, of the Kentucky community, had come up to Sinsinawa from St. Rose's at his earliest opportunity to see that all was well with the family, there is little evidence of close association between the Powers and the priests at the college. That association seemed to lie fallow, waiting for the ploughing of the man who had given up the actuality of the institution he had built but who had not given up his dream of the purpose of that institution. It was only when

Brother Louis, then Father Louis, became President of the college in 1860 that the relationship of his people to the place became marked; and by that time the course of events had brought them in even closer touch with the founder of Sinsinawa.

In the meantime they were making the base of their structure of good citizenship. Bridget Power was a good neighbor. With little to give of material goods, she gave generously of service and sympathy whenever they were needed. She taught her children to do the same. She seldom talked of their rights in a country founded on the assurance of rights. She often talked of duties and responsibilities, translating the philosophic idea into tasks and opportunities of the day. It was, "Annie, help Maggie with her dressing," and "Ellen, help Katie with the water from the spring," and "Katie, take care of Alice while I do the ironing." It was, "Will one of you children see if old Mrs. Trevelyan needs any errands done for her?" and "Have you helped the Steiners with their lessons today?" In Fairplay, as in all the frontier settlements, people gave help more freely than they asked for it.

Holydays and holidays helped in the merging of both immigrant and native-born Americans. On All Souls' Eve Bridget Power made a great cabbage dish that she called "caulcannon," and shared with neighbors who had never before heard of it. At Christmas Mrs. Steiner brought over a box of *pfeffernuesse,* the Christmas cookies she had learned to bake in Saxony. For New Year's, that feast which the French observed so highly, Madame Grignon produced a heaping plate of the doughnuts she called *croquinoles.* On the Fourth of July they all had a picnic which ended with American strawberries!

Undoubtedly, the four Power sisters who eventually joined Father Mazzuchelli's Dominicans had within themselves the voca-. tional spirit of self-sacrifice and community living; but there can be little doubt that their simple, friendly life in a little Wisconsin village in no way detracted from their destiny of service. There probably seemed nothing extraordinary about them as they grew into young girlhood; but that may have been because the whole condition of the western democracy was in itself extraordinary.

In the early 1850's western Wisconsin was still frontier. The Black Hawk War, which had raged across its forests and fields, was a vivid memory to men who had shouldered arms in it and women who had watched them join the ranks. Most of the Indian tribes had been moved across the Mississippi, but the smoke of old conflicts still hung on the horizon of men's thoughts. The wilderness remained near, although corduroy roads were beginning to traverse it.

Immigrants from western Europe had come into it, although not in the wide waves of their coming into eastern Wisconsin. There were, however, sizable German and Irish settlements between the Rock River and the Mississippi; and the passionate yearning for political freedom as well as for economic opportunity, which had incited their choice of the United States, made itself part of the general democratic attitude of the region.

The character of the political climate, however, had been largely determined by the earlier settlers who had come, either by covered wagon or by Great Lakesboats, from Upper New York and New England. These settlers, usually designated as "Yankees," were, in large part, descendants of the Scots who had fled from English rule after the disaster of "The Forty-five," as the followers of the Stuart cause called the defeat of the forces of Bonnie Prince Charlie at Culloden. Their grandfathers had served under Ethan Allen at Ticonderoga, their fathers had fought in the War of 1812. The rosters of the first Wisconsin Territorial and the first Wisconsin state legislature show their influence upon the determination of Wisconsin policies.

The mining settlements of the area had brought in numbers of Welsh and Cornish miners, people of independent spirit and a tradition of revolt against conditions they considered unjust. The mines had also brought men from southern Missouri whose political views, in the seething fifties of the past century, made whetstones for the antislavery crusaders.

Racially, southwestern Wisconsin was a heterogeneous community. Socially, however, it was generally homogeneous in its liberalism. Men were free, and were determined to stay free. They wanted order in government; but they intended to remain able to control that order. Either by actual experience, as in the case of the Irish and the German immigrants, or by family tradition, as in the case of the other settlers, they knew governmental oppressions. They were united in opposition to such oppressions. They cherished the reality of American democracy; and they projected the vision of a world made better by it. They were, for the most part, a religious people, and their concept of democracy, like that of the Founding Fathers, was based on their belief in God.

Ellen Power could have had only the vaguest idea that Fairplay, Wisconsin, constituted a nuclear cell in the great American experiment of a free society. To her it was a pleasant village of good neighbors. Throughout her later life she revealed always her interest in people. Sisters who worked with her at the Mound recall that she could remember not only the names but the backgrounds of as many as twenty girls as she introduced them to some visiting dignitary. Throughout her lifetime she remembered the names of her Fairplay neighbors — Owens, Tregatha, Heffron, Macpherson, Streit; and she could state their racial backgrounds as easily as she gave the personal backgrounds of Sinsinawa students. Quiet as she was, she had a gift for association with people. Inevitably, she was influenced by the community application of the Wisconsin spirit of liberal democracy, a spirit that was to assume, in her lifetime, important leadership in the social consciousness of the nation.

The Powers were in Fairplay in 1856 when the question of religious freedom became a political issue. Stephen Douglas, United States Senator from Illinois, had insisted upon inserting in the Democratic Party platform of that year a plank denouncing the Know-Nothing Party, a group violently opposed to the free exercise of their religion by Catholic citizens. The battle in the party convention created a cleavage in the Democratic Party which was one of the factors in the 1860 break. Because the region largely favored Douglas, who was popular because of his aid to the Illinois Central Railroad, then bringing rail transportation to the Mississippi Valley, the issue did not arouse bitterness in the area, although a few sporadic groups, one of them in Benton, tried to exploit it. There is no record and no recollection that Fairplay joined these groups.

The one school in Fairplay was a public school. Five years earlier its teacher had probably been a Catholic for Father Mazzuchelli's records mention a schoolmaster and his wife for the Sinsinawa neighborhood. The change of ownership of the college had evidently changed this condition, and there is no record available of any further association between the college and the village school. Recollections of descendants of some of its students give only a dim picture of the institution.

The three R's were the standard subjects. Choral recitations shouted that nine times nine was eighty-one and that the boy stood on the burning deck. The Readers were McGuffey's, used then in nearly all the public schools of the Middle West; and, although McGuffey's economic philosophy was undemocratic, stressing as it did the idea of "be good, and you'll be rich one day," the books none the less emphasized the moral foundation of the nation and widely contributed to good citizenship.

The Fairplay school was, to say the least, casual, being little better than the "kitchen" schools of the settlements where enterprising women, for the payment of a small sum from their neighbors, taught the neighbors' children with their own. Teachers came but did not linger in the one-room schoolhouse. To Bridget Power, however, starved for education as were nearly all the Irish by centuries of its suppression by the conquerors of their land, a school was a school; and she bundled off to it three of her five daughters under the guidance of the Heffrons. The two boys had already found work in the mines.

All of them were good students, Anastasia probably the best, although the younger Ellen excelled them all in mathematics. Her skill in that troublesome subject brought about her first assumption of leadership. She set out to teach her sister Catherine and two of the Heffron boys the fractions which baffled them. She was holding the class under a tree not far from the road when there drew up near the house a rider on a white horse. "Whoa-a,

Napoleon," he bade his mount and swung down from the saddle.
With a whoop of joy, the two Heffrons deserted the class. "Father
Samuel," they shouted. "Father Samuel!" and, like the serpents of
Laocoön, wrapped themselves around the priest. As if their cry
were a view-halloa in hunt country, there came a flock of boys and
girls, some shouting, others chanting a badly garbled French
royalist song that Ellen Power did not know. She only caught its
meaning in one of its oft-repeated lines,

Napoleon l'mort, Napoleon l'mort.

Why, though, should these children in Fairplay exultantly pro-
claim the death of a long-gone Emperor? Napoleon had died, she
remembered from her father's telling of the story, in the year when
her grandmother had died, in 1821, the year when Ireland had
celebrated the first promise, soon to be broken, of Catholic
Emancipation. "When did Napoleon die?" the priest asked when
the shouts died down.

There was no answer.

"How many years ago?" he asked again.

Ellen Power could stay silent no longer. She did not know this
strange priest who rode gaily upon a white steed of long mane
and longer tail, a priest amazingly different from the solemn
pastors and more solemn curates of Bishop Nicholas Foran's
diocese of Waterford. She was still a stranger in this amazing land
of vast distances and odd customs. She was already a teacher of
mathematics to Catherine and two young Heffrons, and her professional reputation was at stake in her silence. "Thirty-one years,
Father," she said.

"Ah, the little one knows!"

He looked at her with suddenly quickened attention. He saw
a child small for her eight years, with fine, sandy hair and blue
eyes of a remarkable color and keenness. To the casual observer
she might not have seemed notably different from the children
who had transformed the chanson of Napoleon Bonaparte's death
into a jibing welcome for a white horse. But Father Samuel Mazzuchelli was no casual observer. His artist's insight went below

surfaces to find the depth and the wisdom and the beauty of the Lord's creation. "What is your name?" he asked.

She told him as she watched him with straight, solemn stare. Long afterward she was to describe him as "little, and gentle, and kind" but she must have apprehended in him, as he did in her, qualities beyond even those attributes of charity. "Power?" he repeated the name. "You have come. My brother's people have come!" He held out both hands to her. Then his eyes found Catherine, and saw the resemblance. "You, too!" he cried. "Where is the mother? And the others?" he waved the crowding children aside, and started to the door of the double house. "Welcome," he cried. "What is it you Irish say? A hundred thousand welcomes to our country!" Then, almost before Bridget Power could catch her breath, he flung at her the question, "Will your girls be coming to our school?" It was his question to all parents. If they had the money, they could pay for their children's education. If they hadn't money, he'd manage somehow. The important part was not the money but the child.

It was a query he was to raise, over and over again, in the years to follow. Through those years Ellen Power was to begin to learn — not from him as much as from others — the odyssey of Father Samuel Mazzuchelli's apostolate, the true and tragic tale that had already made him one of the most remarkable, farseeing, and constructive personalities in the history of the American frontier.

CHAPTER FIVE

Sinsinawa: First Planting
1847–1852

ELLEN POWER first saw Sinsinawa on a Saturday that was bright
with May sunshine and white with May blossoms. Brother Louis,
coming up from Kentucky to the college, naturally wanted to
show to his young sisters the place which had been so important
in his own destiny and which was to be so much more important
in their lives. As they drove from Fairplay behind the team of
horses which their neighbors, the Heffrons, had loaned to them
for the occasion, the Power girls saw the white stone structure of
Father Mazzuchelli's building rising proudly above the smaller
houses of the estate.

Ten years earlier Sinsinawa had been the estate of Colonel
George Wallace Jones, one of the first tycoon statesmen of the
frontier. Even in that land and time of picturesque characters
Colonel Jones had been, and still was, notable for both achievements and eccentricities.

Born at Vincennes in Indiana during the year of the Louisiana
Purchase, he had lived in every commonwealth of the Northwest
Territory but Ohio; and he made up for that omission by adding
Missouri, Kentucky, and Iowa to his list of residences. He had
been in turn, drummer boy, soldier, lawyer, lead miner and smelter,
country merchant, farmer, land speculator and politician. He had
invested some of Daniel Webster's money in his land enterprises,
and by the aid of Webster's influence trebled the investment. As
delegate to Congress from the territory of Michigan, he had brought
about the establishment of the territory of Wisconsin. Then, as

the first territorial delegate from Wisconsin, he had won by one vote — over the opposition of John C. Calhoun who warned him that he'd live to regret his action because Iowa would be settled by Abolitionists, and Jones, like Calhoun, believed in State Rights — the creation of the territory of Iowa. He was Iowa's first territorial delegate. Later, he was the first Senator from the state of Iowa and was still serving in 1852, battling with Stephen A. Douglas about the location of a railroad terminal, when the Power family came to visit the place which had been his home.

Jones had taken up a lead mining claim at Sinsinawa in 1827, worked it profitably, and acquired the property from the government. He had put up a log cabin, shelters for workmen, and a smelter. In 1831 he married Josephine Gregoire, a nineteen-year-old French Catholic of Ste. Genevieve, Missouri, and in the next year brought her and two servants to the larger log house he built beside the Mound.

There were few taverns beside the road and the candlelights gleaming in the log house windows assured travelers of hospitality. Jefferson Davis, a classmate of Jones at Transylvania College in Kentucky, often stopped at Sinsinawa on his way to and from Fort Crawford. So did the Dodges, the Dunns, the Campbells, and scores of other political and commercial leaders. So, too, did Father Samuel Mazzuchelli.

Jones had gone into Galena one day and was making ready to drive home when Nicholas Dowling, mayor of the town, asked if he would take with him a priest who wished to go to Dubuque. Jones said that he'd grant the request, on condition that the priest would stop at his home overnight and in the morning say a Mass which Mrs. Jones and some of their Catholic neighbors could attend. Jones, like thousands of other men who met Father Mazzuchelli, found him a gentleman of great charm. He urged him to make frequent visits to Sinsinawa, an invitation the priest accepted. He baptized all the Jones children and performed marriage ceremonies for several of the Jones and Gregoire Catholic relatives. There he met the men who were determining the course of westward-moving empire. There he talked with them and listened to them about affairs of the day; but his alert, far-ranging mind was even then occupied with a dream of the morrow.

In 1840 Jones, having been voted out of his office as territorial delegate from Iowa by a committee of Congress, was appointed surveyor general for Wisconsin and Iowa. William Henry Harrison's election threw him out of that place, and, in 1843, the colonel was made clerk of the Supreme Court of the territory of Wisconsin. He had to move his family and household goods to Mineral Point. His wife, Josephine, wept to leave the house to which she had come a gay, young bride; but Colonel Jones set off blithely. He could not then have known that he was to be the first United States Senator from Iowa, but he was sure that one day he would return to power.

In the meantime Sinsinawa was to be sold. It was, by all odds, the most beautiful site in the district. Jones had once thought of offering it to the territory of Wisconsin as a future state capital, the capitol building to be set atop the great mound. On it were the excellent farm buildings Jones had erected, including a stone stable and granary. The farm was in good working condition.

Here was Father Mazzuchelli's opportunity to make real his cherished dream of a great educational foundation. From the time he had first seen the place he had envisioned it as the setting for a Dominican convent and college of the type which Bishop Fenwick and Father Wilson had established in Kentucky some forty years earlier. Here could be built an institution, not only to educate young men for the priesthood, but to educate other young men for their places in the life of the laity. To supplement this, he would start a Sisters' convent and a girls' school. For the times this was a grandiose project, but even Father Mazzuchelli did not know its ultimate importance; nor did he know that the plan would work out not in his way, but on a parallel course he would suggest.

To begin it he needed money to buy the Jones estate. He had a shrewd idea of where he could obtain this money, but feared lest Colonel Jones sell the place before he would be able to buy it. Jones, however, hesitated about any sale; and in 1844

Father Mazzuchelli set out for Europe with Bishop Chabrat of Kentucky, who paid most of his expenses. In the same year Ellen Power was born in Ireland, he was promoting on the Continent his plan for Sinsinawa. In Rome he won the approval for the project of the Master General of the Dominicans, the Most Reverend Thomas Ancarani. In Milan he set forth his desire to his sister Josephine and to a friend, Count James Mellario. They financed his undertaking so that on his return he was able to pay Colonel Jones $2,340 cash and give him notes for the balance of the purchase price of $6,500. By March 25, 1845, he had paid off these notes and held entire ownership of the 800 acres of the Mound property.

There was the small wooden Church of St. Augustine which he had built near the place. Father Mazzuchelli had it moved to the upper slope of the Mound and renamed it the Church of St. Dominic. Above, on the long ridge, he started the erection of a stone building. The cornerstone of the building was laid in May of 1846 in the presence of a great crowd of people from all over the lead mining region. Colonel Barry of Galena was master of ceremonies, and young David Wilson of Dubuque, the principal orator of the occasion. The program went according to schedule until it was discovered that Father Mazzuchelli had modestly left out his own name from the documents to be placed in the cornerstone. The indomitable Colonel Jones, who never shrank from giving credit where it was due, protested against what was to him a serious omission. The audience shouted until the builder had to accede to their wishes and set his name in the record. Then, to the strains of music from the Galena band, and to the roar of cannon that had guarded Sinsinawa during the Black Hawk War, the cornerstone was set in place.

This was the building which Ellen Power saw as she came up the slope of the Mound. Built of big blocks of limestone from the quarry which Father Mazzuchelli had opened on the property, it rose in three-storied simplicity which emphasized its dignity of line. Around it clustered smaller structures: a house for the priests, a house for the Sisters, a house for the workmen, and the stone farm buildings of the Jones regime, one of them built over the blockhouse with its portholes for the rifle fire of its former defenders against possible Indian attacks. Set against the towering mass of the Mound and among the massive oaks of the Wisconsin forest, Sinsinawa was even then an impressive estate.

Through the years of his missionary wanderings Father Mazzuchelli, with the high zest of another Milanese, St. Charles Borromeo, had been projecting the plan of a threefold institution, a provincial house, a college for boys, and a convent for Sisters with a girls' school. On his visit to Rome in 1844, he had won the consent for this from the Master General of the Dominicans and from Pope Gregory XVI. He had the approbation of Bishop Henni of the Diocese of Milwaukee. With this backing, and with the money from his family and friends in Milan, he started the ambitious project of the Province of St. Charles, the establishment of the Sinsinawa Mound College and the beginning of a Sinsinawa Female Academy. In 1846 the Catholic Almanac carried an announcement of a "Dominican Convent, or at least a commencement of it," at Sinsinawa.

Practically alone, Father Mazzuchelli kept up the college for a little while. In that time he was able to lay the foundation for the good work done by the priests who followed him. The college was a going concern when, in 1849, he turned over, without payment, to the Dominicans of St. Rose's Seminary in Kentucky, of St. Joseph's Province, all rights to the eight hundred acres, the college, the convent, and to four diocesan missions attended from the establishment. Saddened and discouraged, he went to become the pastor of two small parishes, Benton and New Diggings, in the mining settlements.

He did not give up, however, his interests in the college of his foundation. He remained as secretary of the board, assisting in the physical, mental, and spiritual welfare of the institution. He was both architect and builder of the second division of the Old Stone Building, setting atop it a fine two-story tower and placing iron-fretworked balconies at front and sides which added much to its beauty. He purchased not only books and scientific instruments for its classes but he also bought luxuries which he alone seemed to be able to find for the frontier. Decades before Kipling was to write that

"You cannot pack a Steinway half a mile,"

Father Samuel was bringing in a grand piano by ox-teamed wagon over roads that even the drivers told him would be impossible. Give youth the best, was his educational creed, the best of environment, of culture, of the vision of God. Unquestionably, the knowledge that he could help the children of Benton and New Diggings even more than he could help the boys at Sinsinawa — particularly since he had supplied them with other preceptors — buoyed him up in his self-imposed exile from the place he had loved.

He left behind him at the Mound his third establishment, the Sisterhood he founded in 1847. Made wiser, perhaps, by experience, the founder announced his intention of establishing a group of young women to practice the Dominican rule and obey Dominican authorities and "to consist of members gathered from the part of the country wherein they were to serve since they would better understand the spirit of the people they were to aid and edify." Knowing how his own difficulties had been multiplied by his distance from the headquarters of his Order, he sought to create a community in the place where the great need for it existed. To that end he established a tiny, but entirely separate and individual foundation, with the direct authorization of the Holy Father, a community of Sisters of the Third Order of St. Dominic. In the little Church of St. Dominic, on the fourth of August, 1847, he held the ceremony of admitting to the novitiate Mary McNulty, as Sister Mary Seraphine, and Mary Routanne, as Sister Mary Ermeline.

With these women as a beginning and with the addition of four other novices, he drew up the charter of the Sinsinawa Female Academy, an institution intended to include both Sisters' convent and the girls' school which did not arise at Sinsinawa until three years after his death. After a century, one of the paragraphs of that charter stands out almost surprisingly:

"No religious tenets or opinions shall be requisite to entitle any person to be admitted as a student in said Academy, and no student of said Academy shall be required to attend religious worship in any particular denomination."

Father Samuel certainly was taking a wide view in a wide land.

In the course of his missionary work, especially during the latter years in the lead mine district, the priest had seen the need of Catholic parochial schools. To the best of his ability he had taught the children of the many parishes he had served, even enlisting the aid of non-Catholic teachers of the "kitchen" schools of the settlements to hear the catechism lessons of their Catholic students. He wanted Sisters for these schools, but he was determined that these Sisters should be close in thought and feeling to the settlements they were to serve. Had he held to this qualification for his first recruits he would have been spared some later difficulties; but in his zeal to start the community he took volunteers at hand and lived to regret his choice.

Mary McNulty was a woman of unusual ability, determined will and uncertain temperament. As a member of the Sisters of Charity of Cincinnati she had been superior of an orphanage and of a hospital in St. Louis. For reasons known only to herself and her community she had withdrawn, a procedure easily carried out, since, at that time, the Sisters of Charity took annual vows. She had gone to Milwaukee to ask the newly consecrated Bishop Henni to start a community there, but found the School Sisters of Notre Dame already established. She then crossed the territory and found a job teaching a school near Dunleith, in Illinois, a town later known as East Dubuque. Occasionally going to Mass at Sinsinawa, she met Father Mazzuchelli. His desire for teachers, and her desire to head a community, came together like tow and fire. Her enthusiasm brought from St. Louis her old friend, Mary Routanne, who had also been a Sister of Charity. These were the women whom Father Mazzuchelli received as novices in August of 1847 and who withdrew from the little group early in 1849 after having tried in vain to induce the four Wisconsin girls who had been received by Father Samuel — Sisters Ignatia Fitzpatrick, Clara Conway, Josephine Cahill, and Rachel Conway — to leave with them.

Father Mazzuchelli had located the Sisters in a building entirely separate from the college and the Fathers' home. It was his purpose to make their work exclusively one of teaching in the schools associated with the parishes at, and around, Sinsinawa, as well as at the still unopened Academy. He had emphasized this intention when he held, on August 15, 1849, the first solemn ceremony of Profession, admitting the four Sisters according to the rites of the Dominican Order. Even earlier, he had set the novices teaching in public schools at Shullsburg and New Diggings. Generously, however, he had allowed his successors at the college to enlist the services of the Sisters for cooking and laundry work, as well as for the teaching of the Sinsinawa day school. For three years, although classes were suspended at the college in order to finish the interior of the building and to clear more land for a larger community, the Sisters continued in these tasks. Finally, in 1852 while the Power family was on its way up the Mississippi, Father Mazzuchelli made up his mind to remove the Sisters from Sinsinawa to Benton so they might the better carry on the purpose of his foundation.

On that day of Ellen Power's first visit to Sinsinawa he had come to take the Sisters away.

The child stood watchfully beside her mother, her sisters, and Brother Louis as Father Mazzuchelli leaped from the dusty vehicle he had driven up the winding road. She must have apprehended the drama of his errand, for Brother Louis had always enjoyed the confidence of his mentor. Older than her years and saddened by her father's death and the uncertainties of the family livelihood, Ellen could give the priest understanding sympathy for his disappointment. Even then she knew what it meant to leave a place she had loved. She knew what it meant to wonder what tomorrow might bring in care and want and trials. But despite her youth, no maudlin sentimentality swayed Ellen Power. The look she flashed the priest must have held challenge, for he smiled at her and moved closer that he might put his hand upon her uplifted head. "What would you do, little Ellen?" he asked her, almost playfully.

Still shy in a strange land, she made no answer.

Father Mazzuchelli looked deep into her eyes, those bright blue eyes which had, even in her old age, a strangely electric gleam in their depths. Then, in one of those flashes of vision which at times seemed to lift for him the dark curtain of the future, he spoke. "Who knows?" he said. "Some day, perhaps, you may be over them all." He said no more; but his glance at the high stone building told the rest of his meaning.

"All may yet be well," Brother Louis told him.

"Of course." Once more he was his blithe self. "Is it not the good God's work?"

He turned away then toward the college building to visit with his fellow Dominicans there. After a little while a group of them came out with him, bidding him Godspeed as he went toward the Sisters' house. Then, from that building, came a little procession which Catherine and Anastasia and Ellen watched with fascinated attention.

Sister Clara, the Prioress, carrying two heavy carpetbags, came from the doorway of the Sisters' house. Behind her, laden with bundles, walked Sister Josephine. Sister Rachel, burdened with books, followed; while Sister Ignatia brought up the rear with a battery of kitchen utensils. All of them were clad in the black habit permitted them by dispensation from Rome — "a neat habit," as Father Mazzuchelli called it, although he regretted that the traditional white of the Dominicans had been unavailable under frontier conditions. "They look beautiful," Catherine Power said to Ellen.

"They look brave," Ellen said.

The Sisters had already said good-by to the priests at the college. Now they gave only a glance at the tall stone building as they walked toward the road. Once, and once only, the missionary looked back. Then, bending over the reins, he turned the wagon toward the lower levels of the broad green lands. His work at Sinsinawa was done.

Ellen Power's work there was not to begin for fifteen years.

CHAPTER SIX

Benton: The Mining Country
1857–1867

1

FOUR years after Father Mazzuchelli first asked her to send her girls to his school, Bridget Power entered the two eldest in his academy at Benton. Through those years she had resisted his bombardment, not because she lacked belief in his ability as an educator, but because she lacked money to pay the cost of the education he was offering. With passionate intensity she desired for her children the best possible education, but her Irish pride resented the acceptance of any concessions that might savor of philanthropy. Until the family fortunes bettered sufficiently to promise security the Power girls went to the little public school in Fairplay. Then Michael, who had gone to the Arizona mines, wrote from Tucson that he would send, from time to time, money sufficient to pay for his sisters' schooling at Father Samuel's Academy. With this brightening horizon their mother sent Catherine and Anastasia to the Benton academy.

"You'll go next year, God willing," she promised Ellen.

"I'll stay home, Mother, as long as you need me," the girl said.

Bridget Power looked at her daughter shrewdly. "Why should I be needing you if I can spare Katie and Annie?" she asked. "You'll have their chance," she went on, "as long as God spares me to make it for you."

Catherine and Anastasia did not often come home, but from their infrequent visits and from the neighbors Ellen learned much of the Benton school.

She came to know that the St. Clara Female Academy was, to

the Mississippi Valley, "Father Samuel's School." Set in an un-promising location, off the beaten track of dwindling river and growing railroad travel, surrounded by the ugliness of derricks and diggings, it none the less attracted students from nearly all the valley states and territories. To the older generation of the region, Father Mazzuchelli represented the culture they desired for their children. In spite of distances and inconveniences, and often in spite of differing creed, they sent their daughters to him.

Vicariously, Ellen Power learned the history of the founding years of the academy. Out of her own experience she could supply understanding of some of its difficulties. All frontier life was hard, even when it was not stark. Saint Clara's had been no exception. Father Mazzuchelli and the Sisters from Sinsinawa had followed the pioneer rule: "Do without and make do." There was always enough to eat, enough to wear, and enough to shelter them; but Sister Ignatia, maker of the famous white bread, was sometimes hard-pressed to find flour; Sister Clara Conway, the Prioress, had hard work to acquire woolens for habits; and Father Mazzuchelli had trouble in finding carpenters to finish the buildings he designed.

Other Sisters had come to join the community, her own sisters told Ellen. Four had come, at Father Mazzuchelli's request, from the Dominican convent in Somerset, Ohio. They wore white habits, not the black ones which frontier conditions had imposed upon the Sinsinawa Dominicans. Three of them had not stayed, but Sister Joanna Clark had remained, and Sister Clara had resigned her office in order that Sister Joanna might be made the Prioress.

Another newcomer, Sister Mary Theresa Kevlehen, had come to Benton, but she had declared that she must wear a white habit for the salvation of her soul. Father Mazzuchelli had gone to Galena to buy white woolens and the Sisters had made two habits for Sister Mary Theresa before they bade her Godspeed on her way to St. Catherine's in Kentucky. Even in her brief passage through Benton she had impressed the Power girls with that quality of piety, which was to distinguish her in later years in association with the Washington convent, a future branch of the Sinsinawa institution.

Most of all, however, the talk of Catherine and Anastasia was of their school and their schoolmates. They took great pride in the fact that, in 1853, Father Mazzuchelli had obtained from the state of Wisconsin for the St. Clara Female Academy the first incorporation of any school for girls in the Northwest. He had remodeled an old church building, giving it the appearance of a pillared southern mansion. He had made the ground around it into a garden that was beautiful in summer. Outwardly and inwardly, the Benton school was a place to inspire the pride of its students.

Mary Ann Griffin of Benton, the first of these students, was still there when Catherine and Anastasia arrived. For a little while she had the distinction, which she probably did not enjoy, of being the sole beneficiary of the teaching of the priest and the Sisters. Then other girls came and classes began. They were studying Oleny's *History of the United States, Webster's Dictionary,* Comstock's *Philosophy,* Kirkham's *Grammar,* the Hirney *Compendium of Ancient and Modern History,* and an astronomy textbook which was not half as interesting as Father Mazzuchelli's astronomy lessons.

In 1857 there were forty-nine students in the academy; and it was in this year that Ellen Power entered the Benton school.

She came to the school with no sense of strangeness. She knew Father Mazzuchelli, the Sisters, and some of the students. She knew a great deal about the discipline of the place; and she quickly apprehended the school structure. Father Mazzuchelli was curriculum builder, teacher, principal, and chaplain. Under his direction the Sisters taught the "common branches," arithmetic, grammar, geography, United States history, writing, needlepoint, and *Webster's Dictionary;* the last-named "following every branch, inexorably," according to the academy annalist of that time. Father Mazzuchelli himself taught astronomy, rhetoric, and Christian Doctrine.

In his classes the Sisters often sat with the girls, for the priest never forgot his original intention of having a Sisterhood composed of teachers "native to the soil," and helping their neighbors toward cultural improvement as they themselves attained it. Unquestionably, this procedure was the beginning of teacher training, which has always been so characteristic of the Congregation, and which has often vanguarded the progress of Catholic education in the United States. In addition to the class work with the students, he gave the Sisters courses in higher mathematics, natural sciences, Latin, French, Italian, and philosophy. He hired a certain Mr. Law to teach them music "at five dollars a lesson." On three evenings a week he himself gave lectures on science, history, and Christian Doctrine to both Sisters and girls. On Sunday afternoons he conducted a Bible history class.

This was the academic framework of the school to which Bridget Power finally sent her five girls — Catherine and Anastasia in 1856, Ellen in 1857, and the younger two in the early '60's. Michael, in Arizona, was keeping his promise of money to help the family. Richard was working in the Wisconsin mines, and able to give some aid. With no injury to their mother's feelings the Power girls could go to Benton.

Board and tuition for three months cost twenty-five dollars; bed, bedding, and laundry (done by the Sisters), four dollars; piano music, eight dollars; guitar, five dollars; foreign languages, drawing, painting, or waxwork, five dollars; and astronomy, rhetoric, and philosophy, three dollars. It may be seen that the era set higher value upon the making of waxen flowers, to be placed under funeral glass cases, than on the study of stars, similes, or syllogisms. Day scholars paid four dollars for the quarter. The catalogue announced that all bills were payable in advance; but Father Mazzuchelli's account books show that the parents and guardians of his students seldom took this statement seriously. In time, he usually received what they owed him, but sometimes the waiting dragged wearily for him and the Sisters, who had to keep living even when bills were not paid.

Both tasks and pleasures were simple at the school as were all in that time and that region. There were no motorcars, no telephones, no radio, no electric lights or equipment. Oil lamps had not entirely superseded candles. The cooking range and the heating stove, using coal or wood, had only lately come into the uses formerly assigned to the fireplaces. Pioneer methods of furniture making, of soap manufacture, of laundering were still operative in the West. Galena, like all successful mining towns, had luxuries of New Orleans mahogany, Parisian clothing, London jewels, and even fine paintings which Father Mazzuchelli appreciated, although he could not afford. The Benton school however was only a little better in furnishings and in equipment than its village neighbors. From what it had, it made the stuff of happiness.

Father Samuel, again and again, described his establishment as "a home school." Rejecting the stern ideas of many educators, he assailed repressive methods. At Benton everyone was to be made not only good but happy. To that end the priest-director created an atmosphere of enjoyment in work and play. By his zest he made learning attractive; but he also offered pleasures that were good in themselves. There were wagon rides and picnics in summer — for the school year ran into midsummer months — sledding and snowballing in winter, plays, and concerts and candy pulls, dancing, singing, informal parties every little while, and gay Christmas and Easter festivals for those who did not go home. There was never any letdown in routined discipline, but the routine included recreation that was actually re-creative, a joyous run of hours for both Sisters and students.

2

Ellen Power, thirteen years old now, but still little, slid into the life of the academy with the quiet ease of the cosmopolitan. The place itself was even less like Fairplay than it was like the town outside its gates. Father Mazzuchelli had fenced around the building with double gardens, separated by curving white picket fences which ended, at each side of a stone-flagged walk, with a tall, round white post on which stood a little white angel. In summer the inner garden was gay with flowers, iron furniture, and a fascinating sundial. The outer garden was a place of shaded walks and little groves. Permission to go into it "past the angels" was often sought and usually given to romantic youngsters who found the view of Benton's main street beyond the outer fence exciting and exhilarating, even though it contained none of the wider interests to be found within their own fifteen-acre domain.

Beside the pillared building, known as "the old Wooden Cradle," ran the Arbor, a long archway of green lattice work covered with wild grape vines. Under it, in all weathers, the girls walked with one another or with the Sisters, cementing, by insistent confidences, friendships that would in many cases last through life. Beyond it stretched the orchard and a wide field of clover. Near it stood the rock cottage for the Sisters and the rose-trellised infirmary for the sick. The latter was out of bounds for the well, especially in times of measles, but many girls, Ellen among them, found their way to the cottage to taste Sister Ignatia's newly baked bread or cookies; to help the Sisters there with the peeling of apples or stoning of cherries; and to listen to joyous or thrilling tales of days earlier than their own.

The pillared main building had a few rooms on its first floor: a narrow hall, with a stag-horn hatrack and a framed print of the trial of Catherine of Aragon on its walls; the simple, small chapel; the Sisters' community room; a parlor; a "little parlor" that was Father Samuel's dining room; and a very small room where he kept his galvanic cells, his Leyden jars, and his other — and in that day strange — equipment that led the girls to regard him as "a sort of Albertus Magnus." Off the parlor was a music room where the Sisters gave and received lessons on piano, harp, and guitar. Upstairs was the study hall, with its long rows of chairs and walnut-topped, cherry-legged tables, with deep drawers that could look neat to passing inspection. On its platform the teaching Sisters or Father Samuel presided, either over studies or classes. Some girls — like Clara Stevens, "the little Presbyterian" of her own memoirs, who came later to Benton and afterward became Sister Charles Borromeo — actually quailed before that desk of authority, regarding it as a sort of Sinai while others took it with casual consideration.

The forty-nine girls at the Benton school, in that first year of Ellen Power's residence, represented a cross section of the Mississippi Valley. The list for the year is about equally divided between names identifiable as Irish and French and those denoting English ancestry. Most of the latter either came from the South — Adaline Lamar from Louisiana, Mary Louise Sibley from Tennessee, Melvina Forbes from Missouri, Elizabeth Chapman from Kentucky — or were the children of men who had come from the South into the lead mining country. There was one girl, Dalila by name, mentioned on the roll whose record page is torn from the book of accounts. What happened? And who took out the page? Probably every one of her forty-eight schoolmates knew, in the way girls at a boarding school know so much more than their superiors ever realize, but no one of them seems to have passed on the tale, tragic or otherwise, of the lost Dalila. To Ellen the most romantic of the registrations seemed that of Jane and Julia McEvoy, of Ireland, whose accounts were looked after by one William Lindsey of St. Louis, European agent. The general run of girls in the enrollment seemed to be not unlike the general run of their successors through ninety years: good, studious youngsters in tune with their substantial backgrounds and eager to make use of their special opportunities.

Inevitably there was a girl, like Isabel Irving, with the aura of the theater around her. Always, however, Father Mazzuchelli and the Sisters maintained a standard of simplicity in dress and deportment which equalized the social status of their students. The uniform for winter was a black serge dress, for summer a black skirt with "a white sack." No jewelry was permitted.

Perhaps nothing better shows that simplicity of life than the entry for Ellen Power in Father Mazzuchelli's account book for 1859. It reads:

7 mos. tuition (Sept., 1859–Apr., 1860) $70.00
Mending shoes, $.15. Paper, $.32. Paper, $.50. Embroidery, $.10
7½ yds. serge for a dress 3.00
Silk and cotton thread 10
10 stockings 20
Pens, ink, and pencil 1.00
Catechism, $.15. Paper, $.44

Any woman would be curious about how a small girl in her

teens required that amount of serge for a dress until she remembered that it was an era of very full and very long skirts. But, even in that time, how did hosiery cost so little?

There are entries in the book of money sent by Michael Power from Arizona for his sisters. There seems to be one period when the Power payments, like so many others due at the time, were slow in coming. The youngest of the three Power girls must have been conscious of this situation; and doubtless it was one of the reasons why Mother Mary Emily, as president of St. Clara Academy and St. Clara College, was especially lenient to the orphans or half-orphans whose accounts were slow in payment and, as Superior over hundreds of mission Sisters, always stressed the need of charity in considering parochial school bills due and unpaid.

The schedule of work for her, as for the other students, was inexorable; but Father Samuel lightened it with the radiance of his own joy. He loved to teach and he made learning a happy adventure. In Bible History he dramatized the great figures of the Old Testament. In Ancient History he painted verbal murals of Greece and Rome until the Acropolis and the Colosseum gleamed for his listeners. In Mediaeval History he chanted the glories of Paris and Chartres, of Canterbury and Cologne, and of his own beloved Milan. To his structure-building mind the story of civilization could be told by architecture. To him Modern History, more concerned with the building of empires than with the building of cathedrals, was a tragic tale that would one day take its toll from mankind. All this he somehow managed to put into the minds of girls from whom even their parents did not expect erudition.

His classes in higher mathematics were arenas of close reasoning. Ellen Power shone in them from her first day in the school. Before she had finished the course at the academy, Father Louis, coming into the presidency of Sinsinawa College, took her over to one of the classes there to demonstrate to some laggard young men that Solid Geometry could be learned by a girl who did not seem much more than a child.

Astronomy was, however, the favorite subject of school study. Father Mazzuchelli conducted these classes at night, whenever weather permitted, under the stars which shone so brightly over the valley. There might be a bona fide foot tapping because of the cold, and an induced chattering of teeth to win the pity of their instructor, but no class ended until every girl in it knew the location of the planet or star, or group of stars that had constituted the essence of their classroom instruction during the day. "Where is the Little Dipper, Ann Long?" he would question. Ann would hesitate over the answer. "Show her, Ellen Power," he would direct. Obediently, Ellen pointed out the constellation. Then, he would question Christine Rosmyer on the Belt of Orion and delay the longed-for ending of the session.

For all his interest in science — he had brought in instruments at heavy expense and spent hours of time explaining the principles of physics and chemistry — his most important self-imposed task in secular studies was his teaching of secular subjects in the light of Christian principles. To him all study was related to religion. God had made everything. God was in everything. No one could consider the wonders of science, the methods of mathematics, the course of history, the splendors of art, of music, and of literature without apprehension of the greatness of the Creator, without consideration of the debt owed the Creator by His creatures. That debt must be paid by service in God's honor, service for one's fellow man. For the giving of that service the girls must be educated. They must know the needs, the problems of their own world. To that end he instituted weekly discussions, training the girls in material for use, standards for estimating this material, and manner of presentation.

Some of the topics discussed at the school's public "exhibitions" show the trend of the founder's thought. At the exercises of July 30, 1858, Catherine and Anastasia Power expounded the thesis that "the study of Creation was of utmost importance, even for ladies, as a means of elevating the mind to the Creator and to establish peace and unity in the world." Margaret Gaffney spoke of the obstacles in the way of female education, the lack of good teachers, shortness of time allowed, and the distractions forced upon young women. The emphasis on feminism must have been a new note in the convent education of the Victorian era, savoring not a little of New England institutions for women; but it must be remembered that Father Mazzuchelli came of a race that cherished the traditions of St. Catherine of Siena and of the great women professors of the mediaeval universities.

A record, though set down meagerly in the annals of the school, shows the anxiety with which school executives watched the progress of events:

December 20, 1860. This day the Ordinance of Secession from the Union has been passed by the Confederate States. There is great unrest on the question of slavery. Father Mazzuchelli predicts civil war.

March 4, 1861. Abraham Lincoln of Illinois inaugurated as sixteenth President of the United States.

April 12, 1861. Fort Sumter attacked by Confederates. The Civil War has begun.

April 19, 1861. The Sixth Massachusetts Regiment attacked by a mob in Baltimore. The first blood of the war has been shed.

For long years the Mississippi Valley had been the geographical arena, as the Senate of the United States was the rostrum, of the conflict of political opinions concerned with secession and slavery. The Missouri Compromise, the Kansas-Nebraska Bill, the Land Grants, and the Western Railroad developments made gigantic backdrops for the sharper drama of the Lincoln-Douglas debate. In every city and town of the valley there grew keen awareness of the corroding causes as well as the certain inevitability of the conflict. For the most part, the line of demarcation of political thinking ran close to the old Mason and Dixon survey; but there were some sections north of this line where opinion was so sharply divided that embryo wars were fought every day upon street corners and public meeting places. One of these was the old lead mining area, particularly around Galena and its subsidiary towns of northwestern Illinois and southwestern Wisconsin.

Galena, in spite of its later contribution of nine generals to the

Union Army, with Ulysses S. Grant topping them, had its own group of Southern sympathizers. Little Benton was proportionately even more prosecessionist. By 1860 the quiet academy reflected the unrest of the nation. Girls of Southern or pro-Southern families began to argue the impending war with girls of Northern bias. It is tribute to the school authorities that the conflicting sentiments of their young charges led to no unpleasantness. Even the director's determined support of the Union seems to have caused no alienation from his school. Through the war years the academy had many more applicants than the eighty it admitted.

Father Mazzuchelli's insistence upon his beliefs was shown by the commencement exercises of July 25, 1861. The Galena *Courier* two days later reported that, in spite of the oppressive heat of the day, a large audience had attended the St. Clara exercises. After a display of needlework, artificial flowers and waxwork, there came a stirring march, played on two pianos, as the pupils, wearing white dresses with black sashes and wreaths of roses, entered two by two. A little girl, Clara Cochrane, gave the address of welcome. Ellen Power, Julia Williams, Mary Cummins, and Mary Rooney sang "Kind Words Can Never Die." After several musical numbers the pupils sang in chorus the hymn that Father Mazzuchelli loved — a hymn that even yet slides around the Gregorian chant in the Sinsinawa chapel — "Mother Dear, O Pray for Me." The playing of polkas and gallops and dances followed, and a song, "Erin Is My Home." There came a recitation, "The Soldier's Joy." Then, apex of the entertainment, arose the discussion on "This Unhappy War and Its Causes." Instantly the eyes of the audience turned to the background of the stage, a huge American flag. The slanting of the debate to give victory to the Union was not needed to assure the auditors of Father Samuel's loyalty to that Union. The flag told its own story. The Galena reporter recorded that "The Star-Spangled Banner" was sung by all. At any rate, no one gave audible rendition of the "Bonnie Blue Flag."

By newspapers and by reports of couriers from Galena, the priest and the Sisters kept in touch with the progress of events through the dark days of conflict. Perhaps Father Samuel's strongest reinforcement — his subscription to it was his one personal extravagance — was Orestes Brownson's *Review*. Brownson, that fiery seeker for faith and freedom, was offending a large Catholic audience by his outspoken declarations that certain Catholic weeklies, reflecting the attitudes of their episcopal mentors, were "secession sheets." He gave medals of honor only to the Pittsburgh *Catholic* and the New York *Tablet* for being "decidedly loyal." His *Review* was officially interdicted in Richmond, denounced in Wheeling, and declared no longer Catholic by the bishops of Philadelphia and of Cincinnati. Father Mazzuchelli, safely on the outer fringe of ecclesiastical consideration, kept on reading Orestes.

Even in war time the priest was projecting enlargement of the institution. Work had begun on a new stone building, directly back of the old one, when a draft-resisting riot broke out in the town. Shots were fired, and one man, a neighbor of the Sisters, was killed. A company of soldiers moved in to restore order. Its commanding officer asked Father Samuel if his men might visit the garden. The priest had the Sisters make ready a musical entertainment for their unexpected guests. The soldiers listened quietly; but the workmen on the new building disappeared "in the twinkling of an eye," and did not return for days.

Although the leading citizens of Benton were Father Samuel's friends (Doctor Ferris was probably his most intimate companion), and the merchants valued the Academy trade, the town, unlike most of the region, had never been notably friendly. There was ill-feeling between the Irish Catholic and the Cornish non-Conformist miners. The Cousin Jacks were not pro-Southern, merely antiwar, although it was a curious fact that the lead they mined was furnishing the bullets for both combatants, as it had furnished it for the American Army in the Mexican War. The feeling beyond the outer fence served to make the school a little island of peace, for Father Mazzuchelli refused to allow any elements of conflict within its walls. Even when daughters of Union officers met daughters of Confederate officers in class or in recreation periods no recriminations ever arose. The only outburst ever audible over a difference in religion came when Clara Stevens went into a passion of tears because she could not go to Communion with the Catholic girls on the Feast of Corpus Christi!

The school kept no records of students' grades. Only through written recollection of some of their schoolmates is there information that all the Power girls were excellent students. Even then they displayed the particular traits which were to mark them in their later lives. Catherine had a stern sense of duty, Anastasia an adventurous daring, Ellen a combination of both these qualities with the addition of an ability to lead that was based on her readiness to accept responsibility. She was not in the school many months before she was taking on duties which would have belonged to the Sisters, had there been Sisters enough to assume them. "You can trust Ellen Power to do whatever she's told to do," became a byword of the community. She delivered messages, she cared for younger children, she helped slower students with their lessons. Always she did her task quietly, serenely, apparently without effort.

She was as popular as she was able, but she never seemed to make those schoolgirl associations which meant so much to her fellows. Catherine and Anastasia had always been united. Margaret, although she came to the school in 1860, was just young enough to be outside Ellen's sphere of interests by that time. Ellen repelled no one and yet she never sought other girls. She moved in a self-sufficiency which must have strengthened her for the human loneliness which is the lot of any leader.

3

There is no way of knowing how Ellen Power met the realization that she must become one of the Sisterhood of St. Clara Convent. Only by studying her character in after years may it be assumed that she realized clearly just what a vocation demanded of her, that she thanked God for her understanding of His summons, and that, prayerfully, earnestly, and determinedly she set out to make herself worthy of it.

Someone once defined a nun as "a little lady." No one who ever knew Mother Mary Emily Power ever thought of enclosing her by such a definition. A lady she certainly was, in the sense of the corollary of Cardinal Newman's definition of a gentleman. But the combination of adjective and noun suggests a person that she never was, a meek, retiring, almost mousy woman who won her objectives by indirection of method. Mother Emily was direct, straightforward, quietly energetic. Her mind was like a tremendous machine so well co-ordinated, and well cared for, that it ran soundlessly but ceaselessly. "Make her strong," one of her Sisters in the Order once bade a commentator-writer of her obituary. "I don't need to," the writer said. "God made her strong. Her works will tell her story."

Certain it was that her elder sisters' course of action did not influence her. It is one of the marvels of their later lives that they should have accepted her authority over them so willingly. They were all young women of determined character, but from the beginning of their association in the Benton school it was apparent that Ellen had a quality of leadership, spiritual and mental, that set her apart even from her own sisters. It was not the result of personal ambition. She never had that. Perhaps the nearest one may come to appraising it is to call the trait comprehension of the force within her as a means of service for God, and willingness to use it for the glory of God.

In the midst of war's alarms the three Power girls joined the Dominican Order. On Easter Sunday, April 8, 1860, Catherine and Anastasia Power were admitted to the novitiate as Sister Gertrude and Sister Veronica by Father Mazzuchelli. Father Louis Power, who had been ordained in Milwaukee by Bishop John Martin Henni in 1856, said Mass. On May 7, 1861, they made their Professions before another Dominican, the Right Reverend Thomas L. Grace, Bishop of St. Paul.

On the Feast of the Assumption of Our Lady, the lovely "Lady Day in the Harvest" of the Irish people, there "was admitted to the novitiate" Ellen Power, seventeen years old, to be known in religion as Sister Mary Emily.

She had been a postulant for many months but it was the custom of that time that the postulants should continue their studies with the other girls, making known their intention only to the priest and to the Sisters. Wearing her school uniform, the all-black of formality (perhaps made from the serge set down on her account), she knelt at the altar rail of the stone church. At the foot of the altar, on the epistle side, stood the Prioress, Mother Joanna Clark, and the Novice Mistress, Sister Clara Conway. On the gospel side stood the Director, Father Mazzuchelli.

He began the ceremony with the words, "What do you ask?"

"The mercy of God and yours," said Ellen Power.

She made her profession a year later, having been approved by the necessary four-fifths vote of the members of the community.

On her knees in the sanctuary she put forth both her hands into the hands of Mother Joanna, that saintly woman who had so valiantly held to her chosen work in the little convent. In a voice which seemed not to lift, but which was audible in every corner of the church, Ellen made her vow:

> To the honor of almighty God, Father, Son, and Holy Ghost, and of the Blessed Virgin Mary, and of Blessed Dominic, I, Sister Mary Emily, known to the world as Ellen Power, before you, Father Mazzuchelli, and before you, Mother Joanna, Prioress of the Sisters of the Order of Penance of St. Dominic, of St. Clara Convent of Benton of the Diocese of Milwaukee, make my profession, and promise that I will in future live according to the form and Rule of said Order until my death.

The long years of her service in the Order of St. Dominic had begun.

Sister Emily's first task was the teaching of the smaller children of the academy. She was certainly a good teacher but evidently no stern one. Clara Stevens wrote of her in her diary, "Sister Emily, the dearest, the sweetest, came into the recreation room where the girls were telling ghost stories." The interest in the eerie tales ended abruptly but from interest in the prefect, not from fear. In a later entry Clara wrote that she and another pupil stayed up with Sister Emily, waiting for some belated incoming students from La Crosse, and had "bread and butter, jam and apples."

There can be no doubt of her influence upon the girls of the school. Sisters who had been with her at Benton talked of it so often that it became a community tradition. The story of Clara Stevens gave testimony to that apparently casual but none the less pervading power.

Clara Stevens was probably the most brilliant as well as the most dramatic student in the school. The daughter of an army colonel at a frontier post, she had run wild during her mother's long illness. Her father, called to service in the Civil War, placed her in the Benton school. Her impressions of the place were so vivid that the account of it she wrote years later in "The Old Wooden Cradle" remains today both a fine presentation of a way of life and a remarkable character study of Father Mazzuchelli.

Even by her own moderated account, the little Stevens girl must have been a highly charged electron of excitement. All the exercises of religion familiar to the Catholic girls were new to her — she had seven close relatives who were Protestant ministers — and she reacted unpredictably to practices and words. She read widely and inquiringly, particularly on matters of dogma, a subject as popular in her time as current events in a later era. One day, as Father Mazzuchelli ended a discourse on purgatory, Clara cried out, "That's the place I've been looking for!" only to be told by one of her witty Irish fellow students, "You can have my share of it."

On another occasion, as Father Mazzuchelli was explaining the use of scapulars, medals, and pious pictures, the girl caught a strong smell of brimstone. Her Puritan conscience, she declared, said to her that this was "just as your grandmamma told you, the devil is very near when one begins to think well of Catholic things." She turned her back on the priest, only to see a dim-witted child amusing herself by rubbing a great bunch of matches on the palm of her warm, moist hand. "Grandmamma's influence in matters of religion was greatly weakened," she recorded.

The longer she stayed, the more convinced the girl grew that the Sisters came direct from heaven. It was fitting, she thought, that they should return there, and therefore she would not grieve for them; but she thought the sun very cruel for shining brightly on the day Mother Regina died. She was emotional, but she was also logical, and her thinking finally led her into a determination not only to join the Catholic Church but also to become a Dominican nun.

Her father was a prisoner of war in Mobile when she became a Catholic. When he came at the end of the war to take her back to Boston, she insisted she wanted to join the Sisters. Although she convinced him that nothing but her own reasoning had brought her into the Church, he insisted that she go to her grandparents in Boston, but he promised: "If, at the end of two years, you still wish to enter the convent, I'll let you come back."

For two years she lived in a sternly Presbyterian Boston household, surrounded by the seven clerical relatives and other Protestant clergymen. Not everyone there was hostile to her desire, but no one had the slightest understanding of what she wanted or why she wanted it. She went to Catholic churches entirely beyond her family's pale but, strangely enough, did not find in them the joy she had known in the little chapel in the Benton school. She sought Catholic books, and found them in a little bookshop but they were not the kind she had read at St. Clara. One priest, after testing her spiritual strength, gave her a book on Lacordaire. This she cherished.

She practiced her religion openly and fearlessly, resisting both direct and indirect attempts to win her back to the family way of worship. Amid the elegance of the gilt-mirrored drawing rooms and book-lined libraries of the houses above the Common, the girl longed for the simple rooms of the convent. Through the conversations of the Emersons, the Lowells, the Wendells, her heart sped to the talk of the Sisters.

After two years she spoke again to her father. True to his promise and realizing that her happiness lay in her chosen course, he brought her back to the West and gave her his blessing at the convent door as she entered to become Sister Charles Borromeo.

With that of Clara Stevens there were other prominent names on the Benton list: Coombs, Hamilton, Rusk, a Washington Williams. There may have been Sisters in the school impressed by the wealth and political power these names represented. If there were, Sister Mary Emily was certainly not one of them. Old Sisters, who had been young Sisters with her at Benton, told others how Sister Emily had always treated everyone with the same quiet courtesy, the same recognition of human dignity. Girls who were her students told their children of her fairness. If she made any distinctions, she made them to favor the poorer, the weaker.

Even before the Sisters moved from Benton a tradition was growing up around their Sister Emily. It was definitely characteristic of her that, while she always valued Sister Charles Borromeo for her intense piety and her brilliant achievements, she had closer association with Sister Benedicta Kennedy, who had been Boston Irish rather than Boston Beacon Street before she came West to teach a public school, and who brought to the Benton community broad and deep classic scholarship rather than a Puritan background. Even when young, Sister Mary Emily had a shrewd sense of values that seems to have been characteristic of the pioneer.

Father Mazzuchelli had always maintained excellent relationships with the communities he served. Inevitably, he inculcated his ideal of service in citizenship into the minds of the Sisters and the students; and probably he had no more zealous follower in this field than was the young Sister Emily. Like him, she had a remarkable gift of genuine interest in people. She was not only acutely aware of the children in school but also of their home lives. When it was possible, she visited their homes. In her later life, she was able to introduce to a visiting bishop thirty girls at one time, not only remembering their names but remembering also facts of their home environments.

In Benton, as later at Sinsinawa, she met strangers with such vital attention that her callers were ever afterward to think of her as a long-time friend rather than as a casual acquaintance. The

combination of keenness of mind and warmth of sympathy was a
natural gift which made easy her following of Father Samuel's
attitude toward the people of their world. No one of those who
knew her from her childhood ever spoke of her as having
been demonstrative; but every one of them mentioned her sure
friendliness.

Bridget Power had moved from Fairplay to Benton. With the
closing of the lead mines Fairplay had nothing to offer her sons,
and they had gone westward. For a few years — possibly until
his mother's death — there is mention of Michael who sent money
for his sisters' education from Arizona; but there is no mention of
the younger brother, Richard. Father Louis Power was steadfast
in his concern for his stepmother and her children; but there is
only an occasional report of his own brother, who settled upon an
Iowa farm.

The three eldest daughters, Catherine, Anastasia, and Ellen, were
in the Benton convent. Their sisters, Margaret and Alice, remained
with Bridget. Margaret must have started teaching almost immediately upon going to Benton, getting a post in one of the
public schools of the neighborhood. She stayed with her mother
until Bridget's death, then entered the convent as Sister Adrian.
Undoubtedly, her earnings supported the small and simple
household.

Thought for her own family must have been one of Sister Emily's
concerns during her years at Benton, for to the last day of her
life she watched over little Alice, that strange little dwarflike
creature who seemed so utterly unlike the rest of her family.
There was, however, little she could do for them in those days of
general hardship for the country and particular hardship for the
Benton convent. Like her mother, all she could do was pray to
God as she did His work of the day.

4

Sister Emily's mind was fertile soil for Father Mazzuchelli's
social teaching. In her early childhood she had seen the workings

of a government hostile to the people it governed. She had come into a new country where she had found a people protected, not oppressed by governmental processes. At a most receptive age she had learned what political freedom could mean. To the country which offered liberty to its adopted, as well as to its native-born citizens, the girl already gave that passionate gratitude which was the payment of the more intelligent of the immigrants of that era. In her later life many of her most important associations were made with men who shared that emotion. She might not have been able, however, to utilize it for a working force had not Father Mazzuchelli pointed the way.

No priest on the Middle Border was more conscious of the pressing social problems of his time than was Father Mazzuchelli. His experience as an Indian missionary, as a builder, as a pioneer priest gave him broad information about the difficulties which beset the average man. His deep spirituality gave him insight for the solution of these difficulties. Because he was a born educator he saw education as the only true solvent of social ills. Undoubtedly, he had hoped to impress his beliefs upon the young men for whom he had planned the Sinsinawa college. Losing them, he took the students now under his guidance: the Dominican Sisters of the Benton academy. For them he began a series of instructions in civic duties, a teacher-training course which was to have wide and far-reaching results, first in the mind of Sister Mary Emily and her associates, then through them in the minds of hundreds of Sisters of the community.

Although he never used the modern term, Father Mazzuchelli was a pioneer leader in Christian social living. Out of the area which he served, there later arose the bishops who laid the foundations of education in the Catholic University of America, for the guidance of Catholic citizens in their relations with other citizens of the nation. Ireland, Keane, and Spalding grew into mature vision close to the rivers and forests and fields which Mazzuchelli had traversed. Not accident, but soul kinship drew them and Mother Emily together, to merge into the wide movements of responsible citizenship which had their awakening in the upper Mississippi

Valley in the twenty years which convoyed the nineteenth into the twentieth century.

Trail blazer that he was, Father Samuel had to set markings in the forest of minds when he could no longer cut through a physical wilderness. Everywhere around him he saw evidence of how human weaknesses were causing human disasters. The Civil War was the result of greed, not only of Southern slave owners but of New England sea captains who had brought the slaves from Africa. Beyond the Civil War loomed the danger of a greater war caused by the greed of the few battening on the miseries of the many. There was only one way to prevent disaster. Men must be taught, not in their age when they would give too little heed, but in their childhood. They must learn in school that they must serve God by loving and serving their fellow men. Only religious teachers could give them that instruction; and it was therefore his task to train the religious teachers under him in the duties of citizenship so that they might, as they went out into their teaching, impart this knowledge to others. The method would be slow but the circle would widen as the years passed. How wide it was to become probably he, with all his vision, did not realize.

The necessity for civic teaching of the Catholics of the United States was acute. Great numbers of Catholics, especially Irish Catholics, had poured into the country during the fifties. This increased immigration brought about a labor and a political problem which expressed itself in the anti-Catholic riots and attempted domination by the Know-Nothing Party. The immigrants, confronted with this hostility and threatened by the imminence of a Civil War whose causes they only dimly understood, needed instruction in civic affairs. They needed it far more, to be sure, in the great cities of the eastern seaboard, notably in New York; but Father Mazzuchelli was hundreds of miles away from that metropolis, and his Dominican Sisters would not be inaugurating their famed curriculum at its Corpus Christi School until more than seventy years later. Good workman that he was, he took the material at hand for the task to be done.

From the beginning of his life on the frontier he had advocated and practiced the integration of Catholics into the American social body. The United States was not a Catholic country, but it afforded Catholics the opportunity, denied them in many lands, of becoming or remaining good Catholics. In addition to being Catholics, they were Americans, owing a debt to the nation. The fact that they were Catholics increased their responsibility in the payment of that debt. It did not set them apart from their fellow citizens. They must not isolate themselves in their Catholicity. Rather, they should use their faith to uplift themselves and help their neighbors in a citizenship which would bring about a general betterment.

"The grand truth of an all-seeing God, supreme Judge and Rewarder of good and evil, obliges man as member of a civil society, to keep the law both in private and in public that he may receive an eternal recompense from the Divine Lawgiver," the priest taught. "Thus does the religion of Christ serve as a solid foundation to human societies, by sanctifying the laws upon which it rests."

In his course of instruction he made a sharp distinction between the intention of the American Constitution and the occasional practices of certain citizens. His understanding of American political documents and institutions would seem amazing did not one remember the similarities which the Constitution and the Declaration of Independence bear to elements in the *Summa* of that great Dominican, St. Thomas Aquinas.

As a teacher, he had the advantage of practical experience. He knew his frontier, and the frontier knew him. There is no record of any missionary — even Father de Smet — enjoying the affectionate confidence of his non-Catholic fellow citizens to the extent that Father Mazzuchelli did. Even in the affairs of the church he had a sense of responsibility toward the entire community. Once he had written in the *Northwestern Gazette and Galena Advertiser*, "I deem that accounts of public edifices, especially those built by liberal contributions of the people, should be made known to the community through the voice of the press."

As early as 1860 he was telling the Sisters that the rapid growth of great fortunes, held by the few at the expense of, and injustice to, the many, would eventually create great disturbances, even anarchy and bloodshed, unless teachers of religion could educate all the people into finding solutions for these pressing problems. "The love of God above all things and of our neighbor as ourselves essentially requires," he taught, "that every follower must not only render unto God what belongs to God, but also that we must live with our equals in that peace and harmony which we ourselves wish to enjoy." It is unlikely that he had come on the phrase that religion was the opiate of the people, but he answered the deistic reasoning that led to its coinage by showing that the Christian religion had inspired and would continue to inspire men to perform their noblest deeds on earth for their country or for the smaller community surrounding them. Morality, he said, teaches us to love one another as friends and brothers so that the relation in which we stand to one another should form the most indissoluble of all unions.

"It is our most sacred duty," he told his eager listeners, "to defend the rights and liberties of this land, even to the cost of our lives, when so required; because having our patriotism strengthened and invigorated by the love of God and our neighbor, we are necessarily inducted into the obligation of becoming useful members of society, of doing good to all around us, of loving all our citizens without distinction as brothers, whether friends or enemies, infidels or Christians, Catholics or Protestants, all being the object of our affection, especially in the defense of their spiritual or temporal privileges. So sublime is the system of Christianity, that it teaches us, while we are engaged in the things of this life, to have our eyes continually turned toward the joys and glories of heaven as the reward of good deeds accumulated in the faithful performance of our civil as well as our religious duties upon earth."

"Unless the Lord keepeth the city," he told his students to set down in their hearts, as well as in their notebooks, "he watcheth in vain who keepeth it."

In her own family Sister Mary Emily had an example of civic

service. Father Louis Power, who had been for three years president of the boys' college at Sinsinawa, was transferred by his Order
to Memphis in 1863. Even then yellow fever was raging there,
although not in the epidemic proportions of four years later. Father
Power did all he could to care for the sick and the dying. He
served as chaplain to men of the Union Army stationed in the
neighborhood. Then, realizing that there were men in the Confederate forces equally in need of his priestly offices, he appealed
to General Forrest for permission to go to them. The general
pointed out that the priest's life would be in danger through every
hour, but he sent him off on a federal gunboat to the point where
he could make contact with the Confederate authorities. One of
the officers of the gunboat continually taunted him about his faith,
but the priest did not even report him to his commanding officer.
The Confederates allowed him to go into their lines where he
gave solace to hundreds of dying men, many of them not of
his faith.

Knowledge of her half-brother's courage, not in one cause alone,
but in the aid to men of differing causes, must have had deep
influence upon young Sister Emily. She herself could always see
beyond immediacies. Unswayed by any inherited partisanship of
North or South, she could, with Father Samuel, look below and
beyond the conflict and see evidences of difficulties which would
not be solved by the War between the States.

In the Benton school she could see the social inequalities which
existed even in this land of the free. The uniform could not make
all girls equal, could not transform different ways of thinking,
of living. God was in His heaven, but in spite of Browning all
was not well with the world. There was a way however to make
it right. Prayer? Yes, and work, the work of teaching. That was
the Dominican ideal. She did not wait until she had authority over
others to put the theory into practice. Sister Emily started with
herself, telling the children whom she taught and monitored that
they should learn to obey Christ's own commandment to love
their neighbors. She showed them how they could prove this
love for one another. They must respect the rights of other

children as well as of their elders. They must respect those who helped them; not only their parents, their pastor, their teachers, but the humbler helpers. They must be kind, but, first of all, they must be honest and they must be just to others. That was the teaching of Christ. If all men followed it, there would be no wars, no dreadful conflicts. Even if all men did not listen and learn, it was nonetheless the duty of these listening children to heed the Word of God.

Women who were children in her classes spoke in later years of her effect upon them. "She could make us want to be good," one of them said. "She never preached to us or at us. She simply talked. But she never went away from us without leaving us the feeling that we could and would do our work better and be kinder to one another."

In the convent, as in the school, heavier duties fell upon her. Her mother could have told her that the Lord broadens the shoulder to the burden, and it was probably with memory of the manner in which Bridget Power had taken on her responsibilities that her daughter assumed her own. In a little while she was one of the most highly valued members of the community, doing her own assigned work, and filling in for others. Before she was twenty years old the Benton convent came to know the meaning of loss as it had already known the meaning of sacrifice. On January 17, 1864, Sister Clara Conway died. Father Samuel entered the statement of her death upon his *Record*. It was the last entry he made.

On February 16 there raged around Benton one of those midwinter blizzards which are long recalled in the regions they strike. Freezing winds tore down from the north over icy roads and high-drifted snow. The storm was at its worst when a sick call came to the priest. Its urgency sped him so that he took no time to guard himself against the snow and sleet as he hurried away with the messenger. When he came back, hours later, he was seized by a chill which turned into a fever. The Sisters sent at once for Doctor Ferris, but pneumonia came even sooner. For a week the physician and the Sisters fought for the life of the priest who meant so much to all of them. By prayer and by nursing they sought to save him. Through that time he spoke sometimes to his nurses, striving to comfort and counsel them. Then, on the morning of February 23, the Reverend Samuel Mazzuchelli set out on his longest journey. His last words were the beginning of that psalm of praise,

Quam dilecta tabernacula tua, Domine.

It was the end of a lifetime of high dedication to the service of God, of daring adventure, of wide service to his fellow men in affairs temporal and spiritual; but, when he died, the one quality for which he was most deeply mourned, and by which he was longest remembered by his neighbors was his kindness. Through his account book run the entries: To an Orphan . . . To a Poor Child . . . To a Family in Need. Nothing, except Brownson's *Review,* for himself. No wonder the old lead mining region loved him. No wonder the sad Sisters grieved for him through the years. No wonder the region he helped to build has cherished his memory for nearly a century.

Father Mazzuchelli's death shocked and grieved not only the Benton community but the whole wide area of his activities. In spite of the storm, mourners came from Dubuque and Galena as well as from the smaller towns of the neighborhood. From farther places came messages of condolence to the Sisters. Governors of three states, senators, congressmen, lawyers, doctors, businessmen, miners, farmers, teachers and housewives paid tributes that mounted into a mighty paean of praise for the good works of his years on the frontier.

Men who had known him in Green Bay, in Prairie du Chien, in Davenport, Burlington, Iowa City, in the legislature at Belmont sighed at his passing, knowing how greatly he had enriched their lives and the lives of their children. Always, from the first day he had come to the Mississippi River Valley he had been their brother in citizenship, sometimes leading them to better standards, always helping them. For them his death was the end of an era that had been hard but happy in its achievements. With him the first frontier of the Middle Border had ended. Others would carry on the work he had begun; but the valley would never know another Father Samuel Mazzuchelli.

Before his burial in the little Benton churchyard Sister Catherine Mey died. Before the end of the year typhoid fever broke out in the school which now numbered more than a hundred pupils. Four girls died, one of them sixteen-year-old Fannie Sterling, whose father, a major in the Union Army, consented just before her death to her plea that he sanction her baptism in the Catholic Church. Then Mother Joanna Clark died.

On Christmas Day of 1864, a day almost as troubled for the nation as for the Benton Convent, Sister Regina Mulqueeny was elected Prioress of St. Clara. The work of the institution had to go on. Even the Annals resumed the recording of events. In them are set down these entries:

"April 9, 1865. This day at Appomatox General Robert E. Lee, Commander-in-Chief of the Confederate forces, surrendered to General Ulysses S. Grant. Nothing was ever so noble as General Grant's conduct. He only asked Confederates to lay down their arms, and let them — in fact, told them to — keep their horses 'for the spring ploughing.' He then had 25,000 rations issued to the starving soldiers. A new kind of victory and surrender for all to remember. America does no small things.

"April 14, 1865. Good Friday. Our President has been shot by a fanatic. The assassin is a Southerner, an actor. This is the greatest misfortune that can befall the stricken South. Lincoln's justice, kindliness, and common sense would have made him their wisest, most powerful friend. Now the North is mad with rage."

On the Tuesday after Easter, Mother Regina was re-elected, and Sister Mary Emily Power was made Subprioress. There began for both academy and convent a period which, although overshadowed by the loss of Father Mazzuchelli, Mother Joanna, and Sister Clara, showed marked progress. The school grew to an enrollment of eighty-nine students, and on July 23, 1865, the Right Reverend Thomas L. Grace, the Dominican Bishop of St. Paul, officiated at the reception of nine novices.

At the Bishop's request and at the end of July, the community sent five Sisters to open the Convent of Bethlehem in Faribault, Minnesota. In years to come the presence of Sisters in the Minnesota town was to create a problem not yet solved. At the time the most important phase of the event for Sister Emily must have been the fact that her two sisters, Catherine and Anastasia, now Sister Gertrude and Sister Veronica, were leaving Benton. Since Mother Regina went north with the five Sisters, her temporary absence left Sister Emily, just twenty-one years old, in charge at Benton. In the weeks of her authority she not only supervised the ordinary routine of the convent, but also the work on the new stone building, started by Father Mazzuchelli and never destined to be completed.

By March of 1867 affairs in Academy and Convent had progressed so well that the Board of Trustees of the Benton Female Academy made a momentous decision.

The Dominican Fathers at Sinsinawa had decided to sell the property which Father Mazzuchelli had turned over to them. The war, taking the services of many priests of the Order, had made the closing imperative. The Dominicans made a legal transfer of the property to the Right Reverend John Martin Henni, Bishop of Milwaukee. He was to hold the place in trust until the sale was accomplished. The sale was made to William Ryan of Galena, who had been Father Mazzuchelli's warm friend. He and his brother used the land for farming but were not using the buildings. Rumor came to Benton that William Ryan was offering the property for sale to several religious communities.

The Board of Trustees at Benton considered the situation. The Sisters had the sentimental thought that Sinsinawa had been their first home, the place of their origin as a community. It was, however, not in a town, and six miles from a railroad. The physical difficulties of establishing and maintaining an academy and convent there were tremendous. Students and supplies would have to be carted and trucked uphill in all kinds of weather. Would the students who came to Benton be willing to go so far from a town? Would the Sisters be able to carry the debt they must incur if they bought the place?

On the other hand, what if another teaching Sisterhood took over Sinsinawa? How would this affect the attendance at the Benton school? And what would their beloved Father Samuel have thought of their letting another group carry on the work in the place of his first choice?

The Board voted to purchase Sinsinawa.

Mother Regina and Sister Alberta Duffy went to the Ryans. William Ryan and his wife welcomed them cordially in the best parlor of their handsome home in Galena. The Sisters expounded their proposition. They had no cash. They had used every cent on the construction work of the new stone building. All they could offer was their promise. William Ryan shook his head. "You'd never be able to carry the debt," he said kindly. They protested their eventual ability but he stood firm. "I'm thinking of you as much as of myself," he declared. "It can't be done, not even by you."

They went away, weeping. Mrs. Ryan, seeing their tears, went back to her husband. "We've seen what they've done in Benton, William," she said, "and when they say they'll do it at Sinsinawa, they'll do it. Give them a chance!"

There is today, on the slope of the Mound, a beautifully kept cemetery, not the Sisters', which arouses the curiosity of visitors. Known as the Ryan Cemetery, it holds, in death, the mortal bodies of the Ryans, William and his wife, their children and their grandchildren, and gives lasting testimony of the Community's gratitude. For William Ryan gave them the chance they sought and for which his wife pleaded. On March 31, 1867, the deeds were signed.

On April 15, Mother Regina died.

Three weeks later, on the Feast of St. Pius V, that illustrious Dominican who foresaw in vision the victory of Don John of Austria in the crucial battle of Lepanto, Sister Mary Emily Power, twenty-three years old, was elected Prioress of St. Clara.

Under arrangements made before her election, the annual commencement of 1867, its thirteenth, was the last one held at the Benton academy. Clara Stevens and Julia Curran were awarded diplomas. Nearly every one of the eighty-seven students received premium awards. By that time there was an array of Powers: Mollie, Amelia, Mary, and Nellie from Iowa, probably all of them daughters of David, the eldest Power half-brother. Alice, the sister of Sister Gertrude, Sister Veronica, and Sister Emily, was registered from Iowa, although at the time Bridget was living in Benton. Margaret, who had entered the school in 1860, was an old graduate, already teaching in a public school. There were, as usual, girls from far places, Washington and Canada, Tennessee and California; and on the list was Minniowa Burns whose first name indicated the settling of the interstate dispute which Father Mazzuchelli had once recorded.

Father Samuel had been dead more than three years but his principles and his methods had not died. Clara Stevens not only read an essay upon the Invisible World, but led the discussion of that ageless though worn topic, *Is the Mind of Woman Superior to that of Man?* The Galena newspaper correspondent seemed to think the decision was a draw; but Clara was fairly well satisfied with her presentation of the affirmative.

The Sisters, who had struggled through four terrible years, knew that this was the final function in the old school. Already another plan had been arranged, another site taken. For the first time they had made a definite, drastic change without the counsel of their beloved Father Samuel. Their only guaranty against a failure that would spell disaster for them was the fact that their Prioress was the twenty-three-year-old Mother Mary Emily.

On August 15, 1867, twenty years after Father Samuel's original foundation of the Community, Mother Emily led back the Sisters to Sinsinawa. What fears, what doubts she must have suffered at apprehension of the trials of this overwhelming venture she never told. There is a story that, leading the Sisters, she knelt down to pray at the threshold of the old stone building, and rose with a smile of strength.

"Every day," she said, "we must keep asking God to help us in this work we have undertaken to do. We must work as if work alone could win for us; and we must pray as if prayer alone could win. I think," she added as her keen gaze went over the buildings and the farm on the wide-stretching hillside, already a little dilapidated for want of care, "that we shall need a great deal of both work and prayer. Let us begin."

CHAPTER SEVEN

Sinsinawa: Second Planting
1867–1877

1

THE way to Sinsinawa, physical as well as spiritual, goes uphill. Everything — fuel and food, implements and machinery, dry goods and furniture, grand pianos and libraries, must be carted from railway stations in the valley up the long, rising miles to the Mound. In 1867 — the year of the return of the Sisters to the site of their foundation — horses and oxen toiled to bear their burdens over the Illinois and Wisconsin roads that were sometimes rivers of mud. Only the association of the American spirit of pioneering with the Dominican spirit of intellectual activity could have successfully endured the difficulties of establishing a girls' school and a convent on the top of a hill miles from town or railroad.

Even today men in the neighborhood recall how in their childhood caravans of coal wagons used to come every autumn from Cuba City, Dubuque, or Galena, bringing the winter supply of coal to the Mound. At the foot of each steep hill one wagon waited for another. The team of horses was unhitched from the second wagon and added to the team on the first. The second waited until its team returned, then, with the team from a third wagon, followed up the hill. Often, a caravan leaving Cuba City at dawn did not reach its destination until dark.

Everything else brought to the Mound came under commensurate difficulties. Purchases made in Dubuque had to cross the Mississippi River before the long climb began. Express or freight from Chicago must be called for in Dunleith, now East Dubuque, or Galena. Students must be met at trains and taken back to trains. Before the happy invention of the telephone, doctors, needed in emergencies, were summoned by hard-driving messengers. Probably no one had greater reason for gratitude to Alexander Graham Bell than had the Sisters at Sinsinawa.

Although the project of return to the Mound had not been Mother Emily's idea, the responsibility of carrying it out fell upon her young shoulders. One of the youngest of the community which included her own two elder sisters, she had to make the momentous decisions upon which depended the continuance of the group. To put these decisions into effect she had to overcome what must have seemed insuperable obstacles. Probably the most significant element in this period of her history is that there is neither record nor tradition that any one of the Sisters doubted her ability to accomplish what they had chosen her to do.

The community was deeply in debt, mortgaged to the Ryans for the purchase price of the institution, and owing several other sizable bills. The only sources of income were student tuition and the small amounts sent by the few mission schools. The Benton records of 1867 show that more than $1,000 was due on student accounts, little of it ever to be paid. The July income, including nearly $350 earned by the teachers in Mineral Point and New Diggings, was less than another $1,000. The July expenditures were over $1,500. The income for August, the month when the Sisters returned to Sinsinawa, was a little more than $500 while the expenditures were nearly $350; but in September and the succeeding months of that year the output again exceeded the income.

In spite of the meager income and in spite of the high prices of this period following the Civil War, Mother Emily calmly made plans for improvement and expansion of the institution. The old stone building, erected by Father Mazzuchelli, required and received complete renovation. In addition, a steam heating plant was installed. Plans for an exhibition hall, to cost more than $9,000, were made and construction started. The amazing circumstance is that all these bills were paid, even though a considerable part of the bills owed by the students was never paid.

Only by the almost incredible self-sacrifice of the Sisters could these results have been achieved. The record books reveal indirectly how little the members of the community spent for their own comfort. Not a single luxury is on the list of what they bought, unless one includes butter which was high in price; but that butter was used for the girls' table, not for the Sisters'. The purchase of pianos, harps, and other musical instruments was in the nature of investment for the future of the academy; and the subscription price of $10 for the Des Moines *Leader* must be counted as payment for that association with current events which Father Mazzuchelli had counseled.

The labor costs were constant, although not high compared with modern standards. Most of these payments are listed under the names of the laborers, except a few set down as "to black- smith" or "to woodchoppers," evidently because these were made through an intermediary. There are several payments for "Jimmie," with notations "for ferriage" or "for purchases." Jimmie Kinsella, thanks to Father Mazzuchelli's direction that the Sisters should not go into the local shops, had become local purchasing agent for the Mound. Sister Magdalen, the bursar, used to give him a list of articles needed, and he would go up and down Main Street in Benton on his shopping errands. Jimmie was also the Mound's horse trader.

"I used to do quite a bit of horse trading for the Sisters," he said later. "One day I had just traded a horse and was going home from Benton when a little girl — Maggie Mallarkey she was — told me that Mother Emily was in town and wanted to go back to the Mound that day. I says, 'She can't go.' Maggie says, 'She must go.' I says, 'Well, if she must go, she goes. But I just traded for a little horse, and he is the meanest little rat on earth. She is liable to have to walk halfway.' Well, I took Mother Emily and a load of trunks. When we were well out of town, two fellows stopped us for a trade again. I used to trade horses every day, pretty near. I says, 'I can't stop to talk to you now. I'll see you tomorrow.' And I did."

Better than Jimmie knew, he paid tribute to Mother Emily in

his failure to mention her reaction to the wild ride he must have given her behind the "meanest little rat." Everyone who knew her spoke of her fearlessness. Jimmie emphasized it by taking it completely for granted. "If she must go, she goes" probably characterized the Mother Emily of 1867 as thoroughly as it would have painted the Mother Emily of the year when she went to Rome or of the year when she added the college to the academy. The incident was also characteristic of the young Superior's effect upon her associates. If she had to do something, they did what they could to help her in the doing.

The going was particularly hard in 1871. Already those storm clouds that were to grow into the thunderhead of 1873 were above the horizon. The number of students had decreased from the 125 of 1867, and payments for them also began to decrease. Some parents and guardians paid in full when bills were due but the great majority either paid in dribbles or paid not at all. With all her amazing ability in other business transactions, Mother Emily seems to have had a soft spot about insisting upon payment for students. Unquestionably, the memory of Father Samuel's kindness to the Power family must have influenced her as much as did her natural Irish generosity. But bills grew and grew, and had to be met.

The price of board and tuition was, to the students, $175 a year, with quarterly charges of $3 each for washing and bedding. Piano lessons cost $12 a quarter, harp lessons $20, guitar $6, singing $5 — but voice cultivation cost double that amount — while drawing cost $5 and painting $2. Latin, French, and Italian each cost $5 a quarter. With an enrollment of seventy to more than a hundred students, this should have brought a considerable income. It completely failed to do so, even in good years, because of the negligence of many parents and guardians.

"Do their other creditors treat them as we do?" Sister Magdalen asked one day. "And listen to what our creditors say to us!"

There was a debt of $1,100, due a man who had sold them cattle. He came, time and again, for his money. Mother Emily was making every effort to obtain it for his payment, but all her labors were unavailing. The creditor came with a final demand. Standing in the hall of the old stone building, he told her that he had now come to do what he had been threatening. He would take away, by legal process, the cattle he had sold them. "If we had the money, we would give it to you at once," Mother Emily said.

"You have the money," the man persisted. "How else can you have this beautiful building and these handsome grounds?"

"But we have no money now."

"Then I'll have the papers served and take the cattle."

"You'll be taking down our fences," Mother Emily said, knowing that the use of the cattle helped to support them.

While they were still talking in the hall, a strange little woman came to the front door. The Sister Portress answered her knock. Still standing outside, and without preamble the little woman drew from the folds of her capacious skirt a heavy black bag. She gave it to the Sister. "Take that," she said. "I want a home."

"Come in," said the Sister and led her to a bench in the hall. Then, still unknowing what the bag contained, the Sister drew Mother Emily away from her angry visitor and into the nearby dining room. Together they opened the bag. In it were gold pieces, enough of them to count up to exactly the $1,100 of the debt. Mother Emily called in the little stranger. The woman told how she had managed to hold this money for her own protection when her brother in Dubuque took everything else she had "to invest for her." She had seen the building at Sinsinawa, and thought it some kind of home. She was not old but she was friendless. "Please keep me," she begged. "We'll keep you," Mother Emily promised. She stayed with them through the rest of her lifetime; and she became Sister Cleophas, one of their most devoted and beloved Sisters. The cattle man, however, knowing less of miracles, gravely doubted the word of the Sisters that the money had just come to them. "You had it all the time," he said ungraciously.

In 1873 there were more than seventy students at the Mound; but in September of that year, the usual time for the first quarterly payments, the bills of only two students had been paid in full, and partial payment made for only four others. In October, only one more student was paid for, in November, only eight more. In these four months however the institution paid bills amounting to more than $5,000; and yet the only apparent contribution to the community was the $11.50 given by one Mollie Power "for tea!"

In spite of struggle, or perhaps because of it, the academic phase of the school — rechartered in 1868 under the laws of Wisconsin as The St. Clara Academy — progressed on an even keel through that difficult decade which followed the War Between the States. Most noticeable, after its change in setting from Benton, was the change in the geographical and social backgrounds of its students. The roster of the Benton school showed plainly the influence of the South. The names of girls — Missouri, Virginia, Georgia, Louisiana, Tennessee — revealed, not only their places of birth, but also the strong political bias of their parents. Children of men brought north by the opportunities for money-making in the lead mines, they seldom identified themselves with the northern countryside, although they maintained persisting loyalty to the school.

With the southerners almost completely eliminated from the upper Illinois and lower Wisconsin countryside by the war and the slowing down of the lead-mining industry, the girls of the mellifluous names and the soft drawls were no longer in the northern schools. Only a little company from Tennessee came into the class which arrived in 1867. To Sinsinawa, in their stead, were coming the daughters of Illinois, Iowa, and Wisconsin farmers and merchants, legislators and judges. Even in its first year of 1867, the academy was attracting the group from which Father Mazzuchelli had dreamed of forming the Sisterhood: young women of the region with natural understanding of American problems. Characteristic of his guidance, too, was his acceptance of the provision of Wisconsin law that "the religious principles of pupils of any denomination are not interfered with." Where Benton had not required it, however, Sinsinawa directed that all students should attend the public religious exercises.

The course of study was much like that of Benton: arithmetic, grammar, composition, ancient and modern history in the first year; higher arithmetic, algebra, ancient history, Latin and French in the second, with a *soupçon* of philosophy; Latin, French, geometry, rhetoric, astronomy, and philosophy in the third year; and Latin, French, botany, physiology, chemistry, intellectual philosophy, miscellaneous writing, and domestic economy in the fourth. Many Catholic schools of this period had, of course, somewhat similar courses. The "intellectual philosophy" and the appellation of "domestic economy" to sewing and cooking courses were unique. These were the courses required for all students. For the Catholic students was added the requirement of Christian Doctrine courses throughout the four years. This was also a requirement for the Fifth Class, better known as the Minims, who were also being trained in the fundamentals of reading, writing, and arithmetic.

Music was stressed, with Sister Alberta Duffy as teacher. Jennie Duffy, graduating with Annie Shane and Annie Reynolds in 1868, won a first premium for "thorough bass and harmony" as well as for Latin and Italian. She also received a medal for superior good conduct and politeness — but so did Annie Reynolds and Annie Shane.

Probably all the girls at Sinsinawa would have qualified for these medals. Mother Emily was insistent upon the maintenance of discipline, not harsh but constant. She also put into practice the precept of Father Samuel, "Never, never, never slam a door!" To her, as to him, rudeness was an invasion of the rights of the other individual. Everyone owed everyone else a pleasant "good morning" and equally pleasant "good evening." Good manners were not taught with formality. The girls learned to curtsy, but, hour by hour, they also learned consideration of others.

The old stone house was amazingly pleasant. Unchanged in structure from the original plan, it had been revised in use. The wide hall of its center was bisected by another hall, a plan which held on its four floors. The kitchen and the girls' refectory occupied the east half of the first floor. On the west side were the parlors, the guests' dining room and the Sisters' refectory. Sister

Romana Spillane, writing years later, said that St. Dominic must have loved that refectory, which also served as chapter room and community room, because it showed the practical application of holy poverty. "If one had a knife," she recalled, "her neighbor boasted a fork or spoon. To have a cup *and* a saucer was more than anyone expected. But this was never a cause for fault-finding. The privation was usually a subject of merriment."

The second floor was divided into a study hall — taking one half of the floor space — the girls' recreation hall, Mother Emily's room and one adjoining, "the Cabinet," where Sister Stanislaus taught art and where treasures brought from Benton were stored.

The third floor, west, was divided into music rooms and classrooms; the east into harp rooms, the minims' dormitory and classrooms, and the lamp room. Only by realization that kerosene oil provided most of the illumination of the 1860's and 1870's, can one understand how important was that room, presided over by old Sister Aloysia Cashman, which also served for meeting place as well as storage space. No one could estimate the friendships cemented by hasty confidences given and received while Sister Aloysia filled the lamps.

In the classrooms, through those earliest years, Sister Benedicta Kennedy held classes in Christian Doctrine, Latin, geometry, history, and chemistry. Coming from Boston, she also slipped in instruction in etiquette, although it was not set down in the catalogue. She was also prefect, on duty from early morn until the last student was in bed. Next to Mother Emily, she was one of the greatest influences upon the lives of the girls under her care. Brisk of manner, quick of movement, she expressed her deep piety in devotion to her task of teaching. She was a born teacher in the best New England tradition; and she made scholars of students by force of her personality.

Mother Emily taught French, Sister Alberta, Italian. Both of them had studied the languages with Father Mazzuchelli, but there must have been days when only prayer and effort kept them ahead of their fast-moving classes. Sister Stanislaus, Sister Boniface, and Sister Gonzaga taught other subjects while Sister

Josephine conducted needlework until the coming of the indomitable Sister Lucina to that task.

The fourth floor had the girls' dormitories, Sister Benedicta presiding over one, Sister Stanislaus over the other. From this floor rose the most distinguishing feature of the building, the glassed cupola with its splendid view of three states. Only occasionally was its door unlocked; but youth sometimes found ways of climbing upward to enjoy both view and the triumph of having accomplished the nearly impossible.

Sister Ignatia had charge of the prayer bells. Sister Catherine, the infirmarian, had a cure-all, a cup of senna which the girls loathed so much that they hated to acknowledge illness. Sister Sabina was the breadmaker, always a most important post in a Dominican convent since the days of St. Catherine of Siena, who herself fasted mightily but who dwelt in a house famous for its bread. Few in number though the Sisters were, they managed not only the school but also, with very little masculine help, the farm which helped to feed and support the institution. In those years the Sinsinawa habit of harvest work in the fields and orchards became part of its tradition. Long before the day of the deep freeze, Sister Martha had to find ways of keeping — without ice — meats and vegetables and fruits for the winter months. She succeeded so well that St. Clara's held the reputation it had established in Benton for giving its students good food as well as a good education.

Education, to Mother Emily, was only partly represented by the courses of study set down in its catalogue. Mental training was excellent, but other trainings must have their place in her scheme. Years in advance of other educators in the same field, she insisted upon using education not as an end, but as a means toward those objectives now recognized as essential in the building of good American citizenship: bodily health, economic well-being, social virtue, cultural development, and moral perfection. Long before Dr. Thomas E. Shields worked out his plan for the betterment of Catholic education, before Monsignor Edward Pace went to Germany to bring back a revolutionary idea of educational psychology, even before Monsignor George Johnson was born, Mother Emily, following the ideals of Father Mazzuchelli, was putting into effect a system based on fundamental relationships, aimed at definite objectives, and designed to train the individual not in part but wholly, in order to fit body, mind, and soul for Christian social living.

Fortunately, both for her and for the plan, she had teachers trained as she had been, by Father Mazzuchelli. With her, they had an awareness of the needs they must meet. They knew that the girls coming to Sinsinawa were, upon graduation, returning to comfortable homes, well above the line of poverty but where their individual efforts would still be needed as a contribution to economic safety.

Most of these girls would marry, sooner or later. Some of them, temporarily or permanently, would become public school teachers. A few would become artists, writers, musicians. All of them must be given the basic training to keep them good Christian members of a democratic society. All of them must be given general training for their probable way of life and special training for the particular way of life for which they thought they had a vocation.

The academy was small enough in its beginnings to solve these problems by individual instruction. Mother Emily herself taught some classes. More importantly, she taught girls. Never sentimental — except, perhaps, when an Irish song was sung — she met the students with a friendliness which let no one step over a certain barrier of reserve. She had, however, an electric quality of challenge which startled and inspired. Those who caught that spark knew ever afterward, even without other testimony, that Mother Emily was a great woman, and they made her personality a yardstick for the measuring of other women leaders of her time.

Her realism, born in the trials of her childhood and not abated by frontier conditions, constantly kept her aware of the future needs of the students. If they were going to put their learning to professional use, well and good. St. Clara had always encouraged the mental development of women. If they were going to use it only for betterment of their domestic life, that also was well and good. William Rainey Harper, coming westward three decades later, was to say that a man might not be a better blacksmith for knowing Greek but he would probably be a happier human being. Mother Emily, in the late sixties and early seventies, was telling the girls at the Mound that they might not need Latin and Italian, French and German to improve the doing of their house-wifely tasks upon Midwestern farms but that they would find the broadening of their horizons of the highest value to themselves and their families. She added bookkeeping to the courses with the declaration that every woman should know it, and she retained needlework with the comment that every woman could use it.

Like the Benton commencement programs, the early records of Sinsinawa show the preoccupation of the headmistress with questions of the day, particularly those related to the condition of women. In 1869 there was a discussion on "Woman Suffrage" given by the senior students at the exercises, a procedure far more revolutionary than can rightly be estimated by the progres-sive debaters of our era. The Eaglets of the Mound, as they called themselves, undoubtedly owed much of their liberalism to their location in a state already rising to leadership on social issues; but they also owed Mother Emily a debt of gratitude in that she did not clip their young wings. Under her shrewd tutelage they studied and talked, and studied more and talked with greater surety; and they usually left the Mound with a clear impression of where they stood on current issues.

There was plenty of work at Sinsinawa but there was also plenty of play. Can anyone imagine such diverse personalities as Victorine Rice and Kitty O'Neill of Tennessee; Susie Earnest, Cora Van Osdell, and Adelaide Brisbois of Wisconsin; Ida Halleck of Iowa; Ada Booker of Illinois; and Julia Farley of Colorado Territory, all set down under one roof without the striking of sparks? To say nothing of Minniowa Burns whose very name suggested the armis-tice of two competing states? But if there was diversity of some opinion there was unity on other points, particularly on the attitude of the girls toward one of the few required articles of uniform.

Each girl was expected to bring an underwear outfit which included six night wrappers, six underdrawers, six pairs of cotton hose, six pairs of woolen hose, six chemises, two bathing gowns, and two uniforms. The winter uniform, worn only on Sundays, was a black dress and cloak, with a white nubia. The summer uniform was a black dress and white Swiss waist. No particular dress was required for weekdays. Veils were worn to chapel six days a week; but on Sundays the girls were required to wear to chapel a white slatted sunbonnet with blue ribbons. This article of dress was most heartily detested by all of them but, in time, out of their detestation, jokes arose about the sunbonnet which made graduates almost nostalgic in their remembrance of the monstrosity. By the end of the seventies the nubia was displaced by a hat, but the despised sunbonnet held into the eighties.

The local stagecoach was one of the few outer-world excitements. The stage from Galena arrived at the Mound every Tuesday, Thursday, and Saturday in the late afternoon, and returned to Galena on alternate days. The daily stage from Dunleith came at varying hours, dependent upon the time of arrival of the train from Chicago, and left in the early afternoon. The coaches brought new students, parents, other visitors. Their coming created an excitement which ran like a current through classrooms and study halls, even though the girls could not see the arriving guests. Visits were officially welcome only on Thursdays and expressly forbidden on Sundays. Nevertheless, the stages seldom came without guests for the Mound, even though Dominican hospitality had often to be strained to meet them.

The isolation of the Mound was both benefit and handicap in its process of education. There seems to have been, in its early years, little of that community association which had distinguished Father Mazzuchelli's school in Benton. The students, coming for the most part from greater distances, had less immediate communication with their own homes and families. Letters to parents were supervised, if not censored, and letters from parents were read by the school authorities, a procedure not used in Father Samuel's time. The atmosphere, like that of nearly all American convent schools of that era, was on the restrictive side, a heritage of French and Irish education, ameliorated only by the personalities of the administrators. There may have been times when the remoteness of the location, in spite of its beauty and healthfulness, pressed down on the spirits of young girls. Even though the catalogue promised in the exuberant language of the period, that "weak intellects will become strong, and the strong will be made stronger," there must have been difficulty in preparing girls for later social responsibility. Only awareness of the problems of the outer world and determination to help these students in solving them could have made the school a success. Teachers had to be always several steps ahead of their students, not only in academic lore, but in its periphery.

Keeping the balance was Mother Emily's particular problem. She had to see that discipline was maintained and also to make sure that it was not upheld at the cost of a pleasant good will. Girls might acquire much useful knowledge in one year at a school, but they did not come back if they disliked the environment in which they were placed.

"Mother Emily is a great Sister," a priest who had long known her once said of her. "She is also a fine business woman." She had to be. Even into our own days, presidents of colleges have been expected to combine academic and administrative abilities.

Unlike many schools of the period, St. Clara therefore offered the girls gay as well as healthful recreation. When the weather permitted they played outdoor games. When it did not, they danced and sang and recited. Some of them used their leisure for writing. The *Young Eagle*, appearing first in manuscript form in 1874, contains in nearly every succeeding issue chapters of delightful — if not literary — serials. Invariably, the story was sad. In one, a western tale, everyone died but the narrator. In another, the hero died so suddenly that the story had to cease. The general tone of the periodical was, in spite of the serials, blithe. The personals, probably the best circulation-builders, were sharply pointed. The advertisements, including those for a local livery stable and veterinary surgeon, were delightfully informal. One of them read:

LOOK HERE! ! !
Sister Josephine
is now ready
to supply her old customers
with
YANKEE NOTIONS! ! !

The advertisement probably enjoyed greater popularity than it would have won seven years earlier; for in 1874 no one of the seventy-four girls at the Mound had come from a Southern state. With the exception of two girls from New York, one from Ireland and one from California, all of them were daughters of the Middle Border. One of them, little Wehake LaBatte, was of Minnesota Indian ancestry.

The child had been brought to the Sisters in Faribault by her mother, a full-blooded Sioux. Her father, a French-Canadian trapper, had been killed in an Indian uprising. The mother, fearing for the life of her child, begged the Sisters to take Wehake. Sister Alberta brought her to the Mound. There she became the Academy delight, the first expression of the interracial good will that was to pioneer in the breaking down of racial barriers, and to distinguish the work of the Sinsinawa Dominicans in later years. She was a special joy to Mother Emily, to whom all children were dear; but she died while still a child, and is buried in the Sinsinawa cemetery. Her story became so much a part of the place that children, coming to the school, usually asked to be allowed to visit Wehake's grave. It was as if she had left, in her brief passing, something of her people's spirit of woods and trees that white children could find and enjoy through this evanescent association with her.

Nearly all the girls, especially those from distant homes, stayed at the Mound for Christmas. No one of them ever forgot the beauty of midnight Mass there. There was no chapel in the house. Sisters and students, as well as the Catholics of the neighborhood, worshiped at the Church of St. Dominic which Father Mazzuchelli had built. On Christmas Eve its windows shone golden with candlelight as the worshipers moved toward it through the clear, cold Wisconsin night. The little organ played softly as they entered. Then, as Christ came to each of them as He had come to earth, they knew the peace that the world has never given. As they went back to the old stone building, they looked up at stars which seemed as bright to them as had the stars over Bethlehem to the shepherds finding the Infant Saviour.

Epiphany brought another celebration, the giving out of the Epiphany cards. The chaplain presided over the drawing. Cards on which were written sentiments, either of piety or of humor, were placed in a bowl. Two of the girls drew them out, one by one, as the candidates waited in line. The chaplain read the card. Whether the sentiment was appropriate or inappropriate, gales of laughter followed his reading.

Some of the events were scheduled, others spontaneous. "Mother Emily gave us a half-holiday," run the reminiscences of students of the time. "Mother Emily gave us a cider and doughnut party. . . . Mother Emily told Sister Benedicta to take us nutting. . . . Mother Emily sent us for a sleigh ride. . . . Mother Emily let us put on a play, all our own. . . . Mother Emily told us we might have a Valentine party."

One of the sleigh rides became historic. Wendell Phillips was to lecture in Galena. Mother Emily decided that the older girls should hear the great orator from Boston. The day was gray and cold, but she had a big sleigh packed with hay and bundled in the senior girls, all warmly wrapped in blankets. They drove off, singing gaily. They arrived safely in Galena, listened to the golden-tongued Phillips, then started Mound-ward. Before they had mounted the first hill a driving snowstorm met them. Before they reached the second hill the road was invisible. The driver, avoiding snowdrifts, sought the higher spots, but unfortunately went into a ravine. For an hour everyone wondered if they could get out of it before the next morning. At last, however, the sleigh arrived at the Mound. "Mother Emily gave us all hot drinks," wrote the recorder. No one ever set down anything at all about Wendell Phillips.

One of the gayest episodes of the school was entirely unrehearsed. General Ulysses Simpson Grant, leaving the White House at the end of his second term, came home to Galena. All the way across the country from Washington he had been welcomed by cheering crowds. He had been in Galena only a little while when he accepted Mother Emily's invitation to visit Sinsinawa. He stipulated, however, that his visit must be entirely informal. He would come at his earliest convenience, but there must be no prepared reception for him. He kept his word, arriving unexpectedly Easter Monday when the girls were enjoying their boxes from home.

Mother Emily met the General and former President at the doorway, summoned the Sisters to the parlor, and then Sister Alberta took Grant and his party for a tour of the building. When they came to the third floor, the general mentioned the cupola which he had noticed from the road, and asked if he might go up to see the splendid view it must give. One of the Sisters opened the door to the heights.

At just that moment the Dolans, Mary and Anna, were striving to straighten the confusion of the tower which had become the scene of their private Easter Monday party. Mary had seized a broom and, with vigor, was using it. At the very moment the Sister opened the door below, an avalanche of dust went down the stairs, right into the face of the man who had been President. Luckily for the Dolans, the General had a real sense of humor. He went away, laughing so heartily that the too-vigorous cleaners received no reproof.

The great event of the year was, of course, Commencement. For months voices sang; and harps, guitars, and pianos — where were the violins? — sounded in preparation for the program that would continue through many hours of what would probably be the hottest day of the Wisconsin summer. The exercises took place in the Exhibition Hall which, in spite of its cost, Mother Emily had caused to be erected in the first year of her office.

In structure, the program of 1877 shows little variation from

Father Mazzuchelli's offerings of the early sixties. There were changes, of course, in the topics presented. "Greetings to Pio Nono," given by the Indian Wehake, and the "Jubilee Hymn" to the Holy Father, sung by all the pupils, had replaced, by 1877, the "Causes of the Civil War." Both choices revealed however an awareness of the association of current affairs with basic principles of philosophy. The freedom of the slave and the freedom of the Supreme Pontiff of the Church were surely not unrelated. If it was the mission of Father Samuel's time to emphasize the problems of the frontier, it was the mission of Mother Emily's time to show wider horizons to the children of that frontier, and on those horizons loomed large the issue of the right to physical freedom denied the Prisoner of the Vatican.

The exercises opened, as usual, with a grand entrance march, played on harps, guitars, and pianos. With twelve players operating on six pianos, the march must have been audible as far as Menominee. There were only six accompanists for the opening chorus. There were vocal solos, and cantatas. Six pianos again triumphed in "Gems of Ireland and Scotland." The Valedictory, untitled, was given by Maggie Tierney of Iowa. Wehake LaBatte played "Kathleen Mavourneen" on the harp. And, what was probably of minor interest that day but which is of deeper interest in the light of Sinsinawa history, Kitty Wall made her first appearance, representing the Minims as she gave the Salutatory.

Kitty Wall was to become the famous Sister Catherine, the artist, whose canvases continue to enrich and inspire the community. Her desire that the Sinsinawa Dominicans have a house for art study in Italy led her to write Myron Taylor, later President Roosevelt's representative at the Vatican, an inquiry about possible sites in Rome. The correspondence, begun in 1934, led the Taylors to give, after Sister Catherine's death, their own villa at Florence to the Holy Father, Pope Pius XII, with the request that the Sinsinawa Dominicans be permitted to use it for a School of Fine Arts. Sister Catherine's part in the foundation is commemorated by the Chapel of St. Catherine of Siena on the

hill of Florence, a long way from the Wisconsin hill of her childhood first appearance.

The day after commencement the girls put away Caesar and
Horace and Virgil, Fasquelle's *French Method,* Ollendorf's *Italian
Method,* and Adler's *German Literature,* together with textbooks
for mathematics and science and rhetoric. The "long" vacation,
then limited to the month of August, had begun. Sometimes a few
remained. These were Mother Emily's special care. Undoubtedly
the remembrance of her father's death gave her particular sympathy for the orphaned and the half-orphaned. When she died,
decades later, the mails to the Mound bore letter after letter
from women who had cherished the memory of her comforting
kindness to them when they had come in lonely sorrow to the
school. "She let me cry while she talked to me," ran their
refrain. "Then she took me to the chapel, knelt beside me, and
prayed with me. I never felt so miserable again."

Even with the happy, the untroubled, she had a closeness of
association which did not depend upon daily meetings. Because
children apprehend justice they knew that quality of her spirit.
She made rules and enforced them, but she never refused to listen
to a defense. She dealt punishments, but she never kept the
account open, once the penalty had been paid. She found latent
talents and forced their custodians to develop them. Waste of a
God-given ability was to her a mortal sin, and "You'll never know
what you can do until you've tried it," one of her mottoes.

As the institution grew, Mother Emily grew. Gifted with the
keen intellect and strong memory petitioned for in the Dominican
prayer, she apprehended and reached the best. With the usual
gravitation of molecules, greatness spun around toward greatness.
At Sinsinawa or away from it, the young Mother-General met men
and women who were setting the pattern of the coming day. It
was characteristic of her that she should know the comers better
than those already arrived in fame. Among these were John
Ireland — as the Reverend John Ireland he gave the crowns to
the 1868 graduates — and John Lancaster Spalding, whose bishop-

rics were still in the future, and Eliza Allen Starr. The Brownson association, too, was regarded as a tradition of the school, with the younger Orestes Brownson (son of the famous Orestes) coming as a lecturer, and with some of the Brownson children as students. Although the elder Orestes Brownson had long since attained reputation, he was still leading American economic thought up ways far truer and saner than most of his contemporaries knew. Mother Emily also met groups of thinkers not so well known but equally forward-looking, whom she would influence and who would influence her in their discussion of social and economic problems of the troubled seventies. It was a time of national travail and of national growth, and the young Superior of Sinsinawa enjoyed the growth even as she suffered the travail.

She drove herself far harder than she drove anyone else. Her light burned hours after she had sent Sisters and girls to bed. Only by reading, when all other tasks were done, could she keep up with what was going on in the world. Almost intuitively she knew that this knowledge of the trends and tendencies of her time was important, not so much to herself as to the community and to the Church. She was never to know how important would be her association of Christian teaching with current events; but then and there, in the eighteen sixties and seventies, on a Wisconsin hillside, miles from any town, she was already building a plan of training which would one day dovetail with the theories of other great educators to create a system for the general betterment of Catholic education in the United States.

2

Thirty-three Sisters, not all of them stationed at Sinsinawa, made up the membership of the community in 1867, the year when Mother Emily was elected Superior. During the next decade eighty-five Sisters were received. The young Mother Emily had the responsibility of their physical, intellectual, and spiritual welfare. Upon her devolved the threefold duty of providing food, clothing, and proper shelter; of training minds according to their capacities and for the special necessary purposes of the institution; and of administering the community's Rule and *Constitutions* as expounded by Father Mazzuchelli.

Hard though it was, provision for the physical well-being of the Sisters was the easiest of the three responsibilities. Market prices of foodstuffs were high; but, with the academy, the convent had the advantage of the farm produce. Some of the Sisters had been reared on farms and knew how to put their knowledge of farm methods to account. As a result, no one went hungry at St. Clara, although there must have been monotony of food during the long winter months.

Finding proper shelter for the community has always been a problem at Sinsinawa, with increasing numbers and restricted housing. The stone building lacked room for all the Sisters and some of them, as soon as the exhibition hall was completed, moved to a dormitory in that building. It was a makeshift dormitory, without curtains and with bed frames made of benches and old chairs upon which had been set straw or husk ticks. Sister Ignatia Fitzpatrick, the bell ringer, was among those who slept there, and she had to arise every morning on guessed time in order to consult the clock in the girls' dormitory, high in the stone building, before she could begin her duties. In time, of course, conditions were improved; but even the erection of a new, and comparatively huge, building years later gave the Sisters breathing space for only a little while, so rapid was the growth of the community.

Despite the facilities for hot and cold baths announced in the catalogue there persisted certain stringencies of living. Sometimes the hot water failed. Sometimes the cold water failed. Then Sisters had to pump and carry buckets of water up flights of steps. Cleaning was constant, but the impending arrival of high dignitaries sometimes caused a needless storm of soap and water. Once, when Bishop Henni of Milwaukee was coming, a complete cleaning even to the white-washing of walls, took place. Father Zara, then the chaplain, was so impressed by the activity that his entire conversation with the bishop as he escorted him about consisted of a reiterated statement, "Look, Bishop, nice and clean!"

There is a recorded memory that Mother Emily did not care for the implication that the place had ever looked other than gleaming.

The training of the Sisters for the work they could do in the community was a graver problem. Father Mazzuchelli had been insistent upon the improvement of teacher-efficiency since teaching was the primary purpose of the community. During his lifetime he himself undertook the major part of this training, although his record books show that he employed lay help at times in certain subjects. Within its limitations, Benton had been a normal school as well as convent and academy. His death had not overthrown his plan but it had left the Sisters without the benefit of his wise guidance. To fill the gap the Sisters had to find their own way, and in turn, show the way to others. The academy teachers — Mother Emily, Sister Benedicta, Sister Alberta, Sister Stanislaus, Sister Gonzaga, and Sister Josephine — had to train their co-workers and successors even while they taught the academy students.

Of these Mother Emily and Sister Benedicta were the outstanding educators, the former as policy maker and general administrator, the latter as an inspired and inspiring teacher. Sister Benedicta, who had come as a public school instructor from Boston to the Galena region, had seen Father Mazzuchelli and been influenced by his sermons, although she did not enter St. Clara until after his death. With a precision of manner which belied her soaring soul she taught the *how* and the *why* as well as the *what* of the material of education. Her endowments made her an exceptional teacher for the girls in the academy. Her ability made her memorable in the training of future teachers.

Sister Borromeo — the Clara Stevens of the Benton school — was another teacher whose outstanding personality and attainments contributed much to the rising power of St. Clara education. Less formal and more inspirational in a classroom than was Sister Benedicta, she possessed a remarkable sense of structure which proved a boon to the other teachers of the community. With Sister Benedicta she worked out a curriculum which was to develop into a tremendous influence. Under Mother Emily's direction they devised a plan which associated the usual secular studies of the period not only with religion, but with Father Mazzuchelli's teaching of the social responsibilities of religion. They continued to operate St. Clara as a classical school; and, realizing that its special function was training girls for successful womanhood, they prepared them to be teachers, writers, musicians, mothers of families, or nuns.

To perform this function the school must give them not only informational material but standards of Christian living. Some of the students might be brilliant, others mediocre, a few poor in mental equipment. To all of them Sinsinawa owed training that would better their lives and save their souls. The teaching Sisters never saw these as separate goals. They were closely interrelated. One should not be taught without the other. Religion, the basis of right living in this world and of salvation in the world to come, must not be pigeonholed into a compartment.

The textbooks of the period gave the teacher little help in the attainment of this objective. She had to get the necessary help from the teacher training of the community. This training, established by Father Mazzuchelli and maintained by Mother Emily, set the Sinsinawa tradition. Sister Borromeo's writing, much of it under the name of Carola Milanis, helped to keep alive the Benton tradition. Sister Benedicta's translation of Father Mazzuchelli's Memoirs, which set down his modest account of his tremendous pioneer struggles, also set in the minds of the Sisters in training their founder's standard of service in American citizenship. Under such direction a Sister student had to become civic-minded. If, in 1870, the graduates of the academy were discussing Woman Suffrage, it meant that the academy teachers were studying the subject in 1869.

In that decade of 1867–1877, there came to the St. Clara Convent young women who made deep impressions upon their associates and their students in the long years of their service for God. The roster of their names tells a story of wide achievement: Sister Raymond Cochrane, who had been the little Clara of Father Mazzuchelli's 1861 program in Benton, and who would be the first of a long line of music evangelists; Sister Alexius Duffy, whose historical perspective was cloudless except for her bias in Irish causes; Sister Reginald Kean, whose administrative ability showed speedily; Sister Seraphica Smith, to be long remembered by her parochial school students as a truly great teacher; Sister Romana Spillane and Sister Gregory Kelly, who would set steel into the minds and hearts of thousands of children in elementary schools; Sister Evangelist Bowman, who would teach a hundred topics as she taught art; Sister Calixta Fitzgerald, who would make literature as well as music a land of adventure and delight; Sister Fidelia Delaney, whose work eventually led her to supervise the training of novices according to the Dominican Rule in the newly founded community of the Maryknoll Missionary Sisters; and the one and only Sister Leo Tierney, who by force of intellect and daring became a tradition of education in the Middle West.

These candidates, for the most part, were young women from communities approximating the environment of Sinsinawa. It had been Father Mazzuchelli's idea to found a community that, while practicing the Dominican Rule, should consist of members gathered from that part of the country in which they were to labor. This young community would grow, as the West grew, becoming inspired with its spirit, adapted to its intellectual requirements, and identified with its religious and educational programs. Here, on the hill of his first choosing, the idea was being carried toward consummation.

Every day the postulants, the novices, and the Sisters at the Mound could look out upon miles of country which either included their own old homes or which bore resemblance to them. The lead mining of the era was coming to a close. Farms were spreading over the great valley. The smoke of trains rose on the horizon where Father Samuel had seen Indian fires. America was moving outward; and they, Americans all, by birth or by choice, were moving with the times and the land. The spirit of progress was in their blood. No one of their generation could look upon that wide vista of three growing states without the consciousness of a personal part in the making of tomorrow. The location of Sinsinawa was not the only factor in its widespread development; but it was a factor in shaping the broad outlook of the future.

With strong characters crowding one another in the limited living spaces of the original stone building, the strength of Mother Emily's leadership was evident. She must have chosen to use her power by indirection. There is no record, no recollection of any harsh imposition of authority upon the Sisters. The bond that united them in unity and harmony was a fervent observance of "the Rule." Father Mazzuchelli had given them this rule, as early as 1848. He repeated it, in printed form, adding commentaries, in 1860. It was his own translation from the Latin of the *Rule of the Brothers and Sisters of Penance of Saint Dominic,* which since the thirteenth century had been the guide in sanctity of countless thousands of men and women living in the world, Brothers and Sisters of the Militia of Jesus Christ. The corporate expression of St. Dominic's lay followers to do penance and save souls, this *Rule* had the approval of the Dominican Master General by 1285, and had received papal approval from Eugene IV in 1439. Adapted to conventual use by Sisters, it needed the abbreviation and clarification which Father Mazzuchelli gave.

The Third Order Dominican *Rule* provided for a democratic institution. Originally planned to sanctify secular life, and founded in a time and place where the workers of towns enjoyed considerable economic security and political power, the *Rule* reflected these conditions. In effect, it was a form of government rigid in basic principle but elastic in adaptation to local conditions in a religious community.

In the knowledge that "the more explicit, simple, and extensive is the law governing a religious society or order, the easier and surer will be the desired result," Father Mazzuchelli formulated a preamble into which he packed a large amount of human wisdom. He pointed out that the government of the convent would be in wise accommodation to the spirit of the country since "the people of this republic could not well sanction a religious body composed of citizens governed by the absolute will of one individual, however good." Ownership of real estate and other property should be by simple ecclesiastical title under the aegis of a duly incorporated society, the Sisters possessing nothing personally but all in common. The election of a prioress, subprioress, and councilors should take place once a year. The balloting was secret, a practice old in the Orders of the Church.

The Council, to consist of five members, would receive candidates, make regulations for them and for novices, vote for reception of professed Sisters to their vows, regulate exercises of piety, purchase land and sell buildings, nominate trustees for local mission incorporations, and have the power to delegate many duties to superioress, prioress or other properly constituted officers of the community.

In his Constitutions of 1860, Father Mazzuchelli anticipated every need of the community for decision and direction: admission of new members; spiritual exercises; care of the sick; suffrages for the dead. Complementing these and showing the reaches of apostolic service he envisioned for the Sisters of St. Clara, he could write:

> In our day, it seems that, as the old enemy of mankind is undermining every Christian truth and striving to bring the world back to paganism by the worship of man instead of God, the spiritual armies of the Church of Christ are called upon to file in battle array, to combat the enemy wherever he is to be met. . . . Every branch of human knowledge has been made more or less subservient to the dark designs of Satan; the press, the schools, the politics, and the literature of the day are in their corrupted state powerful arms in the hands of the enemy to destroy, if possible, all that is sacred in Christianity. . . . This is the principal cause which, in our age, persuaded the various Religious Orders, ancient and modern, to appear in the same field of battle, and fight with the same spiritual weapons. Whether this multitude of believers of every rank, capacity and vocation will be victorious at the end of the spiritual struggle is a secret locked up in the impenetrable decrees of God.
>
> It is certain, however, he continued, that every one who joins this spiritual army and combats valiantly, by teaching, by prayer, and by self-denial until death, will receive a crown of glory from the Saviour of the world, in the day of final retribution. The Dominican Sisters, by joining the army of the Church Militant against error and sin, become active members of the militia

of Jesus Christ, according to their original vocation, which is the most exalted station in human life, and well worth leaving their homes, their relatives, and all worldly affections in the well-grounded hope of that exceedingly great reward, the entire and eternal possession of God the Father, Son, and Holy Ghost.

With this remarkable charter (the more remarkable for being issued in the same year as the Marxian *Communist Manifesto*) Mother Emily had, fortunately for her, the road map for her guidance. As teacher and principal of an academy, and administrator of a large and valuable property, she needed authority of documents as well as of personality for the largest task of all, the spiritual leadership of a band of women dedicated, like herself, to the religious life. It is little wonder that she developed something of the presence of a queen. The marvel was that she did not acquire the "We are not amused" manner of Queen Victoria whom she did not admire. Luckily, her Irish sense of humor saved her; and, although she could stiffen over breaches of discipline, she could laugh away minor infringements.

Realizing that Sisters, too, require variations in a fairly rigorous schedule of everyday living, she provided entertainment for them as well as for the girls. There was the daily recreation hour. There were little plays, written and staged by novices and postulants for the Sisters. There was the observance of Dominican feast days. There was the patron-and-motto card drawing at Epiphany, more serious in application than that used for the girls. There was the traditional celebration of Holy Innocents' Day, when Mother Emily sat at table and prayed in choir with the novices while the youngest novice presided as the Superior. There were joyous assemblies in the winter evenings, Fourth of July and campus suppers in the summer. Routine was difficult, not too arduous when it was broken by the planned recreations which the Superior sponsored, and the occasional unplanned fun which she approved with a twinkling smile.

Afterward, her close associates of that period were to remark on what was probably her outstanding characteristic as a Superior. Never, they said, did she form a judgment until all possible evidence had been brought to the court of her attention. When the record was in, she made decision. If the decision were adverse to the person in question, she saw that the penalty was imposed and enforced; but, in all future relationships with her, Mother Emily "bent backward" to give more than ordinary consideration.

Through some years of this period she had the good offices of a wise half-brother, Father Thomas Louis Power. Father Power had led the family to the United States. He had met and been guided by Father Mazzuchelli. He had become a Dominican and had served as president of Sinsinawa College after Father Mazzuchelli had gone to Benton. After a pastorate in Memphis where he had shown splendid heroism during that city's yellow fever epidemic of 1867, he was returned to Sinsinawa. There, following the short chaplaincy of Father Moses Benedict Fortune, also of the Dominican Province of St. Joseph, he remained for three years. Through this critical period and through the years until his death in 1906, he was to be a tower of strength to his half-sister when she needed aid beyond the resources of her own spirit.

He was, first of all, a true priest. This, and "his gentle disposition, winning ways, imperturbable temperament, social spirit, and a kindness prompting help for others," wrote the Dominican historian, Father O'Daniel, "made him universally liked and won him friends in every walk of life. He had rare good judgment as well as being a splendid theologian. He could easily hold his own with the best of educators." Unquestionably, he gave to his young half-sister the full benefit of his wisdom and experience. His counsel must have saved her from many possible pitfalls in business. There is no record of her appeals to him during his time at the Mound; but later records show how she went to him after he had been transferred to Washington, to Minneapolis, and to New Jersey.

By the year 1877, eighty-six Sisters had been added to the thirty-three who had constituted the membership of the community when Mother Emily had come to Sinsinawa. In view of the fact that the community was comparatively new, that it had as yet few missions, and that its location was difficult of access, the number of newly professed Sisters was large. The demands for service were, however, larger; and only spiritual strength could have upheld their mental and physical health under the strain of their duties. The Sisters had to utilize their abilities and their time with reliance on supernatural help.

Of Mother Emily's qualities, the old Sisters, who knew her in her youth, most strongly emphasize her ability to give just such spiritual fortification. One after another, they recall the almost palpable flow of strength from her when they made their professions before her. One after another, they tell of her great understanding of their spiritual problems. "She took me over every raging river," one old Sister remembered; and perhaps some of the rivers were far harder to ford than they would have seemed to the onlooker. There is no record of what her own gravest problems were in her authority over others.

All that the Annals report is that occasionally — and very, very seldom — a Sister left the community. There are no footnotes, no editorials, certainly no news story. The Sisters have a phrase, "She did not persevere." They make no other explanation, draw up no indictment. Somehow, though, there is a faint implication that anyone who failed to persevere under Mother Emily, however well she served in other ranks of goodness, was no true soldier in the Militia of Jesus Christ. She was their mother; but she was also their captain in the war for the world's salvation; and they looked to her, never in vain, for the courage they needed to follow the plume of her plunging spirit. The giving of that courage, especially in the first ten years of her leadership, was probably her greatest gift to her Sisters. The community would one day grow beyond her farthest dreams, but would never lose the splendor of her endowment.

3

From their beginning the Sinsinawa Dominicans had an association with public school education which was both to benefit and to harass them as time went on. For, if it helped them, both financially and socially, in the early years of their foundation, it also involved them later in one of the most famous educational controversies of Catholic Church history in the United States.

Father Mazzuchelli, with his broad intention of service to the entire community, had approved public school teaching by the Sisters of the Benton convent. The school at New Diggings was a public school. For two years during his lifetime, so was St. Rose's in Galena. There was a public school taught by the Sisters, in addition to the Academy, at Benton. The practice still existed to such an extent that the teaching Sisters of St. Clara were required by Mother Emily, in the late sixties, to take a "teacher's examination" in order to qualify for certificates necessary for teaching in the public schools in their charge.

Sister Borromeo who had spent only two days in public schools during her childhood, took the examination, passed, and was assigned to the New Diggings school. Her description of the experience may be taken as characteristic of those of other Sisters in other schools as well.

> I went forth to do my patriotic and religious best in a small mining town of one short street and wide prairie full of mineral holes. Did you ever see mineral holes? Well, we didn't see the holes, but we saw the piles of yellow clay that encircle the openings to these well-like excavations, and for utter desolation and despairful dreariness nothing could compare with the scenery in the lead regions of Wisconsin in the '60's and '70's.
>
> Our abode was a cottage of four rooms, and our furniture was all that the heart of an anchorite could desire. The Sister who had charge of me and the school and the cottage had been wearing the habit seventeen years. I was young and verdant — oh, very verdant! A fervent zeal and an enthusiasm so ardent that it still glows and often bursts into flame, carried me through the first three months of the school year. Then I had to summon the courage I had inherited from my Puritan forefathers, for from farms about the little town there came to me the stalwart youths who worked in summer and went to school in winter.
>
> How they towered above me! How big and strong and invincible they seemed, but how gentle, simple, and submissive they proved to be. How eager they were to learn, and how respectful

they were, because I was a woman, but more, because I wore the religious garb.

And so Sister and I plowed our way on the bitter winter mornings through the old fashioned depth of snow to the queer, roughly built schoolhouse and did our best for our simple-hearted charges. At noon, we plowed our way back to our icy cold cottage, built a fire in our tiny stove, made a cup of tea, consumed it and a goodly slice of bread and butter with an appetite that regarded quantity rather than quality. I remember that we had only one knife and one teaspoon, but we were quite rich in the possession of two forks and two small cups and saucers (one pink and the other blue), three plates and a few odds and ends of table furnishings. . . .

There is one experience that I find especially amusing to look back upon, though it was not at all amusing at the time. My hardy masculine pupils came long distances, over almost impassable country roads, and they wore boots — boots capitalized and emphasized. To the sturdy calfskin footgear, with the hob nailed soles, the yellow clay of the locality clung in heavy masses and was finally plastered over the great rough planks of our schoolroom floor.

One drizzling, shivery, shaky day, when tawny mud was the principal feature of the scene outside, and the chief adornment of feet and floor inside, there came a genteel tapping on the schoolroom door. Local knuckles never spared themselves when demanding that the portal of their schoolhouse be opened, so I recognized the rap as that of a stranger. I hastened to admit the unusual caller. He was a gentleman of impressive appearance and polished manners. There was naught to be done but to invite him in, but, truth to tell, my heart went out, since my body could not "sink through the floor."

There was only one chair, and the preservation of my dignity demanded that I should keep that, so his broadcloth elegance was invited to sit on a backless bench among the homespun simplicity in the rear of the room against the whitewashed wall.

I taught; the pupils recited; the green wood in the big box stove spluttered; the giggly old clock ticked spasmodic ticks; and the fine gentleman listened and smiled and behaved himself in an altogether charming manner.

After an infinite and eternal hour and a half of deadly torture for me our visitor rose to depart. I accompanied him to the door, and very sincerely invited him to come again. "I certainly shall," he said. "It is my duty to visit schools. I am the county super-intendent." Tableau: small, verdant nun, surrounded by tall, verdant youths, staring at a vanishing gentleman with white-wash on his broadcloth coat and yellow clay on his patent leather boots!

He went back to his own town and chivalrously assured the county officials that an environment of mineral holes and a superfluity of yellow clay were no drawbacks in the pursuit of knowledge; that he never worried over schools in charge of the Sisters.

In another public school Sister Borromeo met a boy who promised her to give up the chewing of tobacco. Later she saw signs of his defection. When she charged him with the breaking of his promise, he told her that he had no breakfast because his mother was ill and there had been no food in the house. He would not go to the neighbors nor would he buy bread lest his mother be criticized. He had gone without food until noon, then, to stave off the ravages of hunger, took the tobacco. She looked at the boy, not really seeing him, for, as she wrote, "We don't see clearly through tears." Then she took him to the convent, and gave him her own dinner.

Her next teaching was done in a school where the pastor had separated boys and girls by the full width of the town, and the Sisters had to travel like shuttles behind horses they never really mastered. After that came a school of full-grown boys and girls in a huge room which the stove could not heat. That was where the Sisters held a night school for boys who worked all day. Sister Borromeo gave up her one free hour, the time from six to seven in the evening, to two girls whom she supposed to be workers unable to come at any other time. When the term was over she discovered that they had been learning from her the lessons they recited next day to the principal of the local high school.

The salaries paid to the Sisters for their services in the public schools meant much to the Mound finances. Again and again, upon the ledger of the first ten years of Mother Emily's headship of Sinsinawa, the salary payments to the Sisters at Benton and

New Diggings stand out for comparative size and surety. Even in larger town parishes, the pastor had difficulty in making the payments for the teaching services of the Sisters. Twenty dollars a month, the largest amount paid, seems a pittance for the work done; but, time and again, pastors groaned that they did not know where they would get the salary. Sometimes, the money due came with assurances of regret that it was not more; but there were pastors who sent it, not only belatedly, but with an air of having conferred an endowment. The stringency was all part of the struggle of maintaining a Catholic school system unaided by any of the money paid by Catholics for school taxes; but the universality of the pinch did not make life any easier for the Sisters.

The work of the Sisters in the mission schools, both public and parochial, never ended at the schoolhouse door. There were Sunday schools to be taught, sodalities to be encouraged, boys and men to be brought to confession, at the special request of mothers and sisters and sweethearts. There were sick to be visited and mourners to be comforted. There were families who needed food and clothing, but who could be given them only surreptitiously lest their human dignity be hurt by the stigma of pauperism. There was, in fact, in this time the foundation of the social service which was to characterize the Sinsinawa Dominicans. If Mother Emily was not responsible for all of it — since much of the service had to be done spontaneously — she was at least always approving. Charity, the care of souls, were her watchwords; and the gleam of her solicitude for others shone across the distance which separated her from the Mission sisters.

Bethlehem Academy in Faribault, the first branch academy of the community, had been established in 1865, two years before Mother Emily's first election. Her two blood sisters, Sister Gertrude Power and Sister Veronica Power, were among the little group of five who set out for the Minnesota wilderness, traveling by stage to the Mississippi River, then by boat to St. Paul, then overland again to the Minnesota town with whose history they were to be so closely linked.

The Dominican Bishop Thomas L. Grace of St. Paul had chosen them for the school. Two children named Murphy had been orphaned when their parents, traveling with them toward California in a covered wagon, died in the town. They had no relatives west of the Alleghenies. Their mother had asked Father George Kellar, pastor of the struggling settlement, to care for the children, giving him money enough to pay for their education in Catholic schools. Father Kellar, wishing to keep the boy and girl together, could find no school for that purpose. He therefore went to Bishop Grace, asking for the establishment of a Catholic school in Faribault. Bishop Grace told him that if he would take the Dominican Sisters from Benton, he himself would buy a home for them to use as an academy and that he would also send them a piano, which, of course, would be an article of revenue to the Sisters as well as of culture to the pupils. Father Kellar consented, and the Bishop wrote to Benton.

The five Sisters, chosen by Mother Regina Mulqueeny, set out from Benton at four o'clock on the morning of July 31, 1865. They reached St. Paul on August 2, and stayed with the Sisters of St. Joseph. On the morning of August 4, St. Dominic's Day, Bishop Grace led them to the carriage he had borrowed for the long drive to Faribault. With them was little Clara Cochrane, the child who had given the welcoming address at Father Mazzuchelli's commencement of 1861. All day they traveled through Minnesota fields and forests. It was seven o'clock that evening when they reached Faribault.

There they took possession of the Fowler residence which the Bishop had purchased. The former owners, although not Catholics, remained for a short time to help the Sisters. Major Fowler, with the aid of his neighbors, made the benches for the basement classrooms, and helped with the carpentry for the chapel. Alexander Faribault, founder of the town, gave generously of his orchard supplies; and Daniel Faribault provided them with a carriage, a team of horses, and a driver.

With Sister Josephine Cahill as Superior, the work of the school began. The academy closely followed the plan of the Benton school.

Its first registered student was the little Murphy girl (afterward to become Sister Macarius) for whom the establishment had been undertaken. The Sisters also taught her brother, according to Father Kellar's promise that the children should not be separated; but Bethlehem Academy was distinctly a girls' school. One of its first pupils, a Minim, was the Nora Fitzgerald who would one day be Sister Calixta, and the first of a distinguished roster of Faribault graduates to join the community, among them Mother Samuel Coughlin.

Sister Gertrude (her contemporaries always pronounced her name with the G as in general) soon took over authority as Superior, which she was to hold until she went to Sinsinawa in 1892 as Novice Mistress. Every recollection of her emphasizes her great holiness. She must also have been, like Mother Emily, a genuine builder: for, in spite of poverty and the other difficulties of a frontier settlement, Bethlehem Academy grew into a civic as well as a religious institution. Whenever the academy celebrated an anniversary, a large part of the town joined in the observance with pride.

The academy, however, could not serve all the needs of a Catholic school in the town. Father Kellar, conscious of these needs, insisted at once that the Sisters open a parish school in connection with his Church of the Immaculate Conception. The pupils of this school were of many nations and races, English, Irish, French, German, and both full-blood and half-breed Indians. Only the children of English and Irish lineage used the English language at home. The French and German parents were particularly insistent upon the use of their own language; but even the occasional friendly visits of the Reverend John Ireland, of the St. Paul Diocese, did not yet raise one of the issues that were to extend far beyond the borders of Faribault.

Sister Veronica Power and Sister Benvenuta McCullough taught in the two dark, damp rooms in the basement of the church which constituted the school. The church was about a mile away from the convent where the two Sisters lived. Every day, in sunshine, rain, or snow they had to walk either the wagon road or a trail over the hills through thick underbrush. For four years, when the thermometer often registered a low of thirty-five degrees below zero, the two Sisters made their way. Only a year before he went to his native France was Father Kellar able to provide them with a convent near the church. Father Ireland, again visiting Faribault, gave the children of the schools literal, and the Sisters figurative, pats on the head for their accomplishments.

No one could foresee that, before the turn of the century, the Faribault school would be the storm center of a controversy which would eventually involve some of the great leaders of the American hierarchy before it would be carried to Rome for immediate settlement; thereafter to go down in history as one of the first in a series of hard-fought local struggles on the question of public funds and Catholic schools.

The plan of an American foundation, as projected by Father Mazzuchelli, had been carried on by Mother Emily. To her, as to him, allegiance to the Papacy carried no implication of subservience to foreign authority, since the Roman Catholic Church is, of its essence, supranational. Direction of the community's affairs by a mother house in a foreign land might have hampered, if it did not nullify, its purpose. Mother Emily, trained in the view, continued to stress the Mazzuchelli idea of germaneness to the locality as well as of teaching service.

Unquestionably, this American origin and spirit must have been a determining factor in the decision of two Chicago priests to bring the Sinsinawa Sisters to the Chicago diocese. The priests were Dr. John McMullen and Dr. Thaddeus J. Butler, members of the Bishop's Council. Both of them belonged to that group of Irish clergy who felt passionate gratitude for the freedom given by the United States to the Irish, who had been driven out of their native land by alien oppressors. Both of them recognized in Mother Emily a kindred spirit, and set out to establish in their city a school of the Sinsinawa Dominicans.

They met, unfortunately, the opposition of Bishop James Duggan, who refused to ask the Sisters. Dr. McMullen and Dr. Butler summoned Father Louis Power to meet the Bishop who, after a long interview, withdrew his opposition. At the request of Dr. Butler the Sisters were assigned to set up a school in the parish of the Immaculate Conception where he was pastor, but where he was soon to be succeeded by his brother, Father Patrick Butler.

The Sisters, five in number, reached Chicago on August 18, 1868. The Chicago of the time was already a city of size and importance, but it still had certain rural characteristics which it was soon to lose. The Church of the Immaculate Conception stood less than a half mile south of North Avenue, then the northern city boundary line. Woods and fields stretched within sight of its spire, and Goose Island, a pleasant residential section, lay within its parish borders. The neighborhood was an association of the families of native Americans and German and Irish immigrants. Nearly all the houses were two-story frame structures, tinder for the blaze that was to destroy the city, but at the time pleasant and adequate, if not luxurious, homes for a hard-working people.

According to the custom of the time, the Sisters purchased a lot, paying for it in installments. The Sinsinawa community furnished them with the money for this and for needs not met by the parish. The parish built and furnished the convent, a small frame building with four schoolrooms and six rooms for use of the Sisters. There was no chapel for the first year. When the Sisters came, they found the schoolrooms unfurnished; and the first classes had to be taught without desks.

Sister Ambrose McNamara, the first Superior, died during the following year. Sister Dominica Byrne, who succeeded her, had to meet the disaster of the Great Fire of 1871. The fire, leaping the river from the West Side of the city, almost completely destroyed the North Side. The Sisters, realizing that their home stood in the path of the rushing flames, had to seek safety. Before they went, they buried what they could of their heavy goods, including a piano. Then, burdened with portable possessions, they joined the crowd of refugees. As they came out of the convent, a frenzied woman thrust her infant into the arms of Sister Augustine McCabe who carried the child for a long distance before the mother reclaimed him. The Sisters made their way in the fleeing crowd to the home of Eliza Allen Starr on Goose Island. Later some of them went to Waukegan, others to Kenosha; but when they returned to Chicago they had to start work upon the building of a new school and convent.

The community at Sinsinawa contributed most generously to the relief of fire victims, as well as to the rebuilding of their own property. In a time of its own stringency, the Mound sent hundreds of dollars immediately to the sufferers, and helped to raise thousands of dollars for the rebuilding. Mother Emily wrote an appeal to Bishop Allemany of San Francisco. The Bishop replied that he had sent all the money he could spare to Bishop Thomas Foley, who had succeeded Bishop Duggan. He intimated that, since he had earlier promised money for the convent, he thought that Bishop Foley might be willing to allocate the amount, five hundred dollars, to the Sisters. Bishop Foley was anything but willing. He was, he told Mother Emily, pressed to the wall for money. Her plea must have impressed him, however, for he sent her a check for the money Bishop Allemany had subscribed.

A little later, Sister Borromeo, assigned to the Immaculate Conception School, also had a difficult interview with Bishop Foley. The Sisters, trying to raise money for the many costs of the rebuilding, arranged to give a musical program at North Side Turner Hall. They trained pupils, held rehearsals, and sold tickets. On almost the last day before the entertainment someone suggested to them that they invite Bishop Foley to preside. Sister Borromeo and the music teacher undertook the errand.

The bishop was all affability until Sister Borromeo answered his question about the time set for the meeting. "Eight o'clock in the evening!" he exclaimed. "Religious in a public place at eight in the evening! Surely you are not planning to be there!"

"But we must be there, your Grace," Sister Borromeo explained. "The children cannot do their parts without our direction from back of the scenes. No one will see us from the audience, and we shall go to the hall in a closed carriage."

"But you will be outside your convent," the bishop declared.

"Yes, but we shall be seen only by the children."

"The children must get along without you."

"But — but we wanted the entertainment to be a success."

"Is success to be preferred to merit?"

"No, Bishop, but we never thought of comparing the two," Sister Borromeo said. The music teacher began to cry. "We just worked hard for the one and hoped we were gaining the other. But we will recall the tickets, and give the program in the daytime, although our parish is in a neighborhood where it is hard for the parents to come during the day."

"No, you can't do that," the bishop capitulated. "Have your program, as you planned."

"But will you come, Bishop?"

He smiled suddenly. "Yes," he said. "I'll come, if you come in the covered carriage."

Bishop Foley was no niggard when he kept his promises. He came, bringing with him ten priests and Bishop John Lancaster Spalding; and he praised the Sisters — luckily hidden back of the scene — for their efforts for the betterment of school and parish.

Although the parish extended eastward to the lake and included one of the fashionable sections of the city, the Church and School of the Immaculate Conception profited little, materially, from its location. Most of the Catholic families east of Clark Street, the social dividing line of the neighborhood, went to the Cathedral and sent their children to private schools. A jest, warmly appreciated by the loyal parishioners, is told of Monsignor Thomas Kearns, one of the later pastors. Monsignor Kearns went to see the bishop who had his residence in the lake shore neighborhood of the parish. A servant at the door questioned him. "Tell the bishop," said the monsignor, "that his parish priest has come to make a pastoral call."

If there was a line of demarcation among the parishioners, there was none in the attitude of Mother Emily's Sisters. To them a mind was a mind, and a soul was a soul, and the manner or garb of the governing body was of far less importance. They taught the children in school, holding their own with the best schools of their day. They taught Sunday school. They formed sodalities. They started a parish library. They organized parish social affairs. At the request of Father Patrick Butler, the painfully bashful pastor, they visited the sick and prepared them for the coming of the Blessed Sacrament. Sometimes they found poor homes spotless in anticipation. At other times they had to do the necessary cleaning. Here, as in other parishes as time went on, they came in direct contact with the conditions resulting from the social and economic evils of the time. It was laboratory training; and it was to help make them ready for the kind of teaching that would one day put their community in the forefront of Christian social education.

Through the years the parish was to retain the tradition of its foundation. Its later pastor, Father Thomas Pope Hodnett — a descendant of the famous Irish patriot, Thomas Pope, who gave his life for the cause of Irish freedom in the uprising of 1798 — was a fiery believer in human rights. He was also a fiery orator, but unfortunately without terminal facilities. Many a helpless auditor at school entertainments on hot June nights wilted under his apparently endless paragraphs. He was, however, a genuine scholar and a true American patriot.

In a big city parish, divided between wealth east of Clark Street and poverty west of that thoroughfare, Father Hodnett built bewildered boys and girls into respectable, responsible citizens. He taught them their rights and often fought for recognition of these rights. He also taught them their duties. As a result, the Immaculate Conception parish of Chicago was a hard core of somewhat militant Catholicity.

St. Jarlath's in Chicago was a parish of somewhat different type when Mother Emily sent her Sisters there in 1873. The pastor was Father Thomas F. Cashman. Before his ordination, he had come to Savanna, in Illinois, after Father Mazzuchelli's death. Hearing that there were Irish women among the Dominicans in the little Wisconsin mining town of Benton he set out on horse-back to visit them. His coming began a friendship with Mother Emily which lasted through the rest of her lifetime, more than forty years.

Father Cashman was still a very young man, but he had already shown the temper of his steel. He had been born in Ireland and had studied for the priesthood at Maynooth but, refusing to take the oath of allegiance to Queen Victoria, he came under British suspicion. His mother helped him get away to the United States by hiding him in a great basket and driving him to seaport. He arrived in New York while the Civil War was raging. Immediately he applied for his first citizenship papers, and at once enlisted in the Union Army. After the war he entered the seminary of St. Mary's of the Lake in Chicago, and was there ordained for the diocese of Chicago.

Father Cashman and Mother Emily had much in common. Both had been born in Ireland, both had suffered under British rule, both had found freedom in the United States. They both loved Ireland deeply and tenderly, and wished for her the self-determination of government under which they now lived. They had, however, a deeper sense of gratitude to their adopted country. Both of them were almost passionately patriotic. They held consciousness of the world-wide unity of Catholicity — both of them were pioneer promoters of the Society of the Propagation of the Faith — but they ardently believed that their first obligation in citizenship was payment of the debt which they, as immigrants, owed to America.

Father Cashman's parish ran almost from the south branch of the Chicago River to the Des Plaines River. There he extended his acquaintances as well as his field of endeavor. He won the friendship of many of the public men of his time: Civil War Generals Sheridan, Meagher, Barry; and James Shields who was United States Senator from three states; and in later days, Demo-crats, like the younger Carter Harrison, and Republicans, like Mark Hanna and Medill McCormick. In the Church he kept up friendships so widely scattered that St. Jarlath's Rectory was an inn of all nations, with Chinese and African missionaries sharing rooms with Maltese pastors and Brazilian bishops.

St. Jarlath's was, in its earlier days, a parish of upper middle-class people with the usual respect for material success. It was the pastor's job to instill in his congregation a different set of values. He did this not by any fulminations against the rich, but by insistence that they should enjoy no special ecclesiastical favors. St. Jarlath's allowed no canopies, no church step carpets for fashionable weddings. The pastor seldom visited parishioners, rich or poor, unless illness, death, or disaster had overtaken the household. He upheld the Sisters in his school in their recognition of individual merit as the only criterion of distinction. A multi-millionaire's daughter had a part in an entertainment only because she sang well. (Her attendance at the school gave testimony that her parents agreed with this method of education.) By establishing and maintaining a genuine standard of democracy, Father Cashman and Mother Emily's Sisters accomplished something of a miracle within a sphere of almost unconscious snobbery. Even before they came to St. Jarlath's the Sisters had been indoctrinated in the Christian social philosophy interpreted by Father Mazzuchelli and the spirit of Mother Emily. The net result of the integration of Father Cashman's teaching of American history, and the Sinsinawa Dominican method of education was a course in citizenship noteworthy in its time and place.

Unquestionably, Father Cashman's interest in the school greatly benefited its program, but at times the manifestations of the interest must have been a little hard on his friend at Sinsinawa. Year after year, he sent her a letter insisting that Sister Paul, the first-grade teacher, be returned to the school. Once, he came back from a visit to Ireland to find that Sister Paul had been transferred. Without waiting to transact any other business, he set out for Sinsinawa. On that occasion he won, and Sister Paul went back; but there came a time when Mother Emily made up her mind that Sister Paul must be given a change of pedagogic scene. Not even Father Cashman's stubborn insistence changed her decision.

They parted, but with the victory definitely on the distaff side.

Sister Paul, a marvelous primary teacher, was so much a drill-master that one wonders what she would have done in the modern school; but her pupils came out of first grade knowing how to read and even knowing that there was a "w" in the word answer. She overawed some of them so much, however, that their first recollection of Mother Emily has to be set against the background of Sister Paul's austerity to stand out in proper focus. Once a class had just gone through a fearful, if not a tearful session when the door of the room opened, and a small Sister unexpectedly entered. They struggled to their feet. Here was, they thought, another Sister, come to enforce Sister Paul's rigid discipline. Someone said, "Mother Emily." The name meant nothing to them. Then she smiled, a radiating smile which looked like the coming of sunshine. Everyone there smiled back at her. From that day she was their "Mother Emily."

The combination of her influence with Father Cashman's equal democracy of mind must have been the cause of a condition more remarkable than their pupils knew. The end of the last century was a time of bourgeois ascendancy. All Catholic schools did not escape this secular influence. But in St. Jarlath's School students neither saw nor heard anything of those financial and class distinctions which were fabric of the period. That they were living, in school hours, at least, the Christian democracy of the social encyclicals was due to a force outside their general environment; and that force must have been the associated intention of the Sisters from Sinsinawa and the priest from the County Cork.

The nearness of the city's great hospitals took the Sisters afield from the school. The Cook County Hospital, one of the largest in the world even then, had no resident chaplain. Most of its calls for priests came to the rectory at St. Jarlath's. A young curate, coming back from a summons to a dying man in one of the hospital wards, stopped at the convent. "Won't you Sisters go over to the County Hospital once in a while?" he asked. "If you will only walk through the wards, you will do something for the souls of the poor unfortunates who lie there, friendless and forgotten." The Sisters wrote that night to Mother Emily. She sent permission at once. After that, there was hardly a day when two of the Sisters did not go, as soon as school was over, to the great gloomy building. There they did far more than walk through the wards. They took messages, wrote letters, brought luxuries they had begged from charitable friends; and they solaced the dying, holding before their misting eyes the vision of a world far better than the sad one they were leaving.

Because of Father Cashman's wide range of acquaintances the pupils of the school had early training in national and international interests. General Philip Sheridan was its first visitor. Archbishop Ireland was a frequent informal lecturer. Once Archbishop Satolli, the Papal Legate to the United States, gave a speech in English which his youthful hearers thought was Italian. Missionaries from Alaska, from Borneo, from the Mauritian Islands, from China, from Nagasaki in Japan told of their faraway mission fields. Father Iris, the Babylonian archaeologist, described ruins of ancient cities, and Monsignor Adar talked of modern Bagdad, that fabulous city of the Caliphs. Bishops from Australia and Mexico appeared. So did the Vicar-General of Athens. The star visitor, however, was the priest from Dahomey who illustrated the tribal dances of his mission charges. Certainly, attendance at St. Jarlath's was the foundation of a liberal education, perhaps as much for the Sisters as for the pupils.

Undoubtedly, this situation existed comparably in other schools. If Sinsinawa acted upon the city schools of Chicago, these schools, in turn, reacted upon Sinsinawa, both culturally and socially. Young teachers who had known only the quieter and more secure ways of life on Wisconsin, Iowa, and Minnesota farms came to realize the problems, as well as the educational advantages, of the city. It was all part of the process of growth, and both Chicago and Sinsinawa were growing fast.

Outside Chicago twelve other schools began to operate during the first decade of Mother Emily's authority. These were established in the Wisconsin towns of Mineral Point, Portage, Whitewater,

Milwaukee, and Madison; in Faribault and Austin, Minnesota; and in the Illinois towns of Waukegan, Freeport, and Bloomington. With all these schools Mother Emily maintained close association, not only by reports from the Sisters, but by frequent visits to the scattered towns.

Before the end of the decade she had come into knowledge both broad and deep of the affairs which most concerned the people of the Middle West. She was seeing the passing of the frontier, the development of states upon land that had been territories when she had come to the United States. She was watching economic development, the increase of capitalistic power, that was better on paper than it proved in fact: for already the Granger movement was growing strong in the Mississippi Valley, and paving the way for other and more spectacular sociopolitical parties. She was observing, too, the growth of the Church, with parish after parish dotting the trail of Father Mazzuchelli's footsteps, and diocesan sees doubled in number in the prairie states. She was witnessing the rise of great builders in the American hierarchy: Gibbons, Ireland, John Lancaster Spalding, men with ideals like her own and men with whom she would be associated in part in a great venture.

Like the land of her choice, she was facing a long future; and, like that land, she was unafraid.

CHAPTER EIGHT

Rome: A Pilgrimage
1877–1878

IN 1877 the Sisters at Sinsinawa were living under the *Constitutions* printed for them by Father Mazzuchelli in 1860, an amplified form of the *Constitutions* he had given them in manuscript in 1848. They had made no change in the chapters on government as given in that earlier translation, of which Father Mazzuchelli himself had observed: "The few articles . . . were not intended to answer all the wants of a well regulated community, but simply to form a general system of a Religious Order or Sisterhood which might be combined with all the occupations of life. . . ."

Alert to the needs of her developing community, Mother Emily was realizing this more and more during her first decade of leadership. In addition to the Milwaukee Archdiocese in which it had been founded, the community now had schools, academies, and properties in the dioceses of St. Paul, Chicago, Green Bay, and Peoria. Her problem was: With this extension, which promised to continue progressively, did the community have in its *Constitutions* the proper safeguards of cohesion? No difficulty had as yet arisen with the jurisdictions under which her Sisters were teaching, but she foresaw the necessity of asserting more definitely the permanent affiliation of the present and future Mission houses with the mother house at Sinsinawa.

How to do this? By revising the *Constitutions* to provide for the government of a Congregation of houses inalienable from the central authority. Such revision must have the approval of the

Dominican authorities at Rome and of the Congregation Propaganda Fide, as well.

Wisely Mother Emily turned for advice first to the local Ordinaries — Archbishop Henni of Milwaukee, Bishop Foley of Chicago, Bishop Grace of Saint Paul, Bishop John Lancaster Spalding of Peoria. All responded not only with their approval of the step, but with letters of praise of the Sisters' work which were to be presented at Rome. All remained most friendly through the protracted proceedings. Bishop Grace promoted the cause vigorously; and Bishop Spalding, true to his literary habit of mind, gave advice on the words and wording of various necessary documents.

The method of change threatened, as it later proved, a long, slow process. Undertaken in 1877, it did not become completely effected until 1893. It consumed months of travel, and years of correspondence. It involved the Sisters of the English Congregation of St. Catherine of Siena at Stone, in Staffordshire, England; the Master General and other officials of the Dominican Casa Generalizia, that Convent of Santa Sabina in Rome where Father Mazzuchelli had heard the call to the American missions; and the Holy Father within the Vatican.

With the approval of the chapter, Mother Emily and Sister Alberta Duffy left Sinsinawa in July of 1877. Father Zara, the chaplain, returning to his native Italy and Lizzie Wilmers, one of the pupils at the Mound going to visit relatives in Germany, sailed with them on the *City of Richmond* from New York to Queenstown. The voyage, peaceable and pleasant, must have seemed to Mother Emily a marked contrast to her westward crossing of the Atlantic twenty-five years earlier. Her letters, however, make no mention of the memory of that childhood misery, but emphasize the happiness of the crossing, with mention of the cosmopolitan character of the passengers, although association with any of them seems to have been only through the gregarious activities of Father Zara.

Under the care of the captain of the ship, Lizzie Wilmers went on to England, there to be transshipped to Bremen; but Father Zara remained with the two Sisters while they went through Ireland.

Sister Alberta's Journal, with its almost daily recordings, and Mother Emily's letters to the Sisters at Sinsinawa, give a fairly comprehensive account of their journeying. The Bishop of Queenstown showed them the beginning of the magnificent cathedral. They saw Blarney Castle but did not kiss the Blarney Stone. They drove through the beauties of Killarney; and they came to Waterford.

On August 15, the lovely Feast of the Assumption, the Lady Day in the Harvest of all Ireland, they were in Tramore, visiting one of Mother Emily's cousins and finding relatives of Sister Alberta. "All Waterford seems to be here," Sister Alberta wrote; but, even in her letter to her half-brother, Father Power, Mother Emily made no mention of her reactions to her return to the place of her birth. That she was moved is certain; but she was using neither time nor energy upon sentimental recollections. They went on next day to Dublin, using most of their time in that old gray city in locating the famous Dominican, "Father Tom" Burke, whom they found looking ill and tired; then at Kingston took the boat to Holyhead. From there, while Father Zara went to London, intending to meet them later for the Dover-Calais crossing, the Sisters went to Stone.

The English Congregation of St. Catherine of Siena at Stone was already a well-known Dominican community. From an American standpoint, its principal claim to fame at the time was in the fact that its Prioress was the celebrated Mother Frances Raphael, better known by her name in the world of Augusta Theodosia Drane. She had come into public notice in her teens with an anonymous pamphlet on the *Morality of Tractarianism,* which William Ewart Gladstone attributed to John Henry Newman. She had published the *Martyrs of Stone,* the *Life of Saint Dominic,* a *History of England,* a series of educational sketches and a book of poems before the appearance of her most famous book, *Christian Schools and Scholars,* in 1867. Sister Alberta, writing to Sister Benedicta, was to refer to her in anticipation of their meeting as "that woman at Stone who has written that book"; but Mother Emily, drawn to her as steel to the magnet, was looking forward to their meeting almost as much as to the accomplishment of the most direct cause of her pilgrimage.

The Sisters of the Community at Sinsinawa, in considering the revision of their Constitutions had decided that their best procedure was adoption of the Constitutions in use at Stone. Stone was a Congregation, and Sinsinawa desired to become a Congregation. Stone lived under the Rule of St. Augustine, as did Sinsinawa; but the Stone Constitutions had been approved by the Dominican Master General and by the Holy See. They were available in English. Their adoption would facilitate the undertaking; but only personal consultation with the Sisters at Stone could satisfy Mother Emily on what should be taken from and what left in the Stone Rule for adaptation to the Wisconsin convent.

It is unfortunate that there is no record, in words or in photograph, of the meeting between Mother Frances Raphael and Mother Emily. The points of resemblance and of unlikeness must have been noteworthy, even to somewhat casual observers. Both were Dominican Sisters, dedicated to lives of teaching God's truth to the children of God. Both were women of great personal magnetism, great piety, great vision. But Augusta Theodosia Drane was the product of centuries of English ruling-class intellectualism. In her childhood she had been taught by George Coleridge. She had known Keble. In 1850, in the wake of the Oxford Movement, she had followed Newman into the Church, and had been professed at Stone in 1853, the year after Ellen Power had come up the Mississippi River, an Irish immigrant's child. While Mother Emily had been struggling with frontier finances, Mother Frances Raphael had been dwelling within the ivory tower of book writing. They met, however, upon the common ground of single-minded devotion to their Faith and their Order; and between them grew, within an hour, a friendship that was to last as long as Mother Frances Raphael lived.

Their mutual respect and admiration may have stemmed from their recognition in each other of many of the same qualities. Archbishop Ullathorne said of Mother Frances Raphael that "she could write a book, paint a picture, rule an Order, guide other souls, superintend a building, lay out the grounds, and give wise advice with equal facility and success." Mother Emily never essayed the writing of a book or the painting of a picture; but she did everything else which the chronicler had set down.

The friendship between the two women was to keep alive, by letter, for fifteen years. In 1892, the last year of her life, Mother Raphael was sending to Mother Emily letters of kindly advice and affectionate esteem; and when she was dying she had another Sister write a long letter to her friend.

The friendliness of Stone was to be of great benefit to Mother Emily not only in counsel but in other aid. At the request of the Stone Dominicans, Cardinal Howard took interest in them. Later in Rome he opened gates for Mother Emily and Sister Alberta that would have otherwise remained closed. Long as the campaign proved to be, he undoubtedly helped to shorten it; and in times of crises his assurance of their ultimate success invariably heartened them.

There was in Stone another remarkable woman with whom Mother Emily was to have close association through many years. The contrast in their backgrounds was still more marked. For the assistant — and in a short time the successor — to the Superior was Sister Mary Isabella Howard, who was remembered by most of the aristocracy of Europe as the Lady Isabella Howard. Daughter of a noble family which had, despite its firm Catholicity, remained powerful in the government of Great Britain, Mother Mary Isabella had assumed with her habit a real humility which did not lessen her executive ability.

An American woman, who did not know her identity until later, met her in a crowded third-class carriage on a French railroad and saw her take charge of the half-dozen crying children of a sick mother. Through a long, jolting night the nun held the infant in her arms, told stories in perfect French to two tiny youngsters who clung to her knees, and watched over three on the bench before her.

If there was any overt indication at Stone (and there probably was not) of superiority in age or condition, Mother Emily did not record it. Young as she was, she had then, as later, that quality of greatness which knew neither superiority nor inferiority in anything but service to God. Social lines and national boundaries were invisible to her as she progressed upon her mission. Her visit to Stone was for a specific purpose, and she held to it, completely careless of the atmosphere of age and aristocracy which would have impressed a woman of smaller spiritual stature. She noted that the Sisters there had many of the same problems which beset the Sisters at Sinsinawa: financial difficulties, temperamental readjustments, disciplinary enforcements. Shrewdly, she saw that other difficulties might arise in an American convent out of a complete following of the Stone Constitution. Almost before she left the English convent she was setting about the elimination of certain provisions.

Foremost among them was the section entitled "Of the Lay Sisters," with its special emphasis on their duty of "bodily labour" . . . "to eat their bread in the sweat of their brow"; and the devotional life they were to lead separate from the community.

The Constitutions of Stone stated prayers which the Lay Sisters were to say in lieu of the Office. They were to use a different kind of rosary beads. They would have no voice in elections or in the Chapter; and they could never be admitted as Choir Sisters after having once been clothed in the black scapular, which was the badge of their lay Sisterhood.

Inevitably, Mother Emily rebelled at this provision. Sinsinawa had never had "Lay Sisters." In his *Constitutions* Father Mazzuchelli had definitely provided that "all the novices, unless dispensed by the prioress, shall, like the postulants, attend to the housework; and be told that, however well educated or rich they may have been, every kind of housework, even the most menial, may be assigned to them as their occupation for life, without having the least claim to be employed at anything else." This was certainly a clear enough statement of refusal to allow lines of demarcation based upon manual labor; and Mother Emily was certainly the one to hold to the letter as well as the spirit of such a democratic foundation.

The situation at Stone was, of course, the result of the English social system; but it was a system which had duplications in the United States. Some communities had — as they still have — lay Sisters who are assigned to the manual labors of the institutions. Sinsinawa had never had any. Tasks might be specialized; but the teaching Sisters shared the labors as well as the spiritual exercises of the Sisters who worked in the laundry, made the bread, waited upon table, worked on the farm. There was no separate habit, there were no separate prayers. Mother Emily saw that this democracy, which she considered as much Dominican as American, must continue if the original purpose of the community were to persist. Almost up to the Chair of Peter she fought battles in this war for recognition of Father Mazzuchelli's and her own practice; and there can be little doubt that she would have presented the case to the Holy Father had she considered such a course necessary. She was, she knew, struggling against custom rather than against principle. Unquestionably, the men and women who believed in the retention of lay Sisters believed quite as strongly as she did in the equality of human souls. They did not know, as she did, how repellent the idea of visible differentiation was to the ordinary American mind just as it had been repugnant to Father Mazzuchelli.

Influenced not only by Stone, but by fear that exclusion of this provision might jeopardize their whole mission, Sister Alberta held out for the inclusion of lay Sisters. All the way along the line Mother Emily met those, who not only believed in the establishment of lay Sisters, but who saw absolutely no reason why, even in a Midwestern American community, they could not be successfully included. Temporarily, therefore, she consented. If she had to accept lay Sisters in order to obtain the necessary amended Constitutions then take them she would; but always, in her mind, must have remained the reservation that the war was not yet ended.

Eventually, she won that war. The Constitutions for Sinsinawa, finally approved by the Dominicans and ratified by the Holy Father, contain no mention of lay Sisters. There is a chapter "Of the Work," which states that, in all waking hours when the Sisters are not engaged in prayer, in reciting the Office, or in any necessary employment, they shall be "diligently occupied, either in some manual labor for the common good, or in study, in order to fit themselves for being useful in the schools, according as shall be appointed them." Under this section of the Constitutions, the college graduate and the girl who has not yet seen a college work together in an amity which indicates the perfection of the system's democracy. When need arises, doctors of philosophy wash dishes, and authors of erudite theses work in the laundry. Only the visitor is surprised. The Sisters of Sinsinawa take it as a matter of course.

In spite of the basic difference in social outlook between their communities, Mother Emily and Mother Frances Raphael found a wide area of common ground in their zeal for Christian education. There is no doubt that both Mother Emily and Sister Alberta absorbed information of great value at Stone; and a widened educational outlook went into their closely packed little bags when they left the English convent.

Father Zara met the two Sisters in London and convoyed them to Dover. They were held at the channel port by a driving storm but finally ventured the crossing. "It was dreadful, rough and stormy," Mother Emily wrote to Sister Benedicta from Munich. "Sister Alberta and I steadied our heads by resting one against the other, and so escaped what others did not." They landed at Calais, with Father Zara looking after the baggage, and entrained for Brussels.

Mother Emily had arranged, by letter from Stone, that Lizzie Wilmers, having ended her visit to her German relatives, should come to the Belgian city. When the Sisters arrived, however, the girl was not there. The mail clerk at the hotel insisted that there was no letter. Father Zara spent most of the night going from hotel to hotel. The next morning, after the Sisters had spent a sleepless night of worry, he went to the Bureau of Police. The police, too, were unsuccessful. Mother Emily, fearful of the girl's fate sent a telegram to Lizzie's address in Cologne. The answer came. Lizzie was still in Cologne, unable to go to Brussels, although she did not state the cause of her detention. She had sent a letter, she telegraphed, to the Brussels hotel. The hotel clerk still refused to give to Father Zara the letter, which he now found. Mother Emily thereupon decided that they would go to Cologne.

They were driving from the Cologne station to a hotel when Lizzie saw them passing. "She rushed out like a crazy one," Mother Emily reported, but she was probably as glad to see Lizzie as Lizzie was to see her. After a visit to an uncle, who was both blind and deaf, in a household which evidently had no desire for her visit, the girl had come into Cologne, boarding with a respectable family while she had, she said, spent her time "reading German, practicing, and visiting places of interest." Her money gave out, and the bank which had been expected to look after her refused to advance her anything. At Mother Emily's insistence, the bank eventually turned over her money to Lizzie, but the delay was so long that Sister Alberta had plenty of time to examine the great cathedral, and Mother Emily had an opportunity to glimpse the sociopolitical situation of Germany.

Lizzie Wilmers, after all, repaid her benefactor for the trouble she had caused. For Lizzie spoke German well, had been in Germany for some weeks, and was more than ordinarily intelligent. She told the travelers how Cologne had been, for many years, one of the centers of the combat between the Church and German nationalism. The arrest of the Archbishop of Cologne by the Prussian government had driven Wilhelm Emmanuel von Ketteler out of the service of that government and into study for the priesthood. As Bishop of Mainz, he had promulgated Christian social doctrine against the encroaching totalitarianism of the German State and the rising Communism of Marx and Engels. He was leading the workers of Germany into a realization that Christianity was the defender of their rights when the rise of Bismarck throttled the movement. The imposition upon Germany in 1871 of the so-called *Kulturkampf* began an eight-year persecution of Catholic education. This was still in force, with the diabolic Falk as Minister of Worship, in that year of 1877. The Jesuits, the Redemptorists, the Vincentians, the Congregation of the Holy

Ghost, and the Religious of the Sacred Heart had been suppressed. Archbishop Ledochowski, refusing to have religion taught in German in his Polish diocese of Gnesen-Posen, had been arrested, then exiled. Every year restrictions on Catholic worship and Catholic education were being tightened; but Pius IX was arousing the Catholics of Germany to action, and the party of the Center was rising.

Mallinckrodt, Windthorst, the Reichenspergers — Lizzie Wilmers rattled off the names of the leaders. The Center Party was not a sodality, not a church organization. It was a political party, fighting for civil rights. "And they will win," Lizzie prophesied. "They will put Bismarck out of power." His power was checked the following year, although it would take the successor of Pius IX to make terms with the Prussian king whom Bismarck had made German emperor. In that August of 1877, the leaders of the Center were in Cologne, planning the course that was to lead them to victory. The Sister from Sinsinawa, listening to the trumpetings of their progress, heard in them an echo of Father Mazzuchelli's teachings, and came to realize something of the great unity of Christendom. In the years to come she was to recall that her lasting impression of the German city was not the gold and silver tomb of St. Engelbracht, but the thought of a people struggling against a persecution that strove to deny them God.

Here was the center of the arena which would, even in her lifetime, extend far into the Western World. Here the theories of Karl Marx were meeting the truths of Christianity. Here the conflict between totalitarianism and Christianity had already begun. Mother Emily may not have apprehended the extent of that conflict, but she did not miss its significance. "Father Samuel was right," she told Sister Alberta, "when he said that there would one day be terrible wars unless men learned to live as Christ bade them live."

The glories of Old World cities impressed and delighted the Sisters as they progressed to Munich and Vienna. Sister Alberta, diligently keeping her journal, seems to have set more store than did Mother Emily upon places. She wrote pages of description, with an occasional mention of people whom they met. Mother Emily's letters are comparatively short. In them she illuminates with a phrase what Sister Alberta uses a page to describe. Throughout the letters, too, runs her interest in home.

"Tell me everything about home," she wrote Sister Benedicta. "Give my love to the girls, Rose McCoy and Cassie, and also to the 'little' novices. How is Sister Antoninus? Have the Sisters of Shullsburg returned? You will commence school tomorrow. Was there much of what was due on last year paid? Are the girls from Clyman returning? Give them love, please, from us. When you or Sister Romana write to Minnie T., tell her that her letter was received and I will write as soon as I can. Is Sister Stanislaus home yet? How is Sister Faustina? And Sister Mechtildus, Sister Aurelia, and Sister Pius? Give everyone my love, and tell them to be good, earnest, fervent Sisters. There are so many things I want to say. I will repeat again, be good and earnest. Do everything for God's glory."

They went on to Trieste, with Sister Alberta still lyrical and Mother Emily impressed, but not carried away beyond the constant consideration of her affairs, both in Europe and back at home.

At Rome there came one day in her mail a note from an overzealous correspondent, reporting a criticism of the one-day visit made by Mother Emily and Sister Alberta to the home of Father Zara's people, near Trieste, a visit motivated by gratitude for Father Zara's kindness. Mother Emily sped to answer the implied criticism of Father Zara. "He has been truly kind all the way," she wrote, "and priestly every moment. This I could say, were I dying." Her assurances seem to have quieted any apprehension the aroused critic may have had that she was devoting too much attention to the Zaras, for no other mention of them appears. The passage indicated however that all the trials of a Superior are not concerned with religious exercises.

On to Naples, and Bologna, and Loretto, and Venice they journeyed, with Sister Alberta describing churches and statues and museums in good guide book style, and Mother Emily writing home letters of deep concern for the affairs there. In Bergamo Sister Alberta devoted her writing to the description of a Rosary procession through the streets; but Mother Emily wrote a letter to all the Sisters, telling of her meeting with "Aunt Rachel," Father Mazzuchelli's only surviving sister.

"Aunt Rachel is just like Father Samuel," she wrote, "cheerful, gentle, kind; and she has so much method about everything. We are getting generally repaired while here — washing done, shoes mended. She is a dear old saint — up every morning at five o'clock for Mass."

They stayed in Milan only long enough to see those places associated with Father Samuel's boyhood. Then, through Turin and Genoa and Pisa they went to Rome.

Rome!

For years Mother Emily had dreamed of the day when she would see the Eternal City on the seven hills. By name she knew its ancient glories: the Forum and the Colosseum; the Catacombs and the Mamertine Prison where St. Peter and St. Paul had been imprisoned; the castle of Sant' Angelo; and the famed churches, San Pietro, Santa Maria in Trastevere, San Clemente of the Irish Dominicans, Santa Sabina, and that shrine of the Wild Geese, the San Francesco a Ripa where the Irish Franciscans had buried Tyrone and Tyrconnel.

Mother Emily's meditative habit and kindly method of correction are apparent in this letter: "You couldn't imagine where we read your letter — in the Colosseum; and it was a meditation, indeed, on life as well as on death: life which should be perfect — real, at least — life which is or ought not to be dearer to us than to these glorious martyrs whose lives were not full of sin, selfishness, uncharitableness, pride, like ours, lives given for Heaven; and it seems almost not just to think that Heaven will be as glorious for us, if we are fortunate enough to gain it, as for them. It proves clearly God's love for all is equal; that He is willing to give us as much as He has given them. Let us not forget it, my sister, that we cannot escape the arena of life. Will our angels welcome us when the battle is over?"

Even under the guidance of the Dominican archaeologist, Father Mulooly, discoverer of the original oratory of Pope Clement III and of the body of the martyred St. Ignatius, she could not entirely lose herself in contemplation of the beauties and the history of the city. Visiting within the enclosure of the cloistered Dominican Sisters of Santa Caterina, she sighed to realize that she had to be Martha as well as Mary, and start upon the work that had brought her to Rome.

The Master General was out of the city for a brief time. As she waited his return Mother Emily became only too well aware of the character of the Roman administration. Soldiers were everywhere in the town, even quartered in part of the home of the cloistered Dominicans. In this last year of the lives of both Pio Nono and Victor Emmanuel, the city was divided into separate camps, the adherents of the Papacy, and the minions of the little Savoyard monarch who had been lifted by the brain of Cavour and the armies of Louis Napoleon to the wearing of the triple crown. The atmosphere of tension added to the concern of the Sisters lest some untoward event prevent the completion of their own project.

The Master General, Joseph San Vito, returned and received the Sisters most graciously, inquiring into their welfare and insisting that they be found better lodgings. Mother Emily realized, however, from his statements, that she would be unable to transact her business with him in any American haste. "Rome moves slowly," Father Mulooly had warned her, accepting the delays with the wisdom of the archaeologist. She chafed under them but understood, as days went into weeks, how little she could do to speed the movements of a great organism.

The Master General assured her, however, that she had already moved forward in the right direction by her visit to Stone. He told her that he and the Council advised her to adopt the Constitutions of the English Dominican Sisters, in view of the fact that these had already been approved. In the first place, he said (as she wrote the same day to Sister Alexius) there must be set down laws to govern a Congregation before any Congregation could be established. "Our Constitution for the Third Order was, as we know, not written for community life, much less for a 'Congregation of Communities,' as we want to be. . . . He proposed the method we talked of last vacation, but it will be an incalculable expense, on the mere supposition of a success. Our Constitutions would have to be translated into French or Italian, then printed, before the Propaganda would inspect it. If approved, re-translation into English and another reprint would be made. Whereas, if we take those already approved (they are Dominican, too) all this will be saved and our matters disposed of sooner. They give us the privilege of changing or amending chapters in these Constitutions which we cannot practice in America. We are expecting a copy of the Rule from England every day, and will be better able to judge — though from what we saw of the proof sheet, there are many sections that we can adopt. . . .

"After we decide what to do, we must then write the Bishops for their consent as to the Congregation; and all this takes time. We are writing to some of the houses today, requesting their opinion. Don't mention this to anyone there — as all are young. We will feel more satisfied to have the opinion of the community — at least of those oldest and who have had some experience in *governing*. We can't, of course, arrange to complete the Constitution before we leave here, as it would take too long; but we want to let the General know about the Constitutions so that we can get the matter started."

Perhaps in compensation for the inevitable delay, when the Master General met the two Sisters three mornings later, on November seventeenth, as they went to Mass at the Dominican Church, he asked them if they wished to go with him to meet the Holy Father. Did they wish to go? They sped after Mass to their hospice to make preparations for the great event, returning to Santa Sabina long before eleven o'clock, the time which the Master General had set as the hour of their meeting. From there, with the

General, three Dominican Fathers and all the novices from San Clemente, "a full corona of Dominicans," as the General remarked, they set off in five carriages to the Vatican.

Within the palace, they fell into a line, but the General kept Mother Emily and Sister Alberta beside him, with the cadets forming a file on either side. Up and up marble stairways they ascended, and on through rooms made bright by the uniforms of the Swiss Guards. Ushered by the courtliest of officials, they entered the audience chamber. Swiftly there sounded the measured tramp of feet. Then, through a wide doorway came four officers in crimson satin, bearing aloft a white chair. Instantly, every man and woman in the audience chamber fell to his knees. Pius IX had come before them.

Pio Nono.

Here was the Bishop of Rome, successor of Peter, Father of Christendom. Here was the leader, the guide, the counselor of millions of people, black, brown, white, yellow, red. Here was the Keeper of the Keys. Here was the servant of the servants of God. Here was the Pope who had re-established the hierarchy in England and Holland, who had worked out concordats and conventions with governments in Europe and America, who had attacked vigorously and courageously the wrong philosophies of his era. Here was the prisoner of the Vatican, the martyr Pope, who had gained recognition of his greatest spiritual power in the very year that he had lost the temporal power of the Papacy. Here was the author of the *Syllabus of Errors,* the document which had aroused the frenzied opposition of the anti-Christian thought leaders of the world. Here was the Pope who had defined the dogma of the Immaculate Conception of the Mother of Christ. Here was the Pope who had wrested from the conflicting parties of the Vatican Council of 1870 acceptance of the doctrine of papal infallibility, probably the most important papal pronouncement of the nineteenth century.

His marble-like face and his haloing hair were as white as his white cassock, but his eyes were clear and his voice strong. The pilgrims moved toward him until, finally, Mother Emily knelt before him. Perhaps realization that the Master General of the Dominicans stood back of her brought to the Holy Father realization that she was no ordinary visitor; but again it may have been that his glimpse of her uplifted face, glowing with reverence, revealed to him something of her own spiritual strength. For he stopped the line to ask her, in an Italian that she could happily answer, from what diocese she had come. When she said, "Milwaukee," he nodded. "Ah, Mexico!" he cried, but before anyone else spoke, corrected himself. "Ah, si, Stati Uniti, Stati Uniti!" He held out his hand to her again, and she pressed it as if she would thereby catch hold upon heaven. The General was still talking of her, and of how far she had come, when she moved onward in the line.

Later that day she wrote to the Sisters at Sinsinawa, "You may imagine how anxiously we watched in the Audience Hall for our first glimpse of the Holy Father's venerable face. If a moment like this was so happily anxious — ah, what will it be when we are waiting at the portals of eternity? The Holy Father's face is more than any picture of him has ever expressed; it is full of heavenly beauty, and it must be that his Angel transferred to him some of the peace of the beatified. He blessed us twice, and as the General asked for a Benediction for the families of the members of the community, he kindly gave it. We sent the blessing and messages long ago by our Angels. I wonder if they feared to cross the ocean, or dreaded the cold of America!"

With misgivings that it might be a long time before they could follow the blessings across the Atlantic, Mother Emily and Sister Alberta settled into the patience of waiting. Up to the end of December the Rule had not come from Stone. To save time, the Sisters studied the French Rule, marking off the sections they would not adopt. As the Rule would have to be translated into French in any case, since Father San Vito could not read English, the time was not altogether wasted, and they planned to check off the results of their work against the Stone Rule when it arrived.

The Master General was the soul of kindness, but there were

some points where he entirely failed to see eye to eye with the
Americans; and no conversation could change his opinion. As late
as 1880, when he was no longer the General, he was writing to
Mother Emily that he believed it necessary that there should be
some lay Sisters in her community, "as there have always been,
and as they are all over in our Order, as much in the Sisters as
in the Brothers. If I were still General, certainly I would pre-
scribe it in the accepting of this Community of yours. But let
us hope that all will be done well, and with patience."

Cardinal Howard, who gave them unstinted aid, opened a little
wider the doors of the Vatican to which San Vito had brought
them. It would be necessary for the Congregation to have papal
ratification as well as Dominican approbation. This ratification
could not be achieved until the full process of approval had
been accomplished; but the paving of the way for it had to be
started. Here Cardinal Howard introduced the Sisters to all those
officials who would, in the course of their duty, be likely to handle
the ensuing petition. Unfortunately for the record, Mother Emily
set down no names of the Vatican authorities whom she met in
the course of the Cardinal's kindly tutelage; but it is most likely
that one of them was the Joachim Cardinal Pecci who, within
the space of a year, would become Leo XIII.

On the twenty-third of December Sister Alberta, seeing the
Christmas decorations going up in the Minerva, broke down and
wept. Mother Emily had to comfort her before she could write
her usual letter to the Sisters at the Mound. On the next day
both of them were happier, for the Master General said the Mass
for them in the chapel which contained the walls of the room
in which St. Catherine had died. On Christmas Day he gave them
the welcome gift of the christening of their Congregation in the
name of Our Lady of the Holy Rosary. The mother house at
Sinsinawa would remain the Convent of St. Clara; but the
entire association of communities would become the Congregation
of the Most Holy Rosary.

If this was not final acceptance, it was at least strong indication that the acceptance would eventually come. Mother Emily

could therefore begin to plan her return to the United States. They were still in Rome, however, when King Victor Emmanuel died on January 9, 1878. Rome was full of rumors which Sister Alberta reported. Victor Emmanuel had, at the last, begged forgiveness from the Pope. The Holy Father had sent his almoner to the Quirinal. He was allowed to give the dying king Holy Communion, but immediately afterward excluded from the room lest he influence Victor Emmanuel. The king's son and successor had also been kept out in fear that his father's dying contrition might affect his future course.

"Some weeks ago," wrote Sister Alberta, "when the Holy Father was quite ill, the 'Liberals,' enjoying in anticipation his death, the Court at the Quirinal had ordered full mourning, even to the liveries of their servants, so anxious were they to manifest their grief for *Pio Nono.* Yesterday the mourning purchased with such a different intent was used at the funeral of Victor Emmanuel."

In February of 1878, after a brief pause in Paris, the two Sisters returned to the United States. Lizzie Wilmers could not have been lost, although there is no mention of her after Trieste, for she reappeared in the school at the Mound in the following September. Certain it is that a Mother Superior who went hundreds of miles out of her course to fulfill her responsibility for a school girl's welfare in a foreign land could have done nothing less than continue to insure it. Father Zara was not returning to Sinsinawa, and the Sisters traveled westward alone.

They brought back with them permission to use the new Rule, although it was not yet officially approved. Sinsinawa rejoiced with them in the immediate change and in anticipation of final ratification; but Rome did not change her habit of slow movement. Added to the usual routine of delay, death hampered the passage of the Constitution. Pius IX died. The Master General, San Vito, died. Father Bianchi of the Order of Preachers, who was working directly upon the project, died. Cardinal Howard died.

From 1878, however, the Constitutions of Stone — without the changes finally set within it — was in effect at the Sinsinawa convent. Against her desire, but in conformity to what she thought was a necessity, Mother Emily gave the order for the creation of a division of lay Sisters. These were to include the nonteachers, those doing the manual labor of the institution. The section would number not only incoming postulants, but also those Sisters already in the community and engaged in such labor.

Not until August 4, 1880, the St. Dominic's Day when the Sinsinawa Dominicans reassumed the white habit of the Order, did the whole community come into realization of the full meaning of such a change. For on that day, while the other Sisters appeared arrayed in the white scapular, the newly designated lay Sisters wore the black scapular. For the first time a social distinction was shown at St. Clara. The result was, as Mother Emily had foreseen, most unhappy.

The lay Sisters themselves raised no protest; but many of the other Sisters did. So did many priests already associated with the Mound and the missions. There is no record of the opinions of Bishop Ireland or of Bishop John Lancaster Spalding; but anyone who knew them would know where they stood in the matter. If Mother Emily had really favored the institution, she would have suffered deeply in the rising storm of protest. Since she had never wanted the change, she used the gale to reinforce her original position. Immediately she started a campaign to convince the Dominicans at Santa Sabina that, for her community, she had been right. Unceasingly she kept it up until on May 12, 1885, the Master General of the Dominicans, the Very Reverend Joseph Mary Larroca, wrote her permission to set aside the clause requiring lay Sisters. All the Sisters then wore the white scapular.

The Larroca decision was somewhat influenced by the fact that the Master General had visited Sinsinawa in 1881. Delighted by his joyous reception, he radiated hopefulness. The Constitution would soon be approved. All was well. But his companion, the Australian bishop of Hamilton, Ontario, the Most Reverend J. J. Carbery, advised them to take the Constitution of Northampton, and make changes "suited to the wants, works, and circumstances of your country." The advice seemed a little late, with everything moving at least a little; and Mother Emily held to the original plan, even while she kept insistently at the elimination of the lay Sisterhood.

In 1885 came the first definite good news. Father E. A. Costello, the Prior of San Clemente, wrote her that he had received manuscripts of the Constitutions, letters of bishops, report of origin of work, the petition to the Holy See, and the book of Rule and Constitutions. He was placing them in the hands of the Procurator General of the Dominican Order, Marcolino Cicognani. "The Holy See never does anything in a hurry," he warned; but the Irish Dominicans of San Clemente must have helped to rush the cause, for only a few months later the Procurator General was writing of the receipt of all the documents and adding, "The Roman Congregations move very slowly." Finally, however, he wrote, that "everything is obtained." Pope Leo had given his approval on July 29, 1888; and Cardinal Simeoni, Prefect of the Propaganda, had signed the Constitutions on the Feast Day of the Blessed Emily Bicchieri, August 17, 1888.

On August 20, 1888, Cicognani wrote, "You are not now under the jurisdiction of the Master General. You are affiliated to the Order. You participate in the benefits of the Order, but you remain subject to the Propaganda, and you live an autonomous life of an Institute approved by the Holy See."

There would be, however, another delay before the decree could be made final. The bishops in whose dioceses were located the Dominican convents which would constitute the Congregation of the Most Holy Rosary must, at the end of three years, write their approval of the change, even though the change would take effect at once.

In the summer of 1889 the Superiors of the missions were called to Sinsinawa to work upon the compilation of the Rule and the Constitutions. In that year, too, the elections were held for six-year instead of the former one-year terms; and Mother Emily was named Mother General of the Congregation.

The bishops, at the end of three years, wrote in unanimous approval, and according to their temperaments: Messmer formally, Feehan piously, Spalding carefully, Ireland enthusiastically; but it was in 1893, fifteen years after Mother Emily went to Rome that she saw the object of her mission accomplished. In that year St. Clara Convent and its branches became a Congregation under direct papal jurisdiction. With insured freedom of action, without lay Sisters, and in the white habit which Father Mazzuchelli had reluctantly laid aside because of frontier conditions, the Sinsinawa Dominicans looked out upon the widening horizon of the Catholic American education to which they were to make so mighty a contribution.

CHAPTER NINE

Sinsinawa: The Blossoming
1880–1900

1

THE red bricks of American architecture came to Sinsinawa in the early 1880's. Academy and convent had far outgrown the old gray stone building. There was definite and immediate need of a new structure; and to Mother Emily, who was, as Mother Superior, a ways and means committee on what to do and how to do it, fell the task of providing the plans and their fulfillment. For, although she never made decision without the advice of the Council, she had to present to that body all the essential facts needed for decision; and when the decision was made, she had to carry it out.

Like some of the members of the Council, she did not particularly like the red brick aspect which was becoming almost standard in ecclesiastical architecture in the Middle West of that era. With them she would have desired to continue the use of the native white limestone; but her inquiries showed her that the cost of such stone was prohibitive. She compromised therefore with necessity; and, at that, set up a brick kiln at Sinsinawa because the cost of transporting bricks was proving larger than the contractors had estimated. The loss would have fallen not on the Sisters but on the builders; but Mother Emily's sense of Christian justice made the decision that the loss should be averted, if this were possible.

Ground for the wing, extending along the hillside westward from the gray stone building, was broken in 1880, and the building, impressive and stately, was completed in the autumn of 1882. It was dedicated on the Feast of All Dominican Saints, then celebrated on November 9. For the first time the bell, Albertus Magnus, gift of the former pupils of Sister Alberta, rang out from the high tower, pealing over the countryside.

The associated old and new buildings were the setting for a long drama of educational endeavor which has been both like and unlike contemporaneous efforts, secular and Catholic. To St. Clara came girls from every state of the Middle West and from some beyond, California, New York, even Massachusetts. At St. Clara they met a group of women dedicated to the service of Christian education. Not by drill but by permeative process, these students learned the formation as well as the forms of this Christian education. More than that, they learned how to make it the base of their daily living. In that achievement St. Clara was not unlike many other Catholic educational institutions of that time; but in certain matters of method and of emphasis it was singularly alone. For understanding of its position it is necessary to review the general problem of Catholic education in the last quarter of the nineteenth century.

By that time the public school system of the United States, which had begun to function some three decades earlier, was already established in American popular esteem. In the Middle West its elementary and secondary schools already made solid the base of a rapidly growing structure. Parallel to it ran the Catholic school system, necessitated by the obligation of Catholic parents to give their children a religious education. It was, in turn, the obligation of the Catholic schools to equip their students with abilities and skills in preparation for their later lives when they would be associated with graduates of the public schools. The problem of Catholic educators was that of striking a balance between the secular and the spiritual. Some of them met the challenge with high vision which made their methods of education more than merely outstanding. Mother Emily was one of these.

Someone, in speaking of her at the time of her death, asked

how a young woman whose only formal education had been compassed by a few years in a small academy in a tiny Wisconsin mining town was able to build a structure of education far in advance of her time. The answer is threefold: she took her foundation from Father Mazzuchelli's plan; she took her goal from his ideal of an American institution training young women for Catholic life within the structure of our American democracy; and she used her amazing executive ability to carry out the plan to reach the goal. It is a long way from the little academy in Benton to the colleges in River Forest in Illinois, and Madison in Wisconsin, and Fribourg in Switzerland, and Florence in Italy, established under Mother Mary Samuel, Mother Emily's long-time associate and successor; but the road to them was always the straight line of purposeful action.

With Irish shrewdness Mother Emily realized that a successful Catholic school in the United States must meet the educational challenge on the secular level of the non-Catholic school. Parents wanted their children to have Catholic instruction; but they also wanted them equipped for life in this world. More and more, industrial conditions were forcing women into gainful employment. Girls who had every expectation of marrying planned to work for a time before their marriages. The era of specialization for jobs had not yet arrived, except in the tendency of young women to take up school teaching. This teaching work was almost entirely in public schools. It became therefore a function of the Catholic academy to prepare its students for this eventuality. At the same time it had to keep itself away from the danger of becoming a training school rather than a cultural institution.

With other Catholic educators of her time Mother Emily met the problem successfully. Her distinction lay in the fact that she brought a wider vision to the problem, had greater freedom of action, lived in a milieu of intense development in political consciousness, and was able to utilize her own talents and the spirit of her community to achieve the result she sought: an integrated Christian education which would prepare students to attain the goals later defined by Monsignor George Johnson as physical health, economic well-being, social virtue, cultural development, and moral perfection. She never listed them; but the recollections of her associates in the work show how she took all these objectives into consideration in planning the activities of the school.

St. Clara was, in the eighteen eighties and nineties, as it had been in the fifties and sixties and seventies, a combination of elementary and secondary school. It sheltered even a few children of preschool age whose training established a kindergarten service. There were "Minims," youngsters in primary and intermediate grades. These children were Mother Emily's special delight. They ran to her when she came among them. They clustered around her. She paused, no matter how busy she was, to talk with them. She knew the background of every girl in the school. She knew their heartaches over difficult home conditions or lack of a home. Sometimes by word, but more often by a smile, a pat on the head, a clasp of the hand, she allayed the trouble of a child's mind. This was also true of the older girls, but her special care was for the younger children.

For these, as for the older students, she established a regime of physical education in a period not yet given to its promotion. She engaged lay teachers who instructed the students in games as well as in exercises. She had tennis courts built, and used the big recital hall of the brick building as a gymnasium. No girl went long to Sinsinawa without realization that her body was a temple of the Holy Spirit, and that she must keep that body pure, using it only for God's intention.

Preparation for economic well-being was simpler in that time than today, but it had its own problems. In spite of its nearness to frontier days, the time set up a false standard for women. The Victorian female was at the height of her vogue. Ladies — defined as women able to keep up an illusion of weakness and complete dissociation from a hurly-burly world — did not work, either by the sweat of their brows or the actions of their minds. It did not seem to matter that, as always, most women washed, and cooked, and sewed for usually large families. The ideal was divorcement from training, even training for that common destiny. Gradually, however, the desire for education was breaking down the vogue of the vapors. Schools were rising. Teachers were needed. Year after year, more young women took up this work. Academies, for the most part, became either normal schools or feeders for normal schools.

This was so much in line with the Sinsinawa tradition that it offered no particular difficulty to the Sisters. There was no need of overcoming a method, used in many academies of the time, whether Catholic or non-Catholic, which stressed a social life remote from the great actualities of poverty and distress which were growing rife in the nation. Sinsinawa was so distinctively an American community that it could not, even if it would have, separated itself from its time and place. An administrator less farseeing, however, might have compromised with the current trend. Mother Emily calmly ignored it, knowing that a standard of Christian womanhood was larger, surer, and nobler than any fetish of ladyhood. She might compromise about the substitution of brick for stone in the building. She could not compromise upon an objective of education.

It followed that the girls who were graduated from the Mound came out not only well mannered, but competent to earn their livelihoods. Most of them married within five years after graduation; many of them worked, usually at teaching, before their marriage. Many of them entered convents, St. Clara or others. A few remained spinsters, nearly always in the teaching profession. A few, a very few, pioneered into other professions, notably of art or music. But, as early as the eighteen eighties, the pattern of achievement in life vocation was definitely set for the students. At the 1884 Commencement, the valedictorian, Miss Ada Reese, told her hearers "What a Girl Ought to Do in the World." The girl of Miss Reese's address was no clinging vine. She was a sturdy oak well able to meet any winds of adversity.

One of the difficulties of such a course was the need of setting it in balance with the objective of cultural development. In one way, it was easier to do this in a boarding school, particularly a school seven miles from town, than in a day institution. In the former, leisure time could be utilized as well as class time. To improve that leisure Sinsinawa imported a long line of cultural entertainers, lecturers, singers, violinists, pianists, and a more miscellaneous crew of whistlers, ventriloquists, and specialized performers. In addition to these came a procession of high dignitaries of the Church: bishops, monsignori, eminent scholars, even a cardinal. All of them spoke; some briefly, some less briefly.

Once, in 1881, at the ending of the school year, the Most Reverend Joseph Maria Larroca, Master General of the Order of Preachers, arrived from Rome. He received a royal welcome as he came through an arch of lights; and he remained through a day of great rejoicing. It was the day on which final examinations had been set, and the students believed that the set tests could not be given later since the Sisters were going on Retreat. To their consternation Mother Emily, after the distinguished visitor departed, announced that she herself would hold the examinations on the next day!

The examinations coming at the end of the school year, were both bugbear and triumph to the classes. Often they were held by outside examiners, notable among them Orestes A. Brownson, Jr., son of the distinguished philosopher. Mr. Brownson, who had enjoyed a career even wider ranging than his father, had come back to the United States, after an adventurous voyage to the Philippine Islands and China, to find his family converted to Catholicism. For a while he raged in disgust at them, then came into the Church. Resident in Dubuque, he found understanding friends among the Sinsinawa Sisters, and soon became the founder of the traditional association of the Brownsons with the Mound.

No one who knew Sinsinawa between 1880 and the time of Mother Emily's death failed to know his son, the kindly Dr. Brownson, physician extraordinary, who drove the roads by day and by night, in his one-horse buggy, and the Brownson girls who were of the student body. To the usual girl there was something of a thrill in knowing that her mind had been examined by one descendant of the mighty Orestes, and her throat cured by another. She knew somehow that she was in touch with one of the great intellectual movements of the Catholic Church in the United States.

She knew, too, perhaps better in later years, that she had some association with another and far greater phase of that movement. Among the visitors at the Mound were James Cardinal Gibbons, Archbishop John Ireland, Archbishop John J. Keane, and Bishop John Lancaster Spalding, the four prelates who founded the Catholic University of America. These dignitaries stood preeminently for the ideal of a Catholic education which would firmly establish the Catholic American as an outstanding, productive, and co-operative citizen of the nation. They sought to attain this ideal by the foundation of The Catholic University of America. Pope Leo XIII had defined the purpose as well as the scope of that institution when he had written to its founders in 1887, "I wish that the University be founded by American means, and conducted by American brains; and if at first you have to call in the help of foreign talent in your faculties, it must be with the view of developing home intellect, of training professors who will gradually form indigenous faculties worthy of the name the University bears."

There is remarkable similarity between the Pope's instruction to the University and Father Mazzuchelli's hope of a community including "members gathered from the part of the country where they are to serve." The Sinsinawa Dominicans might not always be in complete agreement with the Archbishop of St. Paul (the Faribault case brought some differences of opinion) but on basic principles of education they moved forward with him and Archbishop Keane and Bishop Spalding and Cardinal Gibbons toward the goal of an integrated education by which man could serve both God and country.

The courses of study used at St. Clara in the '80's and '90's differed little from the program established by Father Mazzuchelli in the '50's. This was due, not to conservatism, but to the realization that the general trend of education was only catching up with the missionary's wisdom. Comparison of the Sinsinawa course and one used by the Minneapolis Public High School in the

nineties shows considerable similarity in the secular subjects, both
in character and in placement.

St. Clara had, at that time, four departments: academic, preparatory, intermediate, and primary. The primary included grades one
to four. The preparatory and the intermediate carried through
to the academic which had two divisions: the classical and the
English.

The classical course of four years provided:

Year I. Christian Doctrine; Algebra; Latin (Grammar and
Reader); English (study of sentence and paragraph; composition;
simple narration and description); French and German (essentials
of grammar, pronunciation).

Year II. Explanation of Baltimore Catechism; Algebra, Latin
(Caesar); Mediaeval History; English (analysis of essays, narra-
tive and descriptive writing; study of Irving's *Sketch Book*,
Macaulay's *Essays*, selected poems of Milton and Addison); French
(*La Parole Francaise*, grammar); German (*Zur Bruecke* for con-
versation and grammar, reading, stories).

Year III. Christian Doctrine (Wilmer's *Handbook of the Christian Religion*); Geometry; Latin (*Aeneid*); History (History of
Greece); Greek (Harper and Castle's *Inductive Primer*, Hadley
and Allen's *Grammar*); English (Shakespeare's *As You Like It*,
Macbeth, *Merchant of Venice*, *Hamlet*, Chaucer's *Prologue to
the Canterbury Tales*, Milton's *L'Allegro* and *Il Penseroso*).

Year IV. Christian Doctrine (Wilmer's *Handbook*); Mathematics (in review); Latin (Cicero, four *Orations*, sight reading,
prose compositions); Greek (*Anabasis*); Logic; English (Newman's *Idea of a University*, Tennyson's *Princess*, Wordsworth's
selected *Poems*, composition).

The English course required no Latin or Greek, but added
Physical Geography, Botany, Physics, Chemistry, Astronomy, and
Constitutional History of the United States, with electives in
Trigonometry, Geology, Ethics, and special study of periods in
the history of literature. The English course also added instruc-
tion in stenography, typing, and bookkeeping for those desiring it.

The study of Christian Doctrine was required only of Catholic students; but all students in that period were expected to attend Mass on Sundays and holydays of obligation as did the Catholic girls.

The result of these courses was determined by examination. All these examinations were intentionally difficult, but the one given the graduates of the class of 1891 seems more than a little appalling. Tessa Hubbard and Helen Condon, who were graduated then, must have been Minervas to answer a test like this:

Evidences of Religion

What do you mean by Divine Revelation? Where contained? Can the possibility of Revelation be denied by any save atheists? Are not mysteries contrary to reason?

Miracles are part of Revelation but are there not false miracles? How distinguish between true and false? If Revelation is contained in the Holy Scripture, may each one interpret them? Why does it belong to the Church to interpret them?

What is meant by the discipline of the Church in regard to reading Sacred Scripture? Into how many periods would you divide it, and what are characteristics of each period? Present discipline of the Church?

What is the Vulgate? The Clementine Edition? First English version? Characteristics of Tyndale Bible?

Prove that the Church is Apostolic.

Explain the relations of Church and State.

General History

Define History. Universal History. What is meant by true civilization? Can it be studied in any single state or period?

What two elements must enter into true civilization? Can there be civilization without progression? Is progress the means or the end?

How should Literature, Philosophy, Arts and Sciences be judged? Can we call that nation civilized whose physical development is in excess of its intellectual? Whose intellectual excludes duty to God?

What great difference appears in civilization of Ancient nations and Modern? Roman. Greek. Hebrew civilization characteristics.

Parallels and contrasts in English and French History from formation of these nations to tenth century. In tenth and thirteenth, find parallels and contrasts.

Which English ruler would compare to Louis XIV of France?
Outline Victorian reign.
Unification of Italy: Fall of Crispi. Present Ministry.
Mention three Theories of History, and explain one.
Literature
Influencing Agencies of Literature. The East. Greece. Rome.
Christianity, Early Fathers, Golden ages in different nations.
Define Literature and give eight laws in brief.
Name chief writers of Spain, Italy, France, Norway, Russia,
   Flanders.
Name living writers of note of these nations.
Quote from Shakespeare and Dante.

In view of today's discussion on Life Adjustment Education it
is interesting to note that in the late 1890's St. Clara offered, in
addition to the standard academic course a "special academic
course for pupils who wish to devote considerable time to music,
painting, elocution, stenography, and typewriting." The regular
course was divided into departments: Christian Doctrine, Mathematics, English, History, Science, Latin, and Modern Languages.
These ran through four years. The special course required the
full four-year study of Doctrine, two years of History and Science,
one year of English literature, one year of English composition,
and one of reading. For the students in stenography and typewriting were added study in commercial law, bookkeeping, and
special arithmetic. The time taken from languages and more
extensive courses in other subjects was used in the specialties
designed to prepare the students for their chosen vocations, either
cultural or commercial.

Vocal music was taught to all in class, but there were private
singing lessons as well. Piano, organ, harp, guitar, and violin
were also taught. Lessons were given in art: oil painting, water
colors, sketching from nature. Needlework was made a fine art
as well as a social meeting ground under Sister Lucina's tutelage.
Talent was encouraged; but no graduate of the school seems to
have any memory of any girl being urged to take any courses
in which she had neither ability to develop nor interest to start.

Rewards went to the one who earned them. In that democracy

of the meeting of American West and Catholic tradition, worth was the determining factor. A lay teacher of the school remembers that the star performer in the most important play given during her time at Sinsinawa was a girl whose tuition and board bills had not been paid for two years. So carefully hidden was that circumstance that the teacher herself did not know it until years later; and she heard it then from the girl who had been the performer.

Music was a common ground. All girls could not sing solos but all could sing in chorus. They learned not only secular music but liturgical as well. This was not so advanced as it now is at the Mound, but it was in advance of the custom of the time. Sometimes it went a little haltingly, as it did one morning when a chaplain, turning from the altar at the end of Mass, rebuked the choir. As he left the chapel Mother Emily followed him. Everyone could hear the sound of her footsteps as she overtook him. No one ever knew what she said in defense of her students; but thereafter all criticisms of the kind were given in private. As a result, not only every girl in the choir, but every girl in the school knew that Mother Emily was her faithful friend and doughty champion.

In addition to this scholastic regime the school, anticipating Hutchins and Adler and the St. John's Great Books movement in education, put in a course of reading recommended by the Reverend J. A. Zahm of the Congregation of the Holy Cross. The list is of more than passing interest; but it is to be feared that Father Zahm knew more about books than he did about girls. The books were in the Sinsinawa library; but there is no record that any student read very many of them. They are still there, however, as testimony to some of the educational demands of the time:

Theology and Religion
Challoner Translation, The Bible
À Kempis, *The Following of Christ*
St. Augustine, *Confessions*

Gibbons, *Faith of Our Fathers*
Fra de Bruno, *Catholic Belief*
Stone, *The Invitation Heeded*
Faber, *Creator and Creature*

Allies, *Throne of the Fisherman*
Lilly, *Ancient Religion and Modern Thought*

Lambert, *Notes on Ingersoll*
Lacordaire, *Conferences*
Marshall, *Christian Missions*

Science
Mivart, *Lessons from Nature*
Mivart, *Genesis of Species*
Molloy, *Geology and Revelation*
Wiseman, *Science and Revealed Religion*
Miller, *Testimony of the Rocks*
Johnston, *Chemistry of Common Life*

Tissandier, *Scientific Recreations*
Newcomb, *Popular Astronomy*
De Quatrefages, *The Human Species*
Van Beneden, *Animal Parasites and Messmates*
Tyndall, *Fragments of Science*
Huxley, *Lay Sermons*

History
Rawlinson, *Ancient Egypt; The Seven Great Monarchies*
Grote, *History of Greece*
Mommsen, *History of Rome*
Lingard, *History of England*
Janssen, *History of the German People*
Bancroft, *History of the United States*
Digby, *The Ages of Faith*

Montalembert, *Monks of the West*
Darras, *History of the Church*
Shea, *History of the Church in the United States*
Thebaud, *The Irish Race*
Bossuet, *Discourse on Universal History*
Schlegel, *Philosophy of History*

Biography
O'Meara, *Life of Ozanam*
Chocarne, *Inner Life of Pere Lacordaire*
Irving, *Life of Washington*
Ratisbonne, *Life of St. Bernard*
Bowdan, *Life of Father Faber*
Vaughan, *Life of St. Thomas of Aquin*

Knight, *Life of Columbus*
Russel, *Life of Mezzofanti*
De Falloux, *Life and Letters of Madame Swetschine*
Strickland, *Queens of England*
Hurtier, *Innocent III*
Roscoe, *Leo X*
Louis Pasteur, by his son-in-law

Art and Music
Rio, *Christian Art*
Starr, *Pilgrims and Shrines*
Lanzi, *History of Italian Paintings*

Taylor, *The Science of Music*
Von Seeburg, *Life of Haydn* (translated by Rev. J. M. Toohey)

Poetry
Dante, *The Divine Comedy* (Carey's translation)

Tasso, *Jerusalem Delivered*
Milton, *Paradise Lost*

Homer, *The Iliad* (Derby's translation)
Virgil, *The Aeneid* (Dryden's translation)
Shakespeare, *Dramas*

Wordsworth, *The Excursion*
O'Reilly, *In Bohemia*
Goldsmith, *The Deserted Village*
Longfellow, *Evangeline*
Newman, *Dream of Gerontius*

Travel
Kinglake, *Eothen*
Hilliard, *Six Months in Italy*
Lady Herbert, *Impressions of Spain*

McGahan, *Campaigning on the Oxus*
Stanley, *The Dark Continent*

Fiction
Wiseman, *Fabiola*
Newman, *Callista*
Keon, *Dion and the Sybils*
Manzoni, *The Betrothed*
Wallace, *Ben Hur*
Griffin, *The Collegians*
Cervantes, *Don Quixote*

Johnson, *Rasselas*
Lady Fullerton, *Too Strange not to be True*
Reid, *Heart of Steel*
Farrar, *Eric, or Little by Little*
Mrs. Craven, *A Sister's Story*

Miscellany and Criticism
Chateaubriand, *Genius of Christianity*
Archbishop Spalding, *Miscellanea*
Balmes, *Protestantism and Catholicity Compared*
Cortes, *Catholicism, Liberalism and Socialism*
Brownson, *The American Republic*
De Tocqueville, *Democracy in America*
Ozanam, *Dante and Catholic Philosophy in the 13th Century*

Dr. Ward, *Essays and Reviews*
Lilly, *Characteristics of Newman*
Lilly, *Characteristics of Manning*
Macaulay, *Essays and Reviews*
Jeffrey, *Essays and Critiques*
North, *Essays*
Smith, *Essays*
De Quincey, *Confessions of an Opium Eater*
Lamb, *Essays of Elia*
Drane, *Christian Schools and Scholars*

With such curricular and extracurricular standards it is little wonder that St. Clara won academic recognition. In 1896 examiners from the University of Wisconsin made a comprehensive study of the academy for the purpose of determining if it should be granted accreditation. The accreditation was not only granted, but the examiners gave eloquent testimony of the standards maintained. This was the beginning of an association which has continued through a half-century, and which has been an important element in the development of Sinsinawa. Always conscious of its close association with the building of Wisconsin, Sinsinawa has found the bond of affiliation a civic, as well as an educational, advantage.

If the academic requirements were stringent, there was compensation in the social life of the students. A boarding school miles from town produces strong and enduring friendships. It is high tribute to Mother Emily and her associates that friendships made at the Mound continued, some of them for more than fifty years. Sharp quarrels there might be between girls, flashes of hot temper; but the sun, going down beyond the Mississippi, took all wrath with it.

The nubias, required as headdresses, had gone out by the end of the '70's, but the sunbonnets stayed until the '80's. A black hat trimmed in white replaced them both for a few years. Then a white veil, to be worn both in winter and in summer, became the proper headwear for chapel. Other dress requirements remained much the same. The Sunday uniform was a black dress, the daily uniform a navy blue. The only jewelry allowed was a ring, a watch, a brooch, and a pair of earrings. For commencement a plain white dress was prescribed. There is no mention in a catalogue of a party dress; but memories of very old graduates testify that one party dress was always brought and, upon proper occasion, worn.

The question of dancing arose in this period. Some members of the clergy and hierarchy were opposed to the practice, even between girls at a boarding school. Mother Emily, needing advice, did not write to any of those known to hold this view. She asked Bishop Spalding what he thought of the practice. That prelate wisely said that, under such supervision as that exercised at St. Clara, he could see no objection to having girls dance either square or round dances.

Recreation was not all indoors. Tennis courts flourished with springtime, and two baseball nines opposed each other. In winter sleds tore down the hill, and there was the big event of the annual sleighride to Galena. Special occasions brought special entertainments, most of them spontaneous in their creation and carried through entirely by the girls. The day of the Chautauqua was upon the land, and Sinsinawa not far off the main travel route.

There were, as yet, no courses in sociology or in economics. These were then regarded as matter for college teaching. But Sisters trained by Father Mazzuchelli were too conscious of the importance of sociological and economic conditions not to bring study of these into related subjects; and Sisters living under the Dominican Rule knew the meaning of democracy too well not to integrate it into daily living for their students as well as for themselves.

In 1881 the school made trial of some student self-government. "If they don't learn to govern themselves here, where will they learn?" Mother Emily asked in initiating it. "You are now responsible for your own good conduct in study halls, in classrooms, in halls, in dormitories. I trust you, and I am sure that you trust one another."

Under the system the girls worked out the project of printing the school paper, the *Young Eagle*. The paper had been started in 1874, by order of the Literary Society. It had been entirely hand written, but it had been a real news organ. Its anonymous editors had a sharp sense of what constituted news. Its articles were necessarily limited to current local information; but no gossip columnist of our own times does a more comprehensive job of finding out what will interest his readers than did the busy news gatherers of the *Young Eagle*. They reported comings and goings, and even rumors. They brought in advertising. They offset frivolity by editorial. They ran travel articles written by students or Sisters. In short, they got out a newspaper, even though it appeared only occasionally and on lined sheets of ledger paper.

In 1884 the *Young Eagle* appeared in print. "Johnny" Brownson of Dubuque ran it off on a hand press. For production and distribution he had the aid of the entire student body. From that time the periodical has maintained its character as a school project, even while it has progressed — both in material and in format — into one of the leading publications of its kind in the academic field.

The association between Mother Emily and the students was amazingly close, in view of the fact that she had so many duties beyond the headship of the Academy. She had no favorites; but every girl who needed help and guidance felt free to go to her. Her sympathy was both deep and practical. Her phenomenal memory gave her information which led to insight. Her sense of humor bridged situations which might have been trying.

When the time came for the celebration of her silver jubilee as Superior in 1892, she vetoed any particular observance by the Sisters; but she could not restrain the students who themselves decided to honor her. They carried through the project with difficulty, particularly because they had to import all supplies they needed. They knew that if Mother Emily learned of their plan, she would halt it. The classes met in secret conclave, and voted to make the graduating class — Mary Sweany, Elizabeth Venus, Jennie Tracy, May Denton, Cora Wells, and Maggie Condon — a committee of ways and means.

The decorations could not be put up until devotions of the previous evening were over. Then the girls set to work, placing banners and bunting, filling reception rooms and chapel with masses of flowers, setting up in the main hall the legend, *Ad Multos Annos*, 1867–1892. In the parlor they set a design made of Sinsinawa flowers, and forming the initials M E P.

At High Mass next morning, the fourth of May, all the Catholic students received Holy Communion. The chaplain, Father Walker, gave a short discourse. Breakfast was a gala affair. Then, at eleven o'clock Mother Emily was escorted to the parlor by the committee. The big doors were opened wide so that all the students could see and hear the ceremony. Little Maude Barrows of the Minims presented a basket of flowers. Mother Emily spoke briefly but with deep feeling, "in that simple, grand earnestness that is peculiarly her own," the *Young Eagle* reported.

"Mother Emily makes you want to be good," Maude Barrows said.

It was a tribute that every girl there echoed, either then or thereafter.

In the evening came a jubilee concert, with piano solos and duets, and songs and addresses. It ended with everyone singing the *Jubilate*. One of the Sisters who was a student then remembers that everyone was joyously happy, "but there were tears in Mother Emily's eyes."

She had brought the community a long way from the day in 1867 when she had led the little band from Benton to this high hillside. She had carried on Father Mazzuchelli's dream of a school and a community serving the land in which they were set. She had expanded both. She had added a great building to the old stone original, and she already had started another, a second extension to the west. She had joined with the farmers of the neighborhood to bring about the building of a better road from East Dubuque. She had daringly planned a water system so unique that engineers had called it impossible. On the summit of the Mound she had caused to be hewn out of the rock a reservoir for one hundred thousand gallons of water, then had artesian wells sunk. The water was forced up the hill to the reservoir, then piped down. Another of Mother Emily's experiments had succeeded.

For, like every great builder, she believed in the future of the land she loved. She refused to see ultimate failure for either nation or community. Once she had examined all the conditions of any enterprise and decided to enter it, she never faltered in carrying it through to its conclusion.

The story of Edgewood Academy in Madison — now Edgewood High School and College — indicates the trials Mother Emily met and the manner in which she conquered them.

In 1873 Governor C. C. Washburne had bought Edgewood Villa, an attractive property on Lake Wingra at the edge of Madison, in the belief that he would be re-elected governor of Wisconsin. He was defeated, but remained at the villa, although his business interests were in Minnesota. Then his mills burned.

They had been insured in eighty-two companies, all of which fought payment on the ground that the mills had been destroyed by explosion, not by fire. Washburne finally won the suits. In the meanwhile he had given Edgewood to the Dominican Sisters.

In 1881 Mother Emily, Sister Magdalen, and Sister Alexius Duffy went to Madison for the final transfer of the property. They found the house usable but requiring changes to make it suitable for a school. The people of St. Raphael's parish in Madison helped them furnish the house, and the Sisters, led by Sister Alexius, came in August.

There were many difficulties, principally of transportation; but the kindly owner of a carry-all took both Sisters and pupils to Mass every Sunday and holyday; and Charity Rusk, one of the pupils and daughter of another Wisconsin governor, gave yeoman aid.

By 1894 the school had outgrown the old building. A new one was erected. It was almost completed when the old Washburne house took fire. The fire destroyed both buildings. Sister Bertha McCarthy and Sister Marcellina King did heroic service in carrying out children from the flames after firemen had declared no one could go back; but two were dead and one dying.

Mother Emily, hastening to Madison, transferred Sisters and students to Sinsinawa. Then she set about plans for a new building. For five years she pressed a lawsuit against insurance companies, and finally won. Despite all advice to abandon Edgewood, selling the property for its greatly increased ground value, she held to the original project of keeping a school there. It was not many years before her wisdom was vindicated: for Edgewood was the link with the University of Wisconsin that accentuated the beginning of the tremendous work of teacher training that has been notable among the Sinsinawa Dominicans. Edgewood, too, has grown in its own right from academy to college.

The late '90's were trying times, especially for the Middle West, the site and source of the strength of Sinsinawa. After the early boom years came the depression. In the cities, lines formed before soup kitchens. In the rural areas, farmers went bankrupt. It was the time of the Populists, of Bryan, of that definite beginning of protest against a capitalistic system which has waxed and waned and waxed again through the fifty years which have followed. It was a time when it was difficult to maintain standards of living in homes, and doubly hard in institutions. Nevertheless, Sinsinawa kept on an even keel. Only Mother Emily and the Sisters of the Council could have known how hard it was to meet the inevitable bills when payment from students was anything but inevitable. But, just as they had managed at Benton and in the early years at the Mound, they survived. More than that, they survived triumphantly. There was no indication that belts had been tightened. Feast days were gayly celebrated. Commencements raised bright banners under the Wisconsin sky. God was in His heaven, and all was right with the world of Mother Emily.

2

Even though the new Constitutions of the Congregation of the Most Holy Rosary were not approved until 1893, the 1880's saw the beginning of the expansion which the promise of the change made possible. The new Constitutions, by making the congregation papal or exempt, would make for more flexible administration, now that there were branch houses in several dioceses. The prospect of this greater flexibility, coupled with the national expansion of education, brought both new opportunities and new obligations to the Sinsinawa Community.

One of the first of these dualities came to them from Archbishop James Gibbons of Baltimore.

Difficulties had arisen regarding the affairs of a small, independent Dominican Community, semicloistered, in Washington, D. C., and it seemed advisable to Archbishop Gibbons that the Sisters there be incorporated into some other larger Sisterhood. He therefore asked Mother Emily whether she would receive as members of the Congregation of the Most Holy Rosary these Washington Sisters, and accept charge of their Convent and Academy of the Sacred Heart of Mary. This posed a difficult and delicate problem for Mother Emily, and when after consideration and, we may be assured, much prayer, she did accede to the

Archbishop's request, it was with consummate prudence in safeguarding the spirit and traditions of her own still young Congregation. All of the Sisters except two of the Washington Convent were received as members of the Sinsinawa Community, and the adoption included also the deceased members of the Washington group, in that the names of the latter were enrolled for suffrages on the obituary list at St. Clara Motherhouse.

Mother Emily wrote the Archbishop, "We accept the mission, but we do so only in our full reliance upon your Grace's reasonable support in all things conducive to the maintenance of the integrity of our Community as well as the good of religion in general." His Grace fulfilled his part of the compact. The Washington school became the nucleus of a Sinsinawa establishment in Washington that has been of benefit not only to students but to the Sisters as well: for it gave them in later days opportunity for residence in attendance at the Catholic University and access to the educational advantages of the capital.

Archbishop Gibbons' satisfaction with the arrangement he had made was indicated in subsequent letters to Mother Emily. One of these read:

Baltimore,
September 4, 1885

Respected dear Mother:
    I am happy to testify that the Community of Sisters of your Order, established in Washington, have commended themselves by their spirit and discipline, domestic peace and by the zealous and diligent instruction of the children committed to their care.

[Signed]   James Gibbons;
Archbishop of Baltimore

Sister Mary Emily,
Prioress.

A second letter several years later echoed and reinforced his assurance in the earlier one:

Baltimore, Maryland
November 21, 1892

Sister Emily,
Dear Sister:
    From a long experience of the work of your Sisters in this

diocese which has been fortunate in having a community of them in Washington as well as from a former examination of the rules of your order of St. Dominic, I hereby bear cheerful testimony to the efficiency of their labors and to their zeal in the instruction of children. The admirable spirit and love of discipline which characterizes their life and labors, give ample assurance that the order is well fitted to advance the interests of Holy Church and the love and practice of religious perfection in these United States.

I remain, with respect,
Faithfully yours in Christ,
[*Signed*]   J. Cardinal Gibbons
Archbishop of Baltimore

Even without the Washington association Mother Emily would undoubtedly have come into a national consciousness. The institution at Sinsinawa was growing steadily. Not only students but candidates for the Sisterhood were arriving from states all over the Union. To augment this consciousness of growth came preparations for the Chicago World's Fair, planned for 1892 but held in 1893.

Mother Emily appointed Sister Borromeo to direct the Sisters in preparing for exhibits of school work for the Fair. Remembering her visit to Stone, she wrote Mother Frances Raphael Drane a request to send an English exhibit. Sister Mary Isabella Howard answered the letter. "You will think us very ignorant," she wrote, "but what is a World Fair?"

The query seems to have ended the idea of an international showing. It also made a certain diversion in Mother Emily's plan. Consulting the Most Reverend Patrick Augustine Feehan, Archbishop of Chicago, she found him eager to have the exhibit held to represent the Chicago parochial schools. This was a limitation of her plan, but she accepted the responsibility he placed on her, and appointed Sister Borromeo to carry out the project.

Sister did this to such good effect that the *Popular Educator* wrote editorially: "The parochial school system has scored a point at the Fair, giving much good reason for the erasure of the past criticism that parochial schools teach sewing and catechism.

Sewing and beautiful embroideries and water-color drawings are there, to be sure, making the aisle rich with tints, but there is also plenty of good work in the line and apparently according to methods of the public schools." The *Chicago Herald* declared that the exhibit "should attract the attention of all good people, be they Presbyterians, Methodists, Baptists, or the people who are responsible for the show." Dr. Selim H. Peabody, chief of the Liberal Arts Department of the Fair, stated to a Catholic audience that he considered the exhibit the gem of the department. "We may have different views in school policy," he said, "but I feel that all true educators will be greatly benefited by the entire educational exhibit. You may see the result of what you are accomplishing and we may examine the result of your school system."

Mother Emily herself led the attendance of the Sinsinawa Dominican Sisters at sessions of the World's Parliament of Religions, held in Chicago in 1893 in association with the World's Columbian Exposition. Not many Sisters attended any of these sessions, although Cardinal Gibbons, Bishop Keane, and Bishop Spalding were among the promoters of the congress. Notes kept by the Sinsinawa Sisters show their special interest in these speeches: Christianity as a Social Force, by Dr. Richard T. Ely of the University of Wisconsin; Christianity and the Social Question, by F. G. Peabody of Harvard; Relation of the Roman Catholic Church to the Poor and Destitute, by Charles F. Donnelly, of Boston; Religion and Labor, by the Reverend James M. Cleary, of Minneapolis; and the Needs of Humanity Supplied by the Catholic Church, by Cardinal Gibbons.

Cardinal Gibbons, introduced by Bishop Keane, declared, "Montesquieu has well said that the religion of Christ, which was instituted to lead men to eternal life, has contributed more than any other institution to promote the temporal and social happiness of mankind. By its moral code it has purified society in marriage, in the sanctity of human life, in the alleviation of human misery, in its care of the needy, the old, the orphans. It has been a friend to the bondsman, and it has dignified manual labor."

Even her meeting with Edward Everett Hale and Julia Ward

Howe could not have thrilled Mother Emily as much as the hearing of the following words of Cardinal Gibbons which she caused to be repeated to the Sisters who had not gone to the congress: "The result of such intercourse will be a broader conception of education and a larger love for all who are tending to one end, namely, to make our youth holier, truer scholars, and better citizens."

Merriment that would have surprised the academy students often reigned in the convent. For their own enjoyment and for the amusement of the mission Sisters a group of enterprising journalists started a hand-written newsletter which they called *The Western Star*. It ran three columns to a page of foolscap paper and contained both prose and verse. It announced itself as published by "Pat and Dan Malloy & Co." Single copies were listed at $200, but an annual subscription would cost $100. Yearly advertising would cost $25 a line, transient $40 a line.

The gem of the publication, verses long remembered and quoted by those who saw the copy, concerned the departure from Sinsinawa of the man who worked for the Sisters as steam engineer and for the government of the United States as postmaster. The verses, entitled *L'Escapade,* were reportorial rather than literary but they testified not only to the episode but to the lightheartedness of its reporters:

> He went and left us all in the lurch,
> Notwithstanding his many prayers in the church,
> He's skedaddled, and never even resigned
> His P. M. office, but left us to find
> At our leisure the P. M. had run away.
>
> What was now to be done? Not one could dream
> How the Post Master used to make the steam.
> We wanted water, and hadn't a drop
> In the pipes below or the tank on top,
> For the man who had pumped it had run away.

Successful as the World's Fair Exhibit was, Sister Borromeo was already engaged on a far more important enterprise. Sinsinawa had always fostered teacher training. Father Mazzuchelli had

definitely established the tradition, and, even when the opportunities for study were limited, Mother Emily had carried it on.
She would assign each teaching Sister a subject for the year's
study: arithmetic or grammar, Latin or Greek. The Sisters undertook this study and took an examination in the subject during the
following summer. In addition to this, Institutes were held at the
Mound, and lecturers were engaged. There was at the time of the
early eighties no standardization of teacher education; but Sinsinawa was certainly moving toward one.

The first recorded Institute was that given in 1884 when
Professor Orestes A. Brownson was the lecturer. There were one
hundred and thirty Sisters in attendance. As this number represented only part of the teaching force, Mother Emily instructed
the listeners to take copious notes for the use of the absent
members of the Congregation.

These yearly Institutes continued, becoming by 1896 a project
of national interest in Catholic education. Meanwhile, Sister
Borromeo had, in 1893, issued a course of study for the Dominican
parochial schools "under the Superintendence of the Educational
Faculty of the Mother House at St. Clara Academy." The course
had been prepared, its announcement set forth, by a Committee
of Experienced Teachers of the Dominican Congregation of the
Most Holy Rosary.

It is more than casually interesting to examine the course. It
was, its editors stated, merely suggestive. The aim of the work
was to keep constantly before the minds of the pupils *subjects
and principles,* instead of paragraphs and pages, thus practically
solving the vexed question about a diversity of textbooks; to
advance the pupils step by step, to give them credit for work done,
and to lessen the damaging result of changes of teachers; and to
unify the work in the parochial schools of the Congregation, thus
forming a basis for comparing, by means of written examinations
and reviews, the work in the different schools. The method also
hoped "to enable the Reverend Directors of Parochial Schools and
parents of pupils to understand better what the Sisters are accom-

plishing for the children, hoping in this way to meet the approval of the former, and gain the active sympathy of the latter."

The course classified the pupils but provided that in ungraded schools there should be as few classes as possible. During the time of classification, all pupils should be kept interested in general reviews. There should be daily classwork in Christian Doctrine, Reading, Spelling, Arithmetic, Penmanship, Geography, Physiology, and History, according to proper grading.

In Primary Reading the objective should be recognition of written and printed words and pronunciation, writing of single words and combinations into sentences, separation of words into elementary sounds, and combinations of sound into words. Teaching by both word and phonic methods was advocated. There should be frequent exercises on the letters i, n, and o, since these letters form the primary principles of writing.

For Language work in higher grades pupils should reproduce stories or descriptions, orally and in writing. In Geography the idea of time, the idea of place and directions were to be stressed. Numbers should be taught by drill.

The art of questioning drew emphasis. Questioning was imperative. There were four classes of questioning: tentative, catechetical, Socratic, and formal examination. The teacher should use all. Instructions for the teaching of Physiology were definite. Under Etiquette and Good Conduct were included topics now given a wider classification: truthfulness, gentleness, kindness; purity of speech and heart; obedience, courage both physical and moral; good manners; love of country, respect for authority, obedience to law; development of civics to create feelings of patriotism and public sentiment.

All this was being done in 1893, before any formal leadership in civic education was developed. Was it any wonder that parochial school teachers, instructed by this method, became a crusading force among pastors and parents as well as among their pupils?

The location of Edgewood in Madison was to prove another

educational boom for the Sisters. In 1895, in Madison, the Columbian Catholic Summer School held its first session; and from it was born an association which was to influence the Sinsinawa Dominicans strongly and, in time, to help create a vital force in Christian social education.

The school, a six-week course, started under distinguished auspices. Archbishop Sebastian Messmer of Milwaukee was chairman of the board. On the board were Bishop A. Watterson of Columbus, Bishop John S. Foley of Detroit, Bishop James McGolrick of Duluth, and Bishop Camillus Maes of Covington. Also on the board were Dr. John A. Zahm, the Reverend Patrick Danehy, W. J. Onahan, Maurice Francis Egan, Condé Pallen, W. A. Amberg, Charles Mair, and Humphrey Desmond.

The lectures scheduled and given were impressive. Father Danehy, professor of Sacred Scripture at the St. Paul Seminary, gave five on his special subject; Dr. Zahm, five on Science and Dogma; Father Eugene Magevney, S.J., five on the historical background of Catholic popular education before the seventeenth century. Father Eugene Conway, S.J., of St. Louis University, lectured on the Fundamental Principles of Ethics; Archbishop Messmer spoke on Church and State; R. Graham Frost of St. Louis, on Economic Questions; Father J. A. LaBoule, of St. Francis Seminary, on the Eastern Schismatic Church; and Maurice Francis Egan, on Literature from a Catholic Point of View.

The single lectures included:
Magna Charta and the Church, John C. Ewing, Notre Dame.
Christianity and Buddhism, Monsignor d'Harlez, Louvain.
Joan of Arc, Joseph Willstack, Indiana.
Spanish Inquisition, Rev. J. F. Nugent, Des Moines.
Missionary Explorers of the Northwest, Judge William L. Kelly, St. Paul.
Christian Science and Faith Cure, Dr. Thomas F. Hart, Cincinnati.
Savonarola, Condé Pallen.
Hypnotism, Dr. Jerome Bauduy, St. Louis.

Church Music, Rev. Raphael Fuhr, O.S.F., St. Francis College, Quincy.

Present Position of Catholics, Rev. Thomas Ewing Sherman, S.J.

In the second year the summer school repeated many of these lecturers, adding Colonel Richard Malcolm Johnson, Archbishop Keane, and Frank P. Walsh — the last-named lectured on Labor Relations. Dr. Edward E. Pace of the Catholic University was also added to the list for a course on Psychology, and Eliza Allen Starr gave a course on Art.

In the third and last summer, 1897, the group remained much the same, but with two noteworthy additions. Henry Austin Adams, a recent convert to the Catholic Church who flamed for a time like a meteor across the sky, came to lecture on the Oxford Movement; and a priest from St. Paul, Dr. Thomas Edward Shields, arrived to give a three-pronged course. It included: (1) Three Phases of Mental Life; (2) Fundamental Qualities of the Student Life; and (3) Laws of Mental Development.

Even then, with practically nothing but local reputation, Dr. Shields was a dynamic personality. Indifferent to his appearance but keen as a whetted blade, he challenged his audiences rather than cajoled them. But he could say what he had to say, and he had a great message for the saying. The method of teaching in all the schools, Catholic and public, was wrong. Each subject was being taught as an entity, unrelated to other subjects. That was not good teaching. In fact, it was hardly teaching at all. There should be in every school a correlated curriculum which would have a core. In the Catholic schools this core should be the teaching of Religion. That teaching should be related to all other subjects taught. The objective of education was not to cram a lot of information, useful or useless, into a student's mind. The objective should be the making of a good citizen. And what was anybody doing about it?

Practical working teachers who heard him, came away convinced that Dr. Thomas Edward Shields had spoken a great truth. Margaret Haley, who spent nearly fifty years working for the betterment of conditions for Chicago public school teachers, once declared that Shields, in these Madison addresses, was the most inspirational educator she had ever heard. Wrongly, she thought him too many years ahead of his time, since she did not know the field in which he was planting his harvest.

Mother Emily already knew Dr. Shields. His friend, Monsignor Devlin, brother of Sister Ruth Devlin, had brought the young revolutionary to the Mound. Archbishop Ireland had spoken of him and his great abilities. Dr. Shields, a born crusader, needed and wanted disciples. He saw in the already established teacher training system of the Mound the opportunity to spread his theories and put them into actual practice. In 1895 he wrote Mother Emily, asking for a lecture engagement at the Sinsinawa Summer Institute. Mother Emily wrote him to come for one lecture.

He himself later told the story of their meeting. She received him with cordial friendliness in the big parlor of St. Clara, a room that had already seen more dignitaries than there were birds in the trees outside its windows. Dr. Shields spoke of giving three lectures. Mother Emily spoke of the weather. Dr. Shields, a determined man, went back to his subject. He had a triad of talks more effective than one lecture. Would he give the three? Mother Emily spoke of his journey from St. Paul. Again he went back to the idea of three lectures. Again she gracefully veered away from the topic.

"Afterward," he said, "I realized that she had made up her mind that she wasn't going to buy a pig in a poke. She had never heard me lecture, and she was not going to commit herself to taking three talks until she had heard at least one. I gave one, and won the chance to give the other two."

He returned the next year, 1896, and again gave three lectures. It was in 1897, however, that Mother Emily, seeing the result of his Madison course, decided to bring him to Sinsinawa for a longer session. In that summer Dr. Shields gave a course on Physiological Psychology that set off sparks in the minds of his Sister students.

Since no one ever remembered Dr. Shields for his courses alone, many of the Sisters have long held amusing recollections of him. He used many colored crayons for illustrating his work on blackboards, and inevitably covered himself with the multicolored dust. Maurice Francis Egan, also at Sinsinawa, giving a courtly and charming course in English literature, was the pink of sartorial perfection. He liked Dr. Shields and was so greatly troubled by the doctor's shaggy appearance that he followed him around with a small whiskbroom, brushing off the chalk dust.

Year after year, Dr. Shields returned to the Mound for the summer Institute. His influence on the Sisters in attendance was so marked that they established their own plan of a core curriculum. That plan, developing slowly but steadily, came to an apex when Sister Mary Joan, who had never seen either Mother Emily or Dr. Shields, built in the 1930's the curricula for Corpus Christi School in New York City, for St. Thomas the Apostle School in Chicago, and for the School of Saints Faith, Hope and Charity in Winnetka, Illinois. Then, in association with the late Monsignor George Johnson, who had been a student under Dr. Shields and the latter's choice as his successor to head the Department of Education in the Catholic University, Sister Joan and her associate Sister Nona, also of the Sinsinawa Dominicans, built the Curriculum for *Guiding Growth in Christian Social Living.* That curriculum is the base of the work of the Commission on American Citizenship and rapidly becoming the accepted structure for education in the Catholic elementary schools of the United States. Monsignor Johnson brought to it the Shields philosophy of education, mellowed and improved by his own experience. Sister Joan brought the Shields method, tried by years of use by the women to whom he had taught it in the long-past Wisconsin summers.

Edgewood, too, was responsible for another innovation. In the summer of 1896 three Sisters at Edgewood — Sister Benedicta Kennedy, Sister George Adamson, and Sister Clementine Tallon — took courses from a famous professor of Greek then teaching at the University of Wisconsin. The classes were conducted in the "front parlor" of the academy. They began on July 11 and probably continued until August 24, for the Edgewood Annals for that date set down the fact that the professor "was paid in full, $14.50." The professor was none other than the distinguished scholar, Grant Showerman. This little Greek class was the beginning of the university study which was to expand in the next century.

No story of Sinsinawa teacher training would be complete without further mention of Eliza Allen Starr. Miss Starr had joined the Catholic Church and was pouring into her teaching work the wide culture of her upbringing and zeal of her conversion. A real authority on both art and literature, she expansively poured both information and spirit into the minds of her chosen students. They were actually chosen, for Miss Starr temperamentally refused anyone she thought incapable of learning from her. Like Mary Garden in her later years, she sent the dullards and the laggards "back to Walla Walla, Washington." In the Sinsinawa Dominicans she found students who delighted her by their ability of concentration and their aptitude in learning. "Give me more of them to teach," she told Mother Emily when the latter feared the teacher might be overwhelmed by the numbers in her classes. What matter if she talked of Dante when she had scheduled a course on Fra Angelico? What if she limned the glories of Leonardo da Vinci to a class that had expected her to talk of Chaucer? She got around to Fra Angelico and Chaucer eventually. It was all grist for the mill, and she was a picturesque miller. After more than a half century, old Sisters talk of her with pleasure. Certainly she opened to many of them doors to a wide world of pen and brush. "She was more than a good teacher," they remember. "She was a thrilling teacher."

The preparation of teachers for their continuing work was, however, only one of Mother Emily's manifold duties. There were provisions to be ordered and brought up the long road to the

Mound. There were new buildings to be erected, and old ones maintained. There were sick Sisters to be cared for. There was correspondence to be initiated or answered, nearly all of it by hand. There was even a lawsuit to be carried through, fortunately to a successful conclusion. There was a multitude of obligations, some small, others large.

Most important of all to Mother Emily, there was the spiritual welfare of the Sisters. This was her eminent domain. She and she alone had the responsibility for this care of souls. How did she do this, in addition to all else?

Every Sister who knew her still speaks of her astounding personal knowledge of their problems. "I was in the chapel, crying one day," one of them tells. "Suddenly I felt an arm across my shoulder, and I looked up to see Mother Emily. She said nothing to me except, 'Keep praying, and God will help you.' Not until years later did I find out that she knew what was troubling me that day. But her strength and her sympathy helped me at once. I began to see the way."

Other Sisters tell of her magnetic touch. "When she took my hands while I made my vows," one of them recalls, "I felt that a great current ran from her hands into mine."

Still others speak of the electric brightness of her gaze. "A blue flame," one of them remembers, "flashing across the space between us and going to my soul."

Her direct influence extended far beyond the wide acres of the Mound. She kept in almost constant correspondence with Sisters on the Missions, and paid visit after visit. "She seemed to know when trouble came to us," an old Mission Sister says. "Sometimes we'd laugh, and call her the stormy petrel because she always came with a storm, not one she had raised, but one she had come to allay. Sometimes she came before all the Sisters in the Mission house knew what was happening to bring her."

On all special occasions she wrote at length to the Sisters who could not come to the Mound. One of these, a letter written in December, 1893, shows her zeal for the spiritual perfection of her

Sisters. Its unusual seriousness reveals her deep concern that the graces of each Sister's vocation be fortified by complete observance of the newly confirmed *Rule:*

My dearest Sisters,

Soon another Christmas morn will gladden the earth — another year we are permitted to join in the eternal Glorias. How is it with each of us this year, 1893? Does it find us nearer to God, or farther away? I tremble at times when I think of the future, lest some of us should be found wanting. I have seen many of the Community die, I am sure, saints, and I believe them to be in Heaven today as surely as I am writing to you now. Unhappily I have seen others lay aside their habit, lay aside God's love, disregard His call, and refuse Him the little He required, namely their hearts. The question comes to me, why such missteps — is it because there was no vocation in the beginning? No, every director of souls will tell you no, but all owing to want of correspondence with grace. This begins in little things; — disregard of silence, want of love for our ordinary devotions, want of fervor in assisting at the Holy Sacrifice; neglect of it, or indifference to meditation; want of sincerity with God, with ourselves, and with our Superiors; allowing faults within us which we know are displeasing to God, and which we are unwilling to correct; not strict in regard to poverty, keeping and using more than is necessary; indifference in rendering an account of moneys, — every cent, whether for the tuition of children, received as presents, or from any source whatever, should be strictly accounted for. Novel reading, the desire to go — all these things upset the peace of the soul, and we cannot be too careful lest the Holy Spirit leave us, and if we force him from us he will leave us in horrible darkness and desolation. We know "To whom much is given much will be required." Our dear Lord has given each of us a great deal, and can we not generously make sacrifices and offer Him at least a perfect life?

Let each then endeavor zealously and faithfully to live this perfect life. It will not be hard — only occasionally to deny ourselves, and surely for Christ's sake we, His Spouses, will be willing to do this. It would be a beautiful thing, now that the Final Decree is given to the Rule, if each and every member would with one united effort observe perfectly the few laws contained therein: and I would say unless there is this zealous self-sacrificing willingness, it would be better, far better, for

those who are not willing to try to observe it strictly, to with-
draw, because we know from the words of our Divine Lord
the consequences to a tepid soul. . . .

This letter is not a local one — I have written to each house.
This advice, warning, or whatsoever it may be called comes from
a sincere heart.

May God bless, protect and keep you, each and all, and
wishing you all the joys of this blessed season, I remain,

Your ever affectionate,

Sr. M. Emily

There were still difficulties for adjustment in the affairs of the
Congregation of the Most Holy Rosary. Approval of the Constitution on which she had labored with such patience and
determination was being delayed. Archbishop Gibbons and Archbishop Ireland, both powerful friends of the congregation, sought
to speed the process. Characteristically, Gibbons counseled patience
and Ireland blamed their Italian counsel who was, he said, "afraid
he would walk too quickly." The Archbishop of St. Paul also
warned Mother Emily against acceptance of any authority except
that of the Congregation of Propaganda and the episcopate. "The
submission of a congregation of women to one of men had always
been a failure," he declared. Mother Emily assured him that this
provision had already been made.

Throughout the building years of the congregation the Mother
General had the powerful support of the great prelates who were
great leaders of Catholic thought in the nation: Gibbons, Ireland,
Keane, and John Lancaster Spalding. They were the men to whom
she turned for advice and aid, a situation less remarkable than
the fact that they admired and respected both her mentality and
her spirituality. Probably no greater intellectual giants lived in
their era than these founders of the Catholic University of America.
Mother Emily's formal education consisted only of her training
by Father Mazzuchelli in the seven years between her entrance
in the Benton school and his death; and yet she could meet the
mighty minds of the Church in the United States.

One of the points of thought which she held in common with
them was her genuine democracy. To her, as to them, democracy

was not merely a political term. It was a social application of Christian principles. She showed this by her generous co-operation with pastors in providing Sisters for parochial schools. Archbishop Ireland, giving permission to the Sisters to accept a parish school in his archdiocese, wrote, "We have too many academies in the diocese, and as to select schools in a parish I find that it is hard to make them proceed without great prejudice to the parish school."

By wisdom and patience Mother Emily overcame many troubles: the difficulties involved in the separation of the country parish around Sinsinawa from the church at the Mound; problems of tax adjudications; problems of ecclesiastical authority; problems of occasional difficulties within her own community. She passed through them all with the serenity of a majestic liner moving in a stormy sea. Her one request was that an issue should be forgotten as soon as it was settled. The morning sun of her judgment never rose upon yesterday's solved problems. For that quality alone she would have been a remarkable woman.

Her ability as an educator probably came from her keen insight into the needs of education. Her success as an administrator came from her shrewd appraisal of men and women. Her greatness as a Mother General came not from qualities of mind but from qualities of soul: love of true freedom; love of justice; love of all men created in the image of God; and love of God.

This was her great gift to the Sisters of Sinsinawa.

3

The mission schools of any community are the firing lines of its action. In these schools the members of the community come in close touch with parents as well as with pastors and pupils. There they come face to face with the immediate problems of living: poverty, family difficulties, poor housing where it exists, lack of employment when it comes, truancy, delinquency, even with crime. There they meet prejudices and intolerances when these arise. There they see, at firsthand, the great social problems of American civilization; and there they do what they can to alleviate their consequences, even as they seek to find a way to solve them.

Going where they went, it was inevitable that the Sinsinawa Dominicans would run full tilt into the problems of the time and place. Their presence in such storm centers as Faribault in Minnesota, Spring Valley in Illinois, and the Yards district in Chicago may have been accidental; but the consequence of their presence in the crises that centered in these places has been anything but accidental. If the Sisters stanchly stood by their people in these communities, they also learned from the people and the crises. Unquestionably, the knowledge they gained in the mission schools equipped them for the social teaching that has become so marked an element in their educational work.

Steering straight courses through the storms of wildly tossing educational issues, of labor troubles, of community difficulties and dissensions, required no small degree of statesmanship. Probably Mother Emily's greatest service to the community at large, as well as to her own Sisterhood, was shown in meetings that have never been chronicled, in sessions never publicly reported. It is a matter of record that she was in Faribault, in Spring Valley, and at the Chicago mission schools during the troubles which beset them; but what she said and what she did rests in the memories of those Sisters who went with her through these times.

For nearly twenty-five years Faribault had been to Sinsinawa only its first branch academy, with romantic associations of Indian life, exemplified by Wehake LaBatte, and of pioneering hardships recounted by its founders, one of them Mother Emily's own sister, Sister Gertrude. Suddenly, in 1890, Faribault became the arena of one of the most violent controversies that ever shook the Catholic Church in the United States; and, without volition or contributing fault of their own, the Dominican Sisters of the Congregation of the Most Holy Rosary were plunged into the thick of the fray.

In addition to their academy at Faribault the Sisters conducted the parochial School of the Immaculate Conception, across the street from the academy. At first their problems were merely physical or academic. Then they became social.

Large numbers of French came into the town, followed by Germans and Belgians. The children of these families attended the parish school with the children of the English-speaking Catholics. The teaching was in English but occasionally the French, German, or Belgian children insisted on reciting in their own language. The pastor instructed the Sisters to let them do this rather than refuse them credit for recitations.

One day Archbishop Ireland came to visit the school. Sister Eligius, who was a very young teacher at the time, was conducting a class in Catechism when his Grace arrived. Characteristically, he took over the examination. "What is a sacrament?" he asked a little French girl.

"A sacrament is — a sacrament is —" she faltered.

John Ireland, Archbishop of St. Paul, was always impressive; but he was probably never more so to any audience than he was in that schoolroom when he asked the girl, "Don't you know?"

"I know," she said, "in French."

The Archbishop turned to Sister Eligius. "This is disgraceful," he thundered. "These children must be taught their Catechism in English. They are Americans and must know the language of our country."

It was a theme which increased his difficulties when he was embroiled in a controversy which swept both western Europe and the United States. Even though he was to win it eventually, he paid for his victory with scars of battle; and before the conflict was over, the Faribault Plan, endorsed by his Grace, had become part of a larger controversy.

The basic issue of this controversy was that of the reorganization of ecclesiastical jurisdiction in the United States on lines of nationality, rather than by the territorial system outlined by the Sacred Congregation of the Propagation of Faith in 1786. Archbishop John Carroll had his own troubles with French Catholic priests and people for the maintenance of the regulation, but he and the Baltimore Councils had held determinedly to its continuance. Archbishop Ireland therefore was only carrying on an established policy of the Church in the United States.

The rightness of his position was sustained immediately by Cardinal Gibbons, Bishop Spalding, Bishop Keane of Richmond, and Dr. Dennis J. O'Connell of the American College in Rome, and also by the meeting in St. Louis of the archbishops and bishops of the American hierarchy called by Cardinal Gibbons. The archbishops and bishops drew up a strong protest against the division of American dioceses on nationalistic lines, and sent it to the Sacred Congregation of the Propaganda in Rome. The Congregation upheld their position. So did Pope Leo XIII. In June, 1891, Cardinal Rampolla, the Papal Secretary of State, sent to Cardinal Gibbons a letter announcing the final decision against nationalistic division of American dioceses.

In the meantime, however, Archbishop Ireland plunged himself into even hotter water. In June, 1890, he made a speech before the National Education Association convention in St. Paul. The speech was not prudent, although the Archbishop intended it to help in reconciliation of Catholics and non-Catholics in the field of education.

In the address, entitled "State Schools and Parish Schools," the archbishop advocated the possibility of union between the two educational agencies. Citing the burden borne by Catholics in their double taxation for education, he advised the adoption of either the English plan or the so-called Poughkeepsie plan. The English plan provided that the State pay a Catholic school for the secular, not the religious, education of the child the same amount it paid a public school. The second plan provided that a school board should rent the building formerly used as a parish school and conduct it as a state school, with Catholic teachers and Catholic students. It should meet state requirements in secular education and during school hours no religious subject should be taught. "Catholics demand the Christian State School," he declared.

The convention speech, like one given by Cardinal Gibbons at a similar convention a year earlier, won warm applause from the convention audience; but excerpts from it, published largely out of context, brought sharp criticism from some of the Catholic press, particularly the German Catholic press. Certain clergymen, already at odds with Archbishop Ireland on the German question, seized upon the issue and made ready to take it to Rome.

In a letter to Cardinal Gibbons, Archbishop Ireland clarified his statements, and, incidentally, wrote with prophetic vision of conditions now existing. He upheld the right of the State to establish and maintain free schools, instruction being so necessary in America for good citizenship, but he required that "while the State obtain its purposes, the purposes of the Church be not frustrated." He granted to the State school its full quota of merit; but he devoted two thirds of his discourse to exposition of the reasons for justifiable Catholic dissatisfaction with the State school. Confessing the good in the system, he pointed out the defects and sought to show how these defects could be remedied.

He maintained the right of parish schools to exist, but he recognized the difficulties of Catholics in the required support of the State school and the voluntary support of the parish school. Many parishes could not afford schools. They should therefore be given proper participation in the State school, assuring to Catholic children the opportunity of instruction in their own faith. "I demand positive Catholic dogmatic teaching," he insisted, "rejecting mere moral teaching, rejecting totally the so-called 'common Christianity' theory."

The Archbishop pointed out to the Cardinal that his most salient statement had been, "I am a Catholic, of course, to the tiniest fiber of my heart, unflinching and uncompromising in my faith. But God forbid that I desire to see in America the ground which Protestantism occupies exposed to the chilling and devastating blast of unbelief. Let me be your ally in stemming the swelling tide of irreligion."

Through the early months of 1891 the resultant dispute grew so acrimonious that Archbishop Ireland, in a letter to Cardinal Gibbons, expressed his fear that he would be called to Rome to debate the educational as well as the nationality issue. The fear proved groundless but the issue remained volcanic.

Inevitably, the St. Paul speech not only gave heavy ammunition to the German nationalist advocates but also added to the number of the Archbishop's opponents; nevertheless Cardinal Gibbons, Bishop Spalding, and Bishop Keane stood by him valiantly. Many Catholic newspaper editors scorned him, but Maurice Francis Egan declared him years ahead of his time. The issue, interlocked with the German question, had greatly broadened. Even the decision of the Propaganda did little to abate the storm.

Cardinal Gibbons, while keeping away from personalities, none the less rebuked Archbishop Ireland's critics indirectly in his sermon in St. John's Cathedral of Milwaukee in August, 1891, on the occasion of the bestowal of the pallium on Archbishop Katzer. Speaking of the unity of the clergy of the nation, the Cardinal declared, "Woe to him, my brothers, who would destroy this blessed harmony that reigns among us! Woe to him who would sow tares of discord in the fair fields of the Church of America! Woe to him who would breed dissension among the leaders of Israel by introducing a spirit of nationalism into the camps of the Lord! Brothers we are, whatever may be our nationality, and brothers we shall remain — we will prove to our countrymen that the ties formed by grace and faith are stronger than flesh and blood — God and our country! This our watchword — Loyalty to God's Church and to our country!"

The Cardinal's sermon, statesmanlike though it was, did little to allay the bitter feeling against Archbishop Ireland. The dispute continued even after the Congregation of the Propaganda had spoken. The summer of 1891 seemed no time for Archbishop Ireland to take any decisive action on a question of relationship between public and parochial schools; but the summer of 1891 was exactly the time when Father Conry, pastor of the poor parish of the Immaculate Conception in Faribault, Minnesota, in the Archdiocese of St. Paul, went to his Archbishop.

The parish of the Immaculate Conception had once been prosperous. A fine stone church had been built in 1858, a fine stone school in 1874. In time the Germans, French and Belgians withdrew, setting up their own churches. They did not, however, set up their own schools; and for many years their children continued to attend the School of the Immaculate Conception. Finally, in 1887, a school for French and German children was built in the parish of St. Lawrence. Two Sinsinawa Dominicans, Sister Hildegarde Ohnhaus for the German children, and Sister Joseph Kane for the French, were assigned there. After two years, with the death of the French pastor, the French school was closed, and its two rooms turned over to the German children.

By 1891 the parish of the Immaculate Conception was in dire straits. The number of parishioners had been reduced from 3500 to 1500. There was a parish debt of $16,000. Yearly church expenses came to $2,750. Even though the Sisters received only $250 a year each, the cost of the school was $1,260. The newly appointed pastor, the Reverend James J. Conry, faced a constantly growing debt and no apparent way to meet it, to say nothing of reducing it.

In this dilemma he appealed to Archbishop Ireland for decision on the future of the Faribault school. Without money it could not remain open. If it were closed, what should be done about the children of the parish? Were they to go to the public schools of the town?

The Archbishop, who knew Faribault quite as well as did the pastor, looked first at the local situation. Was there any possible way of raising money to keep up the school? If not, what would the community do about the education of the children? Would the school board of Faribault be willing to make an arrangement for this education? And what arrangement could be offered that would satisfy both parish and school board?

With Father Conry, Archbishop Ireland studied details of the Martin plan then in use in Scott County, Minnesota. Under this plan Sisters taught secular subjects in a parochial school building, supplementing this by religious teaching outside school hours. The school board paid the teachers and the rental for the building. The plan seemed to be working with success in Scott County, and the Archbishop authorized Father Conry to offer a similar plan to the Faribault school authorities.

Unquestionably, he must have known that any such action on

his part would pour oil upon the flames of the controversy raging around him. He was, however, always utterly fearless, speaking his mind and letting the chips fall where they might. A less courageous man might not have taken on the Faribault difficulty. To him it was both challenge and responsibility. He believed that it was both morally and legally right to ask for wider distribution of public money to Catholic schools. He believed that this course was not only a matter of justice to the Catholic citizen, but a factor for unity in all the citizenry of the nation. A family had the right to determine the kind of education its children should receive. The State had the obligation to give that kind of education by support of both public and parochial schools. He had held out for this belief theoretically in speeches and in letters. Being the man he was, he had to put his conviction into action when the occasion arose in his own archdiocese.

Father Conry went back to Faribault in late July. The teaching Sisters were then in retreat at Sinsinawa. Had Father Conry consulted them, they might have helped him avoid some of the mistakes which later wrecked the project. The community of St. Clara until 1886 had a few Sisters teaching in Wisconsin public schools. They had accepted the work because it had been a choice between that method and no teaching of the children, but they did not like it, particularly when it separated the teaching of religion from the teaching of other subjects. The Sinsinawa Dominicans had gone a long way on the road of an integrated core curriculum, with religion as that core; and they did not like the separation of religion from all other subjects. They had no chance to make known their views, however, before the Faribault Plan had been made an accomplished fact.

In August, with the Sisters still away, Father Conry went before the Faribault school board. There were, he stated, two hundred students in his school, with four teaching Sisters. The school building was in excellent condition, the teachers of highest pedagogic standing. If his school were closed, the board would have the problem of caring for these 200 children the first week in

September. Could they solve that unless they accepted his offer to make his school, with its teachers, part of the public school system of Faribault?

Two members of the school board, one of them Keeley, a Catholic, voted to accept the proposition. Two others voted against it. The meeting adjourned until next day. Then Father Conry presented a letter to the board. He wrote:

> That the children at present enrolled in the school of the Immaculate Conception Parish may receive the benefits that result from American training in all the term implies;
>
> That these children may thus receive in their civic training a perfect preparation for the duties and responsibilities of American citizenship; thereby enhancing the renown of this city among its sister cities of the commonwealth as a great educational center;
>
> In consideration of the sum of One Dollar I agree to place under the management and control of the Board of Education of the City of Faribault the school building and all its equipments, with the ground, the same to be used for educational purposes under conditions as that Board may best determine is to be for the best interests of all concerned.

"Poor Father Conry!" was all that Mother Emily ever said in criticism of his letter. For he knew, as well as anyone, that the teaching was to be a continuation — except for the separate religious teaching — of what the school already had. The preparation for the duties and responsibilities of American citizenship had been going on ever since the school had started. The Sisters had long been impregnated with that ideal of civic service. The pastor knew all that, and more; but his desire to say kind words to a group from which he sought something had led him into a statement that was to plague him and the archbishop.

The board voted thereupon to adopt the proposition. The superintendent of public schools, Willis J. West, was placed in charge. He arranged that the Sisters should qualify for teachers' certificates, that each of them, except Sister Benedicta Kennedy, who was to receive $45 a month, would be given $40 a month.

Next day the Sisters came back to Faribault.

Immediately they were summoned to a meeting of the board. The four teaching Sisters went, led by Sister Benedicta Kennedy and fortified by Sister Leo Tierney. Only those who once knew Sister Leo can completely understand what a stalwart fortress she could be. A tall, broad-shouldered woman, deep-voiced, with Irish laughter that rippled over her words, with Irish blue eyes that twinkled or flamed, she had spent her childhood and girlhood in the camps of the Western railroads that her father, a construction foreman, was helping to build. Deadwood in its wildest days had been one of her childish playgrounds. There was little in human nature she had not seen, good or bad; and she insisted on believing in the best. Somewhere along the line of her adventures she had picked up a passionate love of good literature. She was unquestionably one of the great English teachers of her time because she was more than that, a tremendous personality. She could leave an assembly uplifted or stricken. The Faribault school board did not know her potentialities when they included her in the roster of their meeting.

With the other Sisters she listened in silence to the terms of the contract being explained by Mr. West. Then a member of the board raised a question. Was it proper that these Sisters should wear their religious garb when they taught in a public school?

The question brought confusion to the meeting. Sister Leo did not even rise to answer it. "I infer," she said, with a smoothness which would have been warning to those who knew her, "that the gentleman desires uniformity of garb in all teachers. He may be right in that, although it does not seem quite the American way. But if you will decide upon a garb which all your teachers will wear, we will accept it — with the others."

No motion about any garb for teachers was made.

In spite of the misgivings of the Dominicans, the school, renamed the Hill School, got off to a fair start. Archbishop Ireland, coming to Faribault, found no fault with it, but he endeavored to justify it at a meeting of the Sisters which he called. Sister Benedicta was outspoken in her continuing opposition to the plan. It took away, she declared, the constant religious training necessary for children;

it took away the devotional aspect of the rooms. Inspectors had allowed a few pictures to remain on the ground that reproductions of paintings by Michelangelo and Raphael and Fra Angelico were art, not religion, but these were not enough. The plan also took away the sense of responsibility of both parents and students.

"I know, I know," said the Archbishop, "but this is a necessity. It is a matter of financing. The Church has not the money to do what we want to do."

Sister Leo arose, her eyes glinting. "Your Grace," she purred, "I have lately come from a western city where I saw a magnificent sight. It was the stairway of a church. It had been erected at a cost of $70,000, people told me with pride. How many little parochial schools could be supported in a year on that amount of money?"

The Archbishop did not answer. Father Conry gasped. "I'd never have dared say that to him," he told Sister Leo later. "If I had, I wouldn't have a parish tomorrow."

With public school inspection of the school came publicity, apparently favorable. A reporter for a local newspaper sent a story of the plan to the New York *Times.* The publication of the story started the attack. The first firing came from *Church Progress,* a weekly edited in St. Louis by Condé Pallen, the poet laureate of Georgetown University. "The priest of this parish," the editorial said, "simply carried out what he had heard argued and defended in places where he had the right to look for light and guidance, and where he should have found unswerving allegiance, invincible principles and uncompromising courage." The weekly later declared: "The Faribault School Plan is but a cheap imitation of Catholic education; it is the shell without the pearl, the body without the soul. It shuts out the sunlight of faith and leaves the heart and mind in the outer darkness of secularism."

The attack was stronger than Sister Benedicta's words of criticism but they hit the same target. The difficulty for the Sisters, however, lay in the fact that their lips were sealed except in closed meetings with the ecclesiastical authorities. They did not like the plan but obedience required that they follow it. The only alternative would have been their withdrawal by Mother Emily. Evidently she did not for a moment consider this. The idea would have outraged her sense of obedience to the head of a diocese.

With the attack from within Catholic circles growing there came attack from the outside. The Minneapolis Protestant Ministerial Association, evidently agreeing with Father John Conway of the *Northwestern Chronicle* that the Dominican Sisters had produced a religious atmosphere "as distinctive as any to be found in a convent," went into court to dissolve the school agreement. They found, however, that they had to pay for the litigation out of their own pockets and they let the case die.

Someone in Faribault, however, made the mistake of putting Father Conry's name upon the ticket for membership on the school board. The uproar that rose was so great that, in spite of an ordinary Catholic majority, the priest was defeated. As far as Faribault was concerned, this was the beginning of the end of the experiment. The school remained within the public school system for two years only. The Sinsinawa Dominicans — and probably Father Conry — breathed sighs of relief when the contract was dissolved.

Archbishop Ireland was not yet through with the results of the plan which had somehow become associated with Cahenslyism. Early in 1892 he wrote a memorial to the Holy See, setting forth his belief that "as long as Catholics lived apart from the great mass of the American people, wrapped up in their own national customs and using a foreign language, they would not be trusted by the Republic." His adversaries raised against him the cry that he was selling out Catholic schools to public schools, and cited Faribault.

As Archbishop Ireland later wrote to the Cardinal Prefect of Propaganda, the Faribault plan provided that the school was a public school, taught by the Sisters, between the hours of nine o'clock in the morning and three thirty in the afternoon. At three thirty the children began their religion lessons. The Archbishop thought that the only change from parochial to public school was in the hours of the recitation of Catechism. Sister Benedicta, Sister Leo, Sister Eligius, and the other teachers knew that the change was far greater. They agreed with the Archbishop that the school should be supported from public money as was the public school, but they wanted no compromise to weaken Catholic school curriculum and Catholic school atmosphere.

On the surface the Faribault Plan seemed so successful in its local operation that the Archbishop went on to accept a similar plan for St. Michael's School in Stillwater. The extension of the plan brought on an avalanche of Protestant attacks which brought out a statement from the Minnesota State Superintendent of Schools, which in turn greatly weakened Archbishop Ireland's position. These attacks, however, did not equal the extent and violence of the Catholic attacks upon the plan and the planner.

Catholic newspapers reflected a great mass of Catholic clerical opinion when they tore into the plan. Even the *Catholic Mirror* of Baltimore attacked it until Cardinal Gibbons made known his stanch loyalty to the Archbishop of St. Paul. The *Northwestern Chronicle* of Ireland's own archdiocese and the *New York Freeman's Journal* were almost the only Catholic papers of the country to uphold the plan. Both of them insisted that the enemies of the plan were those who did not understand it.

The publication in November, 1891, of a brochure, *Education, To Whom Does It Belong?* by the Reverend Doctor Thomas J. Bouquillon, professor of moral theology of the Catholic University of America, established another war front. Dr. Bouquillon, a distinguished scholar, had written the pamphlet at the request of Cardinal Gibbons for the purpose of clarifying the issues at stake in the school controversy. Cardinal Gibbons expected the publication of this abstract statement of principles to help bring peace. Instead, Archbishop Ireland's enemies claimed that it had been published in an attempt to influence the American hierarchy, then about to meet in St. Louis. At that meeting the archbishops and bishops discussed the general question of State rights and Church rights in education. Out of the meeting arose storm clouds of publicity calling attention to the wide differences of opinion between Catholic philosophers. Condé Pallen still led the secular attack, using the St. Louis Catholic newspaper, *Church Progress,* to cudgel what he called "the Faribault scandal."

Then, in New York City, Archbishop Ireland, fresh from the St. Louis meeting, gave the *New York Herald* an amazing interview. "The Consecrated Blizzard of the Northwest," as the *Herald* called him, not only stated his own views but lashed out at his detractors. His mention of the Reverend René Holaind, S.J., who had issued a pamphlet in an attempt to controvert Dr. Bouquillon, aroused the indignation of some Jesuits. The nominal leader of the anti-Ireland attack however was Archbishop Corrigan of New York, although the real leader was probably Bishop McQuaid of Rochester. Back of Archbishop Ireland stood Cardinal Gibbons, Archbishop Keane, Bishop Kain of Wheeling, Bishop Spalding, and a majority of the hierarchy, since the St. Louis meeting had delegated him to draw up its findings on the question of education. Even with this backing, the archbishop's position was perilous. It was probably due to Cardinal Gibbons' great tact that the situation did not become worse for both Archbishop Ireland and the Church.

Early in 1892 Archbishop Ireland set out to Rome, bearing explanation and defense of his action in the Minnesota school situation, and preceded by a letter of Bishop Kain of Wheeling giving him complete vindication. The matter dragged, however, although the Archbishop was most cordially received by Pope Leo XIII, who talked to him on social questions, with the Archbishop glad that he knew the encyclical *Rerum Novarum* "almost by heart." In March Cardinal Gibbons wrote the Holy Father a complete, extremely lucid account of the Faribault matter. In Rome Archbishop Ireland found a friend in Cardinal Ledochowski, Prefect of the Sacred Congregation Propaganda Fide, who refused to be swayed by a statement of seven American prelates who did not agree with Cardinal Gibbons in interpreting the action of the St. Louis meeting. But the nationalist advocates were strong in Rome, as were a certain group of Jesuits who opposed Archbishop Ireland. Nevertheless, Archbishop Ireland not only vindicated himself, but also Dr. Bouquillon before the Commission of Cardinals appointed to consider the case. The decision then went to the cardinals of the Sacred Council of the Propaganda. The Cardinals gave decision but its publication was delayed. A rumor, given wide currency by the press and stating that Ireland had lost the case, was welcomed by his opponents.

Then, on April 21, 1892, Pope Leo XIII issued *Tolerari Potest,* upholding Archbishop Ireland and adding that the decrees of the Council of Baltimore still existed in full force. The Council of the Sacred Congregation of the Propaganda met. Cardinal Ledochowski — the Archbishop of Posen who had been held two years in prison for his defiance of Bismarck — gave the verdict. "The Faribault School Plan is allowed and approved so far as the Bishop's arrangement can be approved, and is permitted in all cases where independent parish schools are maintained with difficulty." A little later Cardinal Ledochowski wrote Cardinal Gibbons, urging that the American bishops search carefully for means of supplying the religious needs of Catholic children attending the public schools. Eventually, out of this search, came the establishment of the Confraternity of Christian Doctrine. The Faribault Plan had far and lasting repercussions.

Probably no person, with the exception of Archbishop Ireland himself, stood in a more precarious position than did Mother Emily throughout the course of the Faribault controversy.

On one hand, she owed, through her Sisters in the Faribault school, respect for the Archbishop's authority over them. Had she believed him wrong, however, in his action about the school, she would have been required, by her position as their Mother General, to take the Sisters out of the school. It is certain that she believed the Archbishop right in his demand for an equitable division of public school funds. The tradition of Father Mazzuchelli's placement of the Sisters in public schools around Benton would have been responsible for that belief. Futhermore, she had the same kind of zealous American patriotism that the Archbishop possessed, the same determined desire for national unity. Everything in her own tradition as well as all her philosophic principles put her among Archbishop Ireland's supporters.

On the other hand, Sinsinawa lay within the archdiocese of

Milwaukee where the church authorities favored the nationalist point of view. Had Archbishop Katzer been as prejudiced as Archbishop Ireland thought him to be, the Congregation of the Most Holy Rosary might have suffered. He was, however, a better and kinder man than his brother of St. Paul thought. Even in the midst of the Faribault troubles Archbishop Katzer continued kindly relations with Sinsinawa.

This must have been largely due to Mother Emily's careful maintenance of neutrality. Diligent search of both Sinsinawa and Faribault archives have never produced one line written by her about the situation. Sister Eligius, who lived longest of the Sisters then in the school, remembered that Mother Emily had come to Faribault during the stormy years and that she had advised the Sisters to make no statements of their own opinions to anyone. She had also, Sister Eligius recalled, visited Archbishop Ireland in St. Paul; but no mention of their conversation was ever recorded.

The obituary of the Faribault Plan is written in the annals of Bethlehem Academy of Faribault for 1893. "In September of this year the Immaculate Conception School reopened as a local parish school. There was no Academy graduate this year, a result of the Faribault Plan." Earlier the academy annalist had complained of the effect of the Sister-taught public school upon the attendance at the academy. Since the years were depression years, however, it would seem possible that the poverty of the parish and the drop in academy attendance sprang from the same cause. At any rate, many pupils who had gone from the made-over Immaculate Conception school to the public high school went to the academy in 1895. The Faribault plan was dead, as far as Faribault was concerned.

Relations with public school authorities were not always as friendly even as those in the Minnesota town. Sometimes a definite barrier was raised by public school authorities against Catholic school students. This barrier showed itself in the refusal of the authorities to permit graduates of Catholic elementary schools to enter public high schools without examinations. In Chicago, usually considered a liberal city, this condition existed. In all their schools they met this difficulty; but it took Sister Seraphica and St. Jarlath's School to break down the barrier.

Sister Seraphica was, like Sister Leo, a broad-visioned and determined woman. She was also a great teacher. There were pupils who never forgot the lessons of life, far more important than history or geography, that she taught. Honesty. Respect for yourself and your schoolmates. Fair play, especially with the weaker. She never preached. Wit was her weapon but it was never a searing wit. She had a lovely laugh that was part of her warm humanity.

She used her wit when she stood back of students in a crisis. With hundreds of other graduates of Catholic elementary schools, a St. Jarlath graduate had taken an entrance examination for a public high school. The report eventually told that she had won passing marks in all other subjects but that she had been given a mark of 15 in American History. Her mother took her and the card to Sister Seraphica. Sister Seraphica looked at it disdainfully. Then, in her rich, rolling Irish brogue, she burst forth. "If it were grammar now, I might believe that you had failed," she said, "but in American History — no! Faith, you can write the Constitution and the Declaration and name the Presidents with any of them! We'll go down and talk to the examiners."

They went, the three of them. Sister Seraphica carried her demands all the way up to an annoyed superintendent of schools. Reluctantly, but driven by her persistence, he sent for the examination papers. He stared at the History paper a moment, then darted from the room. He came back angry, but not at the visitors. "I find," he said, "that there has been a mistake. This paper was marked 95. The student's examination number was 515. But Mr. Hicks, who was taking down the marks as Miss Lowry read them, is rather deaf. He caught the 15 on that number instead of the 95. That was all."

"All?" said Sister Seraphica. "And if you have a deaf man to listen, do you also have a blind man to read?"

The girl passed. More than that, so did everyone else from St. Jarlath's; and that was the last year when anyone from the school had to take an examination to enter a public high school. The educational authorities evidently had no desire to let Sister Seraphica learn any more about deaf men and blind men.

Mother Emily's visits to the mission schools took her far afield. She had no favorites among them, as far as anyone ever knew; but she sometimes told with a chuckle stories of what she saw and heard in them. In Kewanee, Illinois, she asked a little boy in the Visitation School, "In what zone do you live?" "In the temper zone," he said. Some of the children laughed, but she said, "I, too, have lived there." Father Crowe, the pastor of the church, gave, to her consternation, a sermon about her. As she went to the train, scores of children ran out of the school to go to the station with her. "It's just as well she's going," said Father Crowe. "If she stayed, we'd have a perpetual holiday." Even without a holiday, some of the pupils insisted on following her to the railway station.

The Visitation School in Chicago, now one of the great educational institutions of the city, was one of her special cares. The neighborhood was poor. Many of its families were dependent for livelihood upon employment in the Union Stock Yards. Most of them had risen a little above the lowest economic level, but life was still for them a struggle. For the most part, the families of the neighborhood were Irish, and determined that their children would have the advantages an education could give them.

The Reverend D. F. McGuire, the pastor of the Visitation Parish, was also determined that the children of his flock should have this education. He went to Sinsinawa in 1891. He found Mother Emily sympathetic but troubled. "I haven't nine Sisters to send you," she declared.

"Eight," he bargained.

"I have no one."

"Seven," he pleaded, and went down to five.

"If I only had them!" she sighed.

"You'll have them."

"But there are so many requests which have come before yours."

"Come out to my parish," he begged. "Look over the place. Then answer me."

She went, and Father McGuire won. In September of that year she sent seven Sisters to him. They lived in a little cottage so dilapidated that, when rain came, they had to put umbrellas over their cots. The school was a square box of a frame building. As if they were out on the prairies, the Sisters had to bring coal and wood for the stoves. They also had to bring salt to throw on the stovepipes when they overheated. They would have had to carry out the ashes had it not been for the boys, who took this over and eventually other such tasks. There were three pupils for every double seat. When Archbishop Quigley came to visit, twelve years later, he asked the youngsters, "What can I give you?" and thought they would ask for a holiday.

"A new school," they shouted.

They got it.

Some of the sturdiest citizens of Chicago have come out of the old school as well as the new. Visitation, both elementary and high school, has made records in citizenship building and in immediate accomplishment in civic affairs. The later war records of its high school would be amazing. The piety of the parish, growing through the years, has become proverbial. Many girls from the Visitation parish have entered the Sinsinawa community, and many others have joined other Sisterhoods. Many boys have entered the priesthood.

The influence of the Visitation school goes far beyond the confines of the parish. To realize what the spirit of the schools has meant to thousands of boys and girls one must try to visualize what the neighborhood might have been had it been permitted to run down, physically or spiritually. It was truly a day of hope for many when Father McGuire induced Mother Emily to send those seven Sisters.

Of all the Sinsinawa missions Spring Valley, now discontinued, has probably been the most dramatic and significant.

Five Sisters from Sinsinawa and a young man by the name of John Mitchell came to Spring Valley in the same year, 1888. To Mitchell, although he was then but nineteen years of age, the mining town on the Illinois River was an old story. He had been born in Braidwood, another Illinois mining town, and had gone to work in the mines when he was twelve years old. There was nothing new to the future labor leader in the conditions existing in the gray, sodden town where a mountain of culm had accumulated around the tipple of the mine, and where company houses, general store, church and school made a replica of other communities of the bituminous coal industry. To the young Sisters of the mission, however (they were too young to have known Benton and New Diggings in the lead fields), Spring Valley was almost appalling; but it was to be far worse before a year had passed.

The base of bituminous coal labor was, like that of the Pennsylvania anthracite fields, English, Irish, and Welsh. The great bulk of the laborers, however, had been brought from Italy, Poland, Austria, and Hungary. The miners lived in company-owned houses, traded at the company store, and on their pay of about ten dollars a week, with deductions for the powder they used and for tool cleaning, tried to raise their families. The children of the Catholic miners were to be the students in the parochial school of the Church of the Immaculate Conception.

The school was not yet finished when the Sisters came in September of 1888. The Sisters lived in one section and found privacy difficult to attain until the doors were set up. They found, too, that their preparations for 150 pupils had to be extended to the care for 250. "With some of them it was a desire for education," Sister Theodosius, one of the original group, recalls, "but with others it was a desire to keep warm through the day. They came from houses where there was no heat, even though they were set right there on the coal fields."

The parents of the children were, for the most part, so poor that they could not afford to pay tuition; but the Reverend Patrick Power, the pastor of the church, gave of his personal fortune to maintain the school. The winter was hard, as all winters were in Spring Valley; but everyone, miners, children, priest, and Sisters, kept looking forward to spring.

In May, 1889, with the countryside beyond the town burgeoned into green fields, the lockout began which was to make labor his-

tory in the United States and to result, eventually, in the formation
of the United Mine Workers. The coal operators, to cut down
expenses in a slack selling season, laid off the miners. They demanded, however, that the men pay rent for their use of company
houses and pay monthly for all supplies bought at the company
store. The miners had no money for such payment. At the salaries
they had received they had lived from hand to mouth. They had,
it was true, frequented the saloons in too great numbers, to Father
Power's distress and to the misery of their wives and children.
Their condition now, however, was pitiable; but there was no pity
in the minds of their masters. When the men could not pay rent,
eviction orders were issued.

The responsibility for the evictions was set on the broad shoulders of the mine manager, Charles J. Devlin. Devlin had himself
come up the hard way. His mother, the penniless widow of an Irish
immigrant, had taken in washing in order to educate her son. He
had found work as an accountant in Chicago, then in St. Paul,
then had been hired by the Spring Valley company. He was known
as a hard-working, hard-hitting businessman in a time when no
holds were barred. But Devlin could not carry out the order. He
refused to evict the miners' families, and was immediately dis-
charged by the company. Later, he became a coal operator in
Kansas, but, probably with remembrance of the Illinois town,
managed his own mines so well that he received an amazing tribute
which he could not have envisioned. For, on the day of his funeral
in La Salle, Illinois, the whistles sounded for work in all Kansas
mines, but there was no response from the miners. The men, his
own employees and those of other mines, with uncovered heads
and wearing mourning badges, were marching to churches for
memorial services for the man who had been their friend. "When
we were in doubt," the *Miner's Journal* wrote, "he gave us counsel;
when we were sick or in distress, he gave us help."

Devlin, however, was one of the few bright spots in the Spring
Valley situation, and his discharge by the operators removed him
from effective aid. Twelve hundred heads of families were out of
work. Seven out of ten families were ill. Malaria, diphtheria,

cholera morbus, ague and pneumonia stalked through the gray houses. Men, women, and children were starving. "Men are dying to escape slavery," wrote the correspondent of the *New York World*. There were two unions to which some of the men belonged: the Knights of Labor and the National Progressive Union; but they bickered for power, and gave little help. Already young John Mitchell was trying to effect better union organization, knowing that only this would give lasting aid to the miners. The only immediate aid, however, for the men and their families was that organized and administered by Father Power and the Dominican Sisters.

Father Power first used his own money to buy food. Then, finding how desperate was the need of greater supplies, he set out to beg. With the consent of Bishop John Lancaster Spalding of Peoria, he went through Illinois, pleading the cause of the miners. He made personal appeals to hundreds of men and women able to extend aid. "Food and clothing," he entreated. "Send us food and clothing!" Food and clothing began to pour into the town. The miners carried it from the station to the school where the Sisters piled, and sorted, and distributed it. The basement of the building became the aid station. From early morning until late evening the nuns worked to fill the requests.

"The people were proud," Sister Theodosius said. "They would not have taken aid from strangers, no matter how great was their need. But they knew us by that time. They knew we were their friends, and so they were willing to come to us."

The Sisters also went to them. They became nurses in those homes where no other help had been given. They divided into squads so that the danger of infection could be minimized. They risked their own lives, hour after hour, "but no one of us died in that terrible year."

The lockout ended in the autumn of 1889, although labor conditions in the mines remained so evil that, on July 4, 1894, three hundred Spring Valley miners offered to go into voluntary slavery for assurance of a "reasonably comfortable home, fuel and clothing." Three years later, the great strike of 1897, one of the tensest struggles in American labor history, had begun in Spring Valley, and John Mitchell, as "the voice of three hundred thousand men," was leading forces captained by W. D. Mahon of the Street Car Unions, James O'Connell of the Machinists, and the redoubtable Mary Jones, known as Mother Jones, and arousing the American public to consciousness of its responsibility in such labor conditions.

In the years between, the school, like the rest of the town, suffered. Father Power's personal funds could no longer extend to meet all the needs of his parish. The school could not continue. Faced by this situation, Father Power went to the public school board. If the Catholic school closed, he said, there would be 250 more pupils to go to the public schools. The public school had no building and no teachers to provide for this contingency. He offered to give the use of the building if the board would engage the Sisters to teach. The board agreed to take three of the Sisters at the salary being given public school teachers for the same experience in the same grades.

This payment took care of the school. The arrangement continued successfully for fifteen years, extending into the time when the employment of Catholic Sisters by public school boards had become an issue of paramount importance in American educational history.

The Spring Valley episode, relatively brief though the lockout was, had a far-reaching effect upon the Congregation at Sinsinawa. In the midst of the period Mother Emily made several journeys to the mining town. Sister Theodosius has remembered that, on these occasions, her Superior not only held long sessions with Father Power, planning ways and means of getting more aid for the miners' families, but also talked to the men, women, and children who came to the school for aid. By her direction the Sisters stayed in the town through a period of vacation when they would ordinarily have returned to the Mound. Characteristically, she worked without fanfare, but there can be little doubt that she went to the heart of the labor troubles. There is no record that she talked with John Mitchell, although the young man was already a friend of Father Power who had deep confidence in his ability. Certainly, however, her intimate knowledge of the circumstances of the Illinois mine lockout deepened her natural sympathy for the men who lived under such conditions, and helped to make her an able and active interpreter of the *Rerum Novarum* when it appeared a few years later. If the Dominicans taught the mission schools, they also learned from them.

In every school taught by her Sisters Mother Emily was known and loved by the children. There was a radiance about her which shone like sunlight entering a dark room. To thousands of children her name, "Mother Emily," meant not a casual visitor, not a superior, but a friend, particularly when teachers who were martinets for order melted under her kindliness. "Come again, Mother Emily," children chanted spontaneously to her. "God willing, I shall come," she always told them.

Unquestionably, it was her deep human interest in the children of the missions which made her so conscious of their problems. To her the pronouncements of *Rerum Novarum* were not academic abstractions. They were living words aimed at those wrongs which she saw as she went from city to city. The children of the poor, saying never a word, cried out to her as she looked down into their pleading eyes. What was it they wanted: Love. Yes, and justice. The only way they could win that justice was by the teaching of others. That was her job. Her teachers, the Sisters of Sinsinawa, must not only know the great encyclical, they must know how to apply it. Education for teachers must be more than academic. It must also be social, with every teacher a missionary of social justice.

To that end she permitted to the mission Sisters a latitude of action unusual in the period. They could visit the sick of the parish. At St. Jarlath's, Chicago, they gave service in the soup kitchen established by Father Cashman during a time of national depression. Everywhere they grew conscious of the association of industrial conditions and poverty. Wisely, Mother Emily let them see the conditions and pointed out — not by sermons but by easy guidance — the remedy. More than twenty years before the issuance of the Bishops' Program, the Sisters of Sinsinawa were writing a social program of their own.

CHAPTER TEN

Sinsinawa: The Burgeoning
1900–1909

THE late 1890's and the early 1900's saw the skyrocketing of higher education for women. State universities and institutions like the University of Chicago had been, for some time, admitting women to both collegiate and postgraduate courses. Vassar, Wellesley, Smith were well under way. Catholic higher education for women lagged, however, although the Ursuline Academy in New Orleans had been the first academy for girls in that area now belonging to the United States, and the Georgetown Visitation Academy, the first in the section which had been the original Thirteen Colonies. Because many Catholic young women were attending secular colleges, largely forced by the exigencies of requirements for teaching certificates, Catholic parents and pastors were beginning to demand provisions for Catholic college education.

To meet the demand, the College of Notre Dame in Maryland had been established in the middle nineties, and Trinity College in Washington in 1900. Mother Emily was quick to see that this need of Catholic higher education in the Middle West could not be served by distant colleges. There must be Catholic colleges for young women established in places to which they could have easier access. Sinsinawa remained, to her mind, the ideal location for such a college. But how could the community finance it? A new convent building, to the east of the Old Stone Building, had just been completed. The debt was heavy, the prospects for greater revenue slight. Characteristically, the Mother General decided to start the project.

St. Clara had a genuine advantage for such a beginning. Father Samuel's Dominican daughters had absorbed his love of scholarship. Some of the Benton Sisters, notably Sister Benedicta and Sister Borromeo, were still living. Both of them had advanced their education notably by study. They had also helped to train a younger generation of teachers. Long before the end of the eighteen nineties, the academy was presenting a course which favorably compared with junior college work in many institutions.

Graduates of the academy had studied, in addition to the ordinary secondary school course of that time, Horace and Xenophon, plane trigonometry, five plays of Shakespeare, plays in French of Racine, Molière and Corneille, and in German of Goethe and Schiller, Newman's *Idea of a University*, Milton's *Lycidas*, history of art, history of music, logic, and ethics. Dr. Knowlton of the University of Wisconsin, examiner for accreditation, gave high praise to the work of the classes and suggested that some of it was actually college work. In a decade when it was not accrediting any other Catholic secondary school, the university accepted St. Clara. Dr. Annie Crosby Emory, dean of women of the University of Wisconsin, after observing the students' sight reading from the *Anabasis* and the *Iliad*, and from the German of Goethe's *Iphigenia of Taurus*, told Mother Emily that the establishment of a college course would present no great difficulty.

Dr. Shields and Maurice Francis Egan had both urged the Sisters to go into college work. Both were convinced that it would be only one step forward for the academy teachers. It would, of course, require preparation and sacrifice — but when had that not been the story of pioneer education, particularly of Catholic pioneer education? Surely Sinsinawa, with its history of overcoming obstacles, would not hesitate at this one!

With this encouragement and this challenge Mother Emily set about the development of the institution. True to the tradition Father Mazzuchelli had set in the Benton school, she applied for charter to the state of Wisconsin on May 1, 1901. This amendment, changing the name of St. Clara Academy to St. Clara College, stated that the purpose of the organization was "to have and exercise all the powers and authority possessed by colleges of the State of Wisconsin, in granting diplomas, degrees, or distinctions for proficiency in the arts and sciences to students of said Colleges and others whom it desires to honor." The document was signed by the president and the secretary of the Board of Trustees, who set down their names as Emily Power and Bonaventure Tracy.

The purpose of the college, announced elsewhere, was "to strengthen and develop the moral character of the student." A true education included the training of the heart as well as that of the mind. The college was without endowment, and its work would be necessarily limited.

It was not too hard to determine a course of studies. These were to be continuations and expansions of the academy subjects. A research college was out of the question. The college would offer the standard materials required in most colleges of its type, place and period. The recounting of these would have daunted a less fearless soul than Mother Emily's. In 1901 they read:

FIRST YEAR — FIRST TERM

Latin. Virgil's Eclogues. Horace, Odes, Epodes, Ars Poetica.
Greek. Demosthenes. Sight reading from Xenophon's Memorabilia.
German or French. Standard novels and plays.
Literature. History of English literature for a connected view of the main facts in its development in the Chaucerian period; the Elizabethan; the Classical. Each period is considered in relation to its contemporary European literature.
Mathematics. College Algebra.

FIRST YEAR — SECOND TERM

Latin. Livy, Book XXI.
Greek. Plato. Sight reading from the Odyssey.
German or French. Work of First Term continued.
Literature. Shakespeare as a dramatic artist. Study of examples of comedy and tragedy.
Mathematics. Plane and Spherical Trigonometry.
(Advanced work in Chemistry or Physics may be elected in place of Greek.)

SECOND YEAR — FIRST TERM

Latin. Quintilian, Books X, XII. Plautus, Captivi.

Greek. Sophocles, two plays. Sight reading from New Testament.
German or French. Study of standard literature.
Literature. Studies in Comparative Literature.
Mental Philosophy.

SECOND YEAR — SECOND TERM

Latin. Cicero, De Amicitia.
Greek. Euripides, two plays. Aeschylus, two plays. Readings
from St. Gregory and St. Basil.
German or French. Work of First Term continued.
Literature. Study of Comparative Literature continued.
Moral Philosophy.
(Geology may be elected in place of Greek.)

In view of the movement in Catholic education today, to sub-
stitute the Latin of the Church Fathers and of later Christian
writers for some of the more flagrantly pagan classic writers, it is
interesting to note that even in a junior college there was a course
in Patristic Greek.

Although the number of students did not greatly increase during
the next few years, there was sufficient demand for third- and
fourth-year college work to have these courses added. By the fall
of 1902 announcement could be made of three divisions of college
study: the Ancient Classical, the Modern Classical, and the English
Scientific. History, English, and Mathematics were the same for
the three divisions. The Ancient Classical required some German
or French, and the Modern Classical, some Latin. All Catholic
students were required to take full courses in Evidences of Religion
and Church History.

The courses in the languages were all greatly extended, as were
the courses in Science. Here again the Mazzuchellian influence
persisted. Few small colleges, especially Catholic colleges, were
giving the extensive courses in botany, chemistry, geology, physics,
and astronomy that St. Clara gave.

The stress on philosophy was unusual. Logic was taught to
freshmen two times per week, psychology to sophomores three times
per week, ethics to juniors three times per week, and the history of
philosophy to seniors four times per week. Unusual, too, even for

Catholic colleges, was the emphasis which Mother Emily placed upon the teaching of Christian social philosophy. This was, of course, Aquinian, but it had been revivified by the publication of *Rerum Novarum*. In both Christian doctrine and philosophy classes the St. Clara teachers emphasized the general trend of the Pope's letter. The presentation was distilled from courses they themselves were taking in their own teacher college, but it showed its efficacy in its effect upon the students, and the entire group of students formed a nucleus of intellectual awareness to social problems which has become traditional with Rosary College, the successor to St. Clara.

Only through the ability, loyalty, and determined devotion of the teaching Sisters was Mother Emily able to carry out this plan, simple enough in the retrospect of fifty years, but elaborate for the time and place. How could it be done by teachers who had never been to college, to say nothing of having no degrees? The University of Wisconsin had the resources of a great state behind it. Like the University of Chicago, it could raid old Eastern universities for its professors. Northwestern University was old enough to have raised its own pedagogic crop. The two Harpers, Capps and Shorey, Herrick and Moody at Chicago offered the summit of American scholarship. Ely at Madison was founding a new school of American social thought. Cumnock at Northwestern was sending out students who could not only read aloud but who knew what they were reading. What could a college like St. Clara, a hope rather than an achievement, offer to the parents of prospective Catholic students?

Fortunately for American education, two ideas persisted in the American mind of the early 1900's. The first was recognition of the efficacy of the little red schoolhouse. The other was consciousness that real education might be attained on a log with a Mark Hopkins at one end and the student at the other. Not size but quality was the important factor. Not reputation but character was the determining element. Women who had, as girls, attended St. Clara Academy took the opportunity to send their daughters to St. Clara College. Women who had attended mission schools or had seen their influence in their towns and cities reasoned that the Sinsinawa Dominicans were not going to fail in any enterprise they started.

Mother Emily repaid their confidence by inspiring the academy teachers. Some of them she had known from the Benton days. Others were comparative newcomers. To every one of them she gave the certainty of her belief in them. "No one could fail Mother Emily," one after another of them has said in speaking of the college foundation.

Certainly the teachers whom she chose for the college were not instructors who would slight any task. Some of them were self-trained in their subjects. All of them had a solid foundation of training. All of them had personality, that subtle element more important than pedagogy in the making of a good teacher. One of the lay teachers of the time at the college described the religious faculty as a mighty powerhouse of intellectual energy.

Mother Bonaventure Tracy headed the staff. She never made any show of authority but no one could meet her without recognition of that authority. She could meet a crisis with quiet calm and with a certain wry humor which might only express itself in a gleam of her eyes, but which sometimes ran into a wit that was none the less sharp for having been expressed in a soft voice. To a student who asked for unusual permission to go home to Chicago during Holy Week Mother Bonaventure quietly asked, "For the *Tenebrae?*" Her tone carried no implication of knowledge that the petitioner had full intention of seeking more worldly entertainment, but the seeker did not press the point.

Sister Benedicta, for all her forty years in the Middle West, held to the accents of her native Cambridge, Massachusetts. She had two outstanding characteristics, a devoted affection for Mother Emily, often expressed in her anxious query as she went through the halls, "Have you seen Mothah?" and her deep appreciation of classic literature. Her translation from the Italian of Father Mazzuchelli's Memoirs was a labor of love. It remains an important document in pioneer history, although the translator made it hard reading by holding too tightly to the original idiom. Just as sternly she insisted that the *Odyssey* be carried over into English words which held close to the Greek original meaning, an exercise which made for exactitude but not for flights of fancy upon the wine-red sea of ancient wanderings.

Sister Clementine, teacher of English, was another tower of strength. She could, and in emergencies did, teach anything in the course, although her innate scholarship insisted on an almost impossible thoroughness. Sister Camillus, who could discipline a language as well as a student, taught Latin. Sister Hyacintha taught English with both precision and fire, a rare combination which inspired students to read well and to write well. Sister Alexius taught history, a little ponderously, perhaps, but with a broad sense of its trends rather than its events. Sister Ruth taught science carefully.

The erudition of the degreeless Sisters was a source of wonder to the young lay teachers whom Mother Emily brought in for those subjects where she had not yet found workers. Graduates just out of large Midwestern colleges, they marveled at the scope of the Sisters' knowledge. "But where did you learn it?" they questioned, not yet knowing what persevering self-teaching could accomplish.

Examiners from the University of Wisconsin wrote glowing reports of the classes they visited. Dr. Paul S. Reinsch, head of the department of political science and later, during the Wilson administration, minister to China, gave high praise to classes he examined.

Every long-established school has a tradition of school spirit, but it seemed to the lay teachers, at least, that the spirit of St. Clara was almost tangible. Every class presented a solidarity of pride in the school. If one girl failed to come up to the standards of the class, her fellows did something about it, rallying either to protect her or to enlighten her. The entire class took responsibility for the misdeed of a member. One girl's slow slip was instantly retrieved by the quick action of others.

There was, too, a general friendliness between the divisions of the school which gave the effect of a big family. There were so few college students that they would have been isolated had they not associated with the girls of the academy. Both groups delighted in the preparatory, particularly in the youngest minims; and although the minims were entirely separated from the other departments, they were the pleasant concern of their elders.

Mother Emily not only knew every student in the three departments but knew a great deal about each one of them. Meeting a girl in the hall, she would remember a sick mother, an aged grandparent, an older sister. Her phenomenal memory recalled small incidents of interest to the girl's family. "Did your aunt like California?" she might ask one. "Did the new reaper do all your father expected?" she might inquire of another.

She watched over their health, too, not only providing the best possible conditions by scientific investigation, but also looking for any evidence of illness. "Mother Emily never sends us to bed when she finds us ill," one of the college students declared. "She takes us there." The infirmarian and the well-stocked infirmary could meet most emergencies; but if anything serious threatened, she herself summoned Dr. Brownson. There were times when that faithful physician came two and three times daily from Dubuque.

Rosary College, successor to St. Clara, graduates at least a hundred and fifty students every year. The Villa des Fougères in Fribourg and the Villa Schifanoia in Florence care for at least a score each. St. Clara College started with two students, Eva Clinton McCarty of Sioux City, Iowa, and Teresa Marguerite Tighe of Omaha, Nebraska. Upon them focused the full force of Dominican teaching: for neither Mother Emily nor the members of her teaching staff would give less to a class of two students than to a class of forty.

The second class to be graduated — in 1905 — doubled the number of the first. Degrees were conferred on Mary Fidele Gleason of Minneapolis, Julia Mary Fitzgerald of Arcola, Illinois, Imelda Bridget Doyle of Cuba City, Wisconsin, and Katherine Loretto Carroll of Joliet, Illinois. At the June Commencement Mary Gleason not only gave the customary salutatory and an argumentation entitled "He is the Richest who gives the Most," but also played a Chopin polonaise. The degrees were conferred by the Most Reverend Diomede Falconio, Apostolic Delegate to the United States. Mother Emily discoursed with him in the Italian she had learned in her girlhood from Father Mazzuchelli.

The class of 1906 fell back to two graduates, Margaret Mary Wigman of Green Bay, Wisconsin, and Marie Margaret Duggan of Sioux City, Iowa, but nine received bachelor degrees in 1908. In 1909 there were thirty-one students registered in the college, most of them from Wisconsin, Illinois, and Iowa, but with Nebraska, Minnesota, South Dakota, Colorado, and Ohio represented.

Throughout the years of building the college the academy was never slighted, nor was it regarded as a merely college preparatory school. During this period it continued its special departments of Art, Music, and Dramatic Art, as well as its Commercial Course. It also established a special literary course "not preparing for college."

As far as anyone remembers, there was no social division between the college and the academy students, nor between the students of regular and special courses. Members of the college classes were frequently the elder sisters of girls in the academy; and many of the closest friendships at the Mound were between girls with different cultural interests.

The semi-isolation of Sinsinawa in the early years of the century not only gave its students unusual opportunity for concentration upon studies but also gave them wider interest in the arts. They could not go to concerts but concerts often came to them. They could not attend plays in city theaters but they could have plays of their own. Even girls who did not take special courses in music, art, or dramatic expression found enjoyment and widened outlook by their interest in the work done by their fellows.

The smallness of the school also helped to break down any possible social distinctions between girls in different courses. There were inevitably small groups in close friendships but there was never any line dividing students either because of home-economic conditions or of scholastic preferment. Sinsinawa was definitely a democracy, on both the convent and the academy sides.

No institution headed by Mother Emily Power could be anything else. She made absolutely no distinctions. She was as concerned over the health and welfare of the humblest as she was over that of the wealthiest student. Her welcome to their families was the same, so pleasant and kindly that men and women, after an hour's visit with her, went away claiming her as a lifetime friend. She knew the history and the problems of the drivers, the farm laborers. Looking over the wide picture, she still saw the details of human difficulties and aspirations.

Hospitality, the unvarying rule of Sinsinawa, sometimes had its drawbacks for its dispensers. Crowds had a way of coming at unexpected times, and individuals a way of staying beyond their allotments. Once, an editor of a Catholic publication arrived on an April day to visit, he said, the chaplain who was then absent. The chaplain, returning, denied that he had issued any such invitation. Mother Emily hesitated, however, to inform the visitor of the denial. The man stayed until mid-August, and might have remained until his death, years later, had not the chaplain finally taken the issue into his own hands and informed the guest that his stay was ended. This was, however, an entirely isolated instance. At all times Sinsinawa was like a western stage station in its panorama of the countryside. A later De Tocqueville would have reveled in its presentation of the American spirit.

Student life at the school was simple but never dull. From the time the tower bell rang for morning rising until it rang for lights out there was constant activity. All the girls went to Mass, although chapel attendance was not compulsory for non-Catholics. They sped back to rooms and dormitories to make beds, to put away chapel veils, to take last-minute looks in the small mirrors. They sped down to a solid Wisconsin breakfast, enlivened by their own chatter. They sped again to classes, some of them taking last-minute glimpses at textbooks. Noon brought dinner and recreation. Afternoon brought more classes, followed by recreation, outdoors in good weather, indoors in bad. After supper came the Rosary and Benediction, then a study hour and a short recreation, usually one of singing and dancing.

The school had plenty of extracurricular enjoyment in concerts and lectures. Some really fine lecturers continued to come, some with religious and moral, others with more worldly messages. Pianists and violinists of national distinction brought programs. Because Mother Emily wanted to lighten the schedule, offerings sometimes backfired.

A lecturer, who aroused the delayed mirth of his hearers, was the priest who was scheduled to talk on literature, but who gave an impassioned lecture upon the evils of strong drink, a vice hardly known to his audience. He portrayed a mythical John who, after a misspent life, died in awful agony. The speaker was nothing if not realistic in the portrayal. He not only depicted John in his death throes, but all his victims who were clustered around him. He ended with a cry of horror as the soul of John departed this life. Scores of solemnly straight faces stared up at him; but in the recreation room later, Mother Emily came on a group repeating the death of John while watchers shrieked in joy. "Now let John rest in peace," was all she said but her eyes twinkled as she turned away.

More interesting to the girls than the lecturers and artists from afar were their own talented performers. Greater pianists may have struck the keys of the Steinway concert grand on the auditorium platform; but for those who heard her no one else played Chopin with the fire and brilliancy of Mary Gleason. No other violinist equaled Martha Matz; and Roberta Goldbeck sang more sweetly than any star of light opera. Part of their reaction was school spirit; but part of it was recognition of really great talent. Even if no one of them ever attained other fame, they played real roles in the progress of their generation.

One of the most popular departments in both academy and college was that of speech and drama. An association with the Cumnock School of Northwestern University was made closer by the St. Clara use of lay teachers in this activity. Among these was Josephine McGarry, later the Josephine McGarry Callan of the Catholic University, whose golden voice and dramatic presentation of classic literature found echoes in scores of voices hardly younger than her own.

The designation of activity program was unknown to the period but the idea was not. St. Clara had Circles — Mount Carmel, Mazzuchelli, Ave Maria, Holy Rosary, St. Agnes, Holy Angels, German — all given to various interests. It also continued the long-established Sodality of the Blessed Virgin, with its annual elective offices. Membership in the circles was based upon age levels and special interests, but they were not held to any special groups in the courses of study. Classic and commercial students associated in them.

Another perennial source of entertainment was the writing, editing, and reading of the school periodical. The *Young Eagle*, which took its name from a translation of the Siouan *Sinsinawa*, was student spokesman for both academy and college. If one considers the smallness of the contributing classes, the issues of the early years of the century show it to have been a noteworthy publication. There were, to be sure, some mediocre verses associating with some real poetry, the latter, usually written by Eva McCarty, Julia Fitzgerald, or Margaret Wigman. As always in such publications, a good deal of reminiscence was indulged concerning the school's past. There was, however, frequent recognition of a world beyond river and hills, a world that was a little frightening but mostly challenging. One of a series of articles on different aspects of Chicago was entitled "A West Side Factory Boy," and showed dramatically the mental and spiritual results of the monotony of work in a great factory, a condition not emphasized by labor itself until the 1920's.

Through the same years the academies in Madison and in Faribault were also advancing in scholarly scope. Any innovation at St. Clara was necessarily reflected in these institutions. After a disastrous fire and a lawsuit over insurance that lasted five years, the Sacred Heart Academy (Edgewood) had taken a new lease on life. At the time of the Catholic Summer School in Madison it had been visited by scores of dignitaries. It had also built a friendly relationship with the University of Wisconsin, which was probably responsible for the fact that, in 1903, there were among the lecturers at the academy Dr. Grant Showerman, of Madison, Dr. J. B. Sterret, of Cornell, Dr. J. H. Robinson, of Columbia, and Sidney Lee, of London.

In 1907 Edgewood was accredited by the University of Wisconsin so that its students could enter the university without examination. Bethlehem Academy in Faribault, after the difficulties engendered by the Faribault school situation, got off to a fresh start under Mother Veronica Power, Mother Emily's sister. She had been one of the pioneer Sisters of the town, and her return to teach their children was hailed joyously by women whom she had taught. In a year that had no graduating class, she started to enlarge the school; and two years later had to hold commencement exercises in the opera house because the new school hall was not sufficiently large. Three years later another addition had to be built. Bethlehem Academy had made itself an integral part of Faribault, building an association so close that, more than forty years afterward, when it was changed to a central high school, the townspeople asked that its original name be retained.

Both by letters and by visits Mother Emily kept in close touch with these academies. Bethlehem, as the first branch academy, was dear to her; but the Edgewood Academy of the Sacred Heart was almost equally dear. Both of them represented the trials of Sisters far from the mother house who were trying to hold to the Sinsinawa standards and who also had to meet local conditions not existent at the Mound. Time and again old Sisters who had been at one place or the other have said, "Just when we were most discouraged, Mother Emily came, and all was well again."

Commencement in 1904 was one of the great days of St. Clara. Not only did it bring to Eva Clinton McCarty and Teresa Marguerite Tighe the first degrees of St. Clara College but it marked the fiftieth anniversary of the first commencement of the Academy, at Benton.

For weeks preparation for it was excited. Earnest piano students practiced the March from Gounod's *Queen of Sheba*. The B Natural

Club of vocalists rehearsed Mendelssohn's "Praise to the Lord." Piano quartets and vocal duets and trios sounded throughout the halls. Mary Gleason thundered the Weber *Concerto in F Minor,* and Martha Matz's violin sang the Mendelssohn *Concerto Opus 64.* Teresa Tighe read, over and over, the essay, "The Touchstone of Literature," and Eva McCarty carefully enunciated her valedictory, "Golden Rosary." For days before the event the school was in a turmoil of preparation for a program that had much of the flavor of the famous 1861 program of the Benton academy. For the change in style of commencement programs from the '60's of the 1800's to the early years of the 1900's was far less than would be the changes in the forthcoming twenty years. Music and elocution still volleyed and thundered in the valley, although the guitars of the '60's no longer thrummed on the platforms.

Then, on the evening of June 14 the ringing of the tower bell, Albertus Magnus, announced the arrival of Archbishop Sebastian Messmer. Already scores of priests from nearly every diocese in Wisconsin, Illinois, Iowa, and Minnesota had reached the Mound. Masses began at dawn on the fifteenth. At nine o'clock all the Sisters and students assembled in chapel for Pontifical High Mass. To the strains of *Ecce Sacerdos Magnus* there entered the chapel the impressive procession of Dominicans, secular priests, and the bishops — Garrigan of Sioux City, O'Gorman of Sioux Falls, Ireland of St. Paul, and Messmer of Milwaukee. Archbishop Messmer celebrated the Mass. Archbishop Ireland gave the sermon.

Thirty-seven years earlier Father John Ireland had spoken to the graduates of St. Clara Academy. On that day of the first commencement at Sinsinawa (the first thirteen had been held at Benton), St. Clara Academy had been a little country establishment, struggling to survive in a land stricken by postwar difficulties. He had been a young priest, secretary to Bishop Grace of St. Paul, a brilliant, ardent but almost unknown young man. Now St. Clara was an educational institution with nationwide recognition, and he was John Ireland, Archbishop of St. Paul, storm center of controversies but easily the most widely known of all the prelates of the American hierarchy.

Probably no other bishop in the United States was better able to sound the keynote of Sinsinawa's achievements. When, standing before the hundreds of assembled students, parents, Sisters, priests and fellow bishops, he rolled out "Sinsinawa! Beyond thee we shall not go in search of ideals and inspiration," everyone who heard his sonorous syllables knew the surety of his statement. "In your labors for God and for fellow creatures you need these ideals and inspiration," he told the students. "A celebration which brings back Sinsinawa's first half century cannot but be an encouragement to holiest ambitions and noblest deeds in the service of God and fellow creatures."

There, in the repetition of the phrase, was emphasis on the social aspect of education. The archbishop believed in active rather than cloistered communities, and the Sinsinawa Dominicans fulfilled his idea of the functions of a community: for God and fellow man. The association ran through all his own thinking. He knew that it ran through Mother Emily's.

"Never before," the archbishop went on, "was there such need of the Sisterhoods of the Church in the work of education as there is in the present age. The age is ambitious of education as other ages never were. It talks ceaselessly of education; it bedecks the land with schools and colleges that education may be within the reach of the weakest as of the strongest, of the poorest as of the richest. The age stakes all its hopes on education; it relies on education for all its strength and all its glory. If words always carried with them the fullness of their meaning, we should say that the age is decidedly right in its worship of education; for true education, the building up of men and women, secures to a people all the blessings that they are allowed to covet. Unfortunately, in its ardor for education the tendency of the age is to think only of mind and to overlook the will, to cut in twain the human soul, bestowing all care upon one half while leaving the other half to struggle for itself as best it can. This is a fatal mistake.

"Schools and colleges where the mind solely is cared for cannot suffice for the education of the children of the land. For the masses of those children the home and the Sunday-school do not supply the moral training refused to them in schools and colleges. The problem facing the country is awful in its portents — what is to happen as the result of the lack of moral training in schools and colleges frequented by the multitude of its children?

"Remedies are proposed but the sole remedy that is effective is feared and shunned — the inculcation of religion in schools and colleges. Moral training, it is admitted, should be sought; but it must be such that religion be not invoked to define and enforce its teachings. But morality without God is void of force, as it is void of sanction. As well you may tell the frail reed of the field to hold up against the passing storm as to bid the human soul, apart from divine support, to withstand the fierce assaults of passion. The peril of the age, the peril of America is secularism in schools and colleges.

"I signalize the peril: how it is to be removed the people of the land will some day declare when the hard lesson of facts will have forced them to realize the gravity of the situation."

The sermon was Ireland at his best, farseeing, nobly patriotic, highly spiritual. It was also the expression of Mother Emily's educational ideals as they had been lived through the years of her leadership of the Sinsinawa Dominicans. It was not mere oratory when the archbishop declared that Sinsinawa gave full and adequate formation of character for life to the children it taught, and "exhibited to the country the ideals and principles of a true education." In the style common to all orators of his period he ended, "Forward, Sinsinawa, in the great work of Christian education! May thy labors be blessed by the Father of light and love; may the fruits of thy labors be ever such as to draw on thee the smiles of earth and of heaven. This is the prayer of those who now throng thy chapel. This is the prayer re-echoed before God's throne by Father Mazzuchelli and the holy Sisters of thy early life and work."

Better than anyone else the Archbishop of St. Paul understood the fundamental spirit of Sinsinawa. Irish-born like Mother Emily, he brought, as she had, to the new land a burning love of freedom that was part of his love of God. He had helped keep the land American just as she had maintained Father Mazzuchelli's idea of an entirely American community to serve the land. Both of them had seen great growth in the land of their adoption. Both of them feared that great dangers would menace her unless moral education, based on religion, built up in the people resistance to the corroding philosophy of materialism. To both of them the golden jubilee of St. Clara was a milestone on the high road of vision.

To Mother Emily it was far more. It was tribute to the Sisters, living and dead, who had labored so hard and so bravely for the building of the school. It was monument to the girls who had come to Benton, to the Old Stone Building and to the new brick building. It was memorial to parents who had made sacrifices to send them there. Most of all, it was a milestone on the highroad of the Mazzuchelli vision.

The little missionary, who had caught the spirit of America more surely than many of her own native sons, had envisioned on the Sinsinawa slope a great school, a foundation where an old religious Order would guide the young of the new world. His dream had seemed ended for him when he had chosen to give up the Mound and lead the few, brave Sisters to a poor little mining town. He had not lived to see it revived by "the little Ellen" he had taught. Not a college for young men but a college for young women stood on the Wisconsin hillside. Not priests but Sisters were spreading his gospel of love of God, love of neighbor. Not as he saw it, but just as surely, Father Mazzuchelli's ideal of service to the nation he loved was moving forward.

Before 1900 the convent grew slowly, compared to its growth in its second half-century. In 1900 there were less than three hundred members of the congregation. Nearly two hundred of the four hundred and seventy-six who had joined the community since Father Mazzuchelli had founded it had been taken by death or departure, although departures were comparatively few. But the time was hopeful, and Mother Emily was constitutionally sanguine. She must have wondered sometimes how she would carry through the plans of the congregation, but she started them bravely.

A new convent building was being erected to meet the needs of the community. Students were crowding Sisters out of the Old Stone Building. The convent, like the brick academy, was to be more than merely adequate. Set at the eastern end of the stone house, it made fine balance for the academy on the western side.

The annalist of its history proudly recorded that it was being built of the best bricks in the world because they were made of the best clay in the world since it contained Wisconsin white limestone, the best stone in the world. The spirit of "On, Wisconsin!" was not confined to the state university.

The construction problems were many, the financial problems greater. None of them equaled the administrative problem of supervising the lives, physical, mental and spiritual, of a large group of women. It is little wonder that the Church has canonized so many abbesses.

There have been institutions within the Catholic Church which have not taken into consideration the wide differences in human tastes. A rule is a rule and no deviations from it are allowed. Perhaps because she had been a pioneer, Mother Emily saw the need of reasonable adaptations. If a Sister had an allergy to milk, she did not have to drink milk. If she were ill, she was sent to bed. If she continued to be ill, she was given care, either at the Mound or in the hospital. Mother Emily was a conserver of the health of her charges.

She was drillmaster but no martinet. Every day, no matter how busy she was with other tasks, she visited all the sick Sisters in the house, comforting them with cheerful words but insisting that they remain in bed until they were entirely well. To the dying she was a tower of strength. Old Sisters now tell with tears how she read the sonorous Prayers for the Dying, her clear voice rising in the *Salve, Regina* as she convoyed her Sister upon a last journey.

When a Sister died upon a mission, her body was brought back to the Mound. Sometimes it was night when the funeral cortege came from the railroad at Galena or East Dubuque. The bearers carried the coffin up the outer stairs of the new convent. Through the lighted doorway the few mourners, relatives of the dead nun, could see the two lines of novices, holding aloft lighted candles, and, beyond them, the white-robed Sisters with Mother Emily, waiting. "When I looked at her face," the brother of a dead Sister once said, "I had the feeling that I was going right up into heaven, and that she was God's own welcomer."

There was sadness, always, in the death of a Sister. If she were young, there was the regret that she had not been longer with them. If she were old, there were years of association to remember. No one looked on the Dominican dead, however, without realization of their departure into a better world. Grief could not last the high tower, did not arouse great sorrow. The time was to come long against that understanding. Even the chapel bell, tolling from when it would, but not while Mother Emily walked in that procession to the God's acre on the hillside.

The usual atmosphere of the convent was quiet contentment. Every Sister had her allotted work, teachers, cooks, postmistress, bursar, prioress. There was leisure, too, and Mother Emily's love of fun sometimes made evenings memorable. There were many lighter diversions in the life of the convent. The custom of Epiphany cards continued. So did the celebration of the Feast of the Holy Innocents when the youngest members of the community took over, for one day, the roles of their elders. There were many evenings of music and song. The annual picnic became an institution which still holds.

With every Sister, every novice, every postulant Mother Emily had personal relationship. Her temperament required that she work through people as well as with them. "I'm depending on you," was her admonition to anyone to whom she gave a difficult task. Once she sent the young Sister Thomas Aquinas on a mission that she knew would be trying. When she welcomed her home she said, "I knew you wouldn't fail me." That surety, amplified to take in every Sister in the convent, was unquestionably one of the most potent factors in the success of her work.

She could be firm and determined as well as genial. For all her resiliency, she had a quality of steel. Few made the mistake of opposing her, once she had made up her mind. She made decisions, however, slowly. Often she asked the young Sisters, the novices, or the postulants about a hypothetical situation which might be a real one. "What do you think?" and "What would you do?" were more often on her lips than "I think." One of her old friends still says, "Mother Emily would take a child's advice if it sounded reasonable to her. She respected everyone, regardless of age or circumstance." To her the farmer knew more about the crops, the engineer more about the steam, the baker more about the bread. She talked with them all as she moved about the place. Her office was on the road, in the halls, in the parlor rather than in its established location.

There were only a few telephones in the buildings, and the distances between the east end of the convent and the west end of the academy was considerable. Mother Emily walked the long hall rather than send a messenger. Sometimes, on the way, she paused briefly in the room she called "the watch tower" but which the girls named "a window in Thrums" because from it Sister Rose, the portress, and Sister Lucina, her friend and neighbor, garnered all the news of the institution. Mother Emily heard some of it from them but, if it was unpleasant, she laughed it off, refusing to judge any cause without complete evidence.

For final judgments she went to the council, the group of five Sisters elected to office as she was, and chosen by the electorate for their wisdom. Among them she found women strong like herself and dedicated to service for God, and among them the young, wise, and farseeing Sister Samuel who would one day be her worthy successor. In these women she put her trust although she did not lean upon them.

Every Sister who remembers her has an almost identical way of phrasing one recollection. "She looked right into my soul." They also speak of her magnetism, her straight look; her powerful presence galvanized others.

In the beginning of St. Clara most of the Sisters were Irish-born or the children of Irish-born parents. As time went on more Germans and French entered. Then the community became characteristically Midwestern. From even farther places came postulants, such as Sister Januarius Mullen, who set out for Sinsinawa from the Nebraska sandhills where she had never seen a Sister of any community. Sisters came from California and from New York. Personalities as diverse as their racial and geographical backgrounds met in the convent with a common purpose; but the maintenance of necessary convent discipline was not always easy for the administrator.

There were occasional difficulties. A group of Sisters at one time in this period definitely opposed the Mother General on a question of convent policy. She could be calmly severe when the occasion required. This was one of the times. She handled the situation with strength and dispatch, and did not, throughout the rest of her life, seem to hold remembrance of it.

She had a strong family feeling but she never allowed it to influence either her judgment or her conduct. With three sisters in the community, she had to steer a careful path. No one ever claimed that she showed any favoritism to any one of them, although it was evident that Sister Gertrude was always more understandingly sympathetic of her than either Sister Veronica or Sister Adrian. Sister Gertrude, who died in 1900, was, like Mother Emily, markedly devout in religious exercises. She had, too, the same warm feeling for people; and her long service in Bethlehem Academy in Faribault endeared her deeply to the townsfolk there.

Alice Power, the youngest of the family — "Little Alice" to both students and Sisters — never entered the community, but lived in the convent until the time of her death. Unlike the others of the family, she was, as the result of a fall in infancy, tiny and malformed. Mother Emily treated her as if her body as well as her mind were normal, and the little woman lived happily under the direct care of Sister Adrian.

Father Louis Power, the Thomas Louis who offered to give up his priestly vocation in order to help his stepmother and her family upon his father's death, had always kept in close touch with his half-sisters, even though he was no longer in their neighborhood. His fellow-Dominicans testified that he was a fine theologian and a wise counselor. Occasionally, after his transfer to Newark, he came west, but less than a year after the celebration of his golden jubilee, he died at Sparkhill where he had been chaplain, and was buried in the Holy Sepulchre Cemetery in Newark on October 23, 1906.

The toll of constant watchfulness, of important decisions, of responsibilities for others sometimes weighed heavily upon Mother Emily. Sister Chrysostom recalls that Mother Emily often came to a fairly secluded music room. "No one will think to look for me here," she would say. Then, after a little while, she would stand up. "I'm going to the chapel to pray," she would sigh.

In prayer she found her strength. She had deep devotion to Christ in the Blessed Sacrament, and made frequent visits, praying before the high altar. With her quick, springing step she would return to the long halls, ready again to take up her duties. Always, to her, the most important duty was the spiritual welfare of her children, the nearly five hundred young, middle-aged and old women who trusted her. To them every little while she sent letters which expressed her concern for them as well as the strong faith which buoyed her own soul. Time and again, she would say to some Sister troubled about her progress in study, "Come with me to the chapel, and we will pray." After their prayer she said, "Now go to your study."

Prayer and study were to her the cornerstones of Dominican life. The study must be organized, purposeful. She had known from the Benton days that Catholic education must, to be successful, not only equal but do better than secular education. It could not do that without knowing what secular education was providing and demanding. She found both good and bad in provisions and demands. Definitely she discovered that American education had come into the era of certificates and degrees. She knew that, both in the academies and in the mission schools, the Sinsinawa Dominicans had teachers of proved abilities, but she realized that to meet the requirements of local boards, particularly in cases of the mission schools, these teachers would require proof of having gone through the mill of regulated processes. She had a shrewd idea that some of her teachers could have instructed their teachers but she conformed to the growing demand.

Characteristically, she started at the top, sending Sisters to universities rather than to normal schools. The first to leave the Mound for study in a college was Katie Smith, a postulant, who set out on December 29, 1896, to the Cumnock School of Northwestern University in Evanston to study with Isabel Garghill. Edgewood provided an entrance into the University of Wisconsin. Sister George lived there while she studied Spanish with Dr. Seynour and his wife, receiving university credit but not attending classes. Sister Gabriella and Sister Grace used the same method in studying German with Hochfeld and Lehman who gave them hard tasks and liberal praise. They also studied French with Fortier, and visited Laird's class in Thucydides, and Dr. Munroe, director of the summer school, regretted that he could not give them free tuition.

Among the first Sisters to wear the white habit of Sinsinawa in American university classes were Sister George and Sister Camillus. Mother Emily had thought of sending them to the University of Chicago, but heard that the Archbishop of Chicago might oppose such a step. She therefore wrote to Archbishop Glennon of St. Louis about the possibility and advisability of sending Sisters to Washington University in his city. After some preliminary correspondence the archbishop sent this letter, revealing both his caution and his general attitude toward secular higher education:

Archbishop's House
St. Louis

June 9, 1908

My dear Reverend Mother:

In response to your favor I would say that I have quite an acquaintanceship with Washington University, its President, some of its Professors and many of its pupils. I have always refused to attend its closing exercises and last year refused to accept an honorary degree it desired to confer upon me. My reasons, however, were not any particular prejudice against the University, but rather because I am living within a block of the

St. Louis University (Jesuit) and it would appear as if I were defaulting in my interest to the one, by accepting or appearing to associate with the other.

This will give you also the key to my diffidence in approving or inviting members of religious communities to come here and matriculate at the Washington University since it might argue a certain inconsistency on my part. But while I may not be enthusiastic in my invitation to your Sisters to come here to study, yet I can readily see that they will not be doing any greater wrong by coming here than by going to the Chicago University, which now has quite a few Sisters studying there; and I know also that Sisters have done Post-graduate work in other secular institutions. I would think, however, that your Sisters would not do well in going to live at the Dormitory on the grounds, not that I know of any decided objection or objectionable surroundings therein, but I am quite convinced that it would not be proper for the Sisters to be there. The Visitation Academy, which is large and not far from the University, might house your Sisters while they attend lectures at the University, but just now I cannot say whether that is their custom or whether it would be their wish.

Sincerely yours in Christ,
John J. Glennon
Archbishop of St. Louis

For reasons remembered by no one and not set down in letters the Sisters stayed at a private residence near the Cathedral. Mother Emily counseled them to concentration. "The sooner you get your degree the better," she wrote them. "If only we can say with truth, our Sisters hold degrees!"

In 1903 Sister Samuel and Sister Joseph matriculated for summer courses at the University of Chicago which granted them free tuition. Mother Emily's opinion of its president, Dr. William Rainey Harper, must have been high, for she certainly approved, if she did not write, an editorial in the *Young Eagle* soon after his death.

"A grand life," it stated, "the life of a courageous gentleman and a true scholar, closed when Dr. Harper gave up the brave fight for time to labor yet longer. . . . Dr. Harper was intellectually a giant, a tireless, indefatigable worker physically, a natural organizer and administrator. His bravest fight was when, facing an agony of pain, he continued his work and prepared the way for future workers. . . . Dr. Harper's forceful character was ennobled by his kindness that made him seek out the poorer student to help him upward, the courtesy that never forgot the rights of others, the love of music that made his life harmonious but above all the vivifying spirit of loving trust in God that prompted his last words, 'God always helps.' "

Nine Sisters went to the University of Wisconsin in 1907. Sister Clementine and Sister Joseph attended a Harvard summer school. Had the Catholic University of America been accepting women students at that time, it is certain that Mother Emily would have preferred to send her Sisters there. She had been in complete sympathy with the aims of the founders of the university, Ireland, Spalding, and Keane. She was the strong supporter of Dr. Shields and was among the first to see the leadership in social thought of Dr. Kerby. Even the Sisters' College of the University was still to be organized, and, since her teachers needed degrees, she made use of the secular colleges.

For degrees but also for wider horizons in art and music she sent teachers abroad. In 1903 Sister Angelico — one of the first of many Dolans who came from Iowa to the Mound — and Sister Catherine Wall went from the art department. "Do not stint yourselves," Mother Emily wrote them in November when they had written her from Italy. "Let me know if you need more money. Do not be stingy with yourselves. Get what you need. Rest when you need it." Then, as if she feared she might have omitted a needed command, she added, "Commence the study of Italian." The Sisters probably paid more heed to the last injunction than to the others. At any rate, they returned with standards of art which did much to establish the prestige of their institution.

In 1905 Sister Chrysostom and Sister Hyacintha went to Italy and Germany. After the grand tour of Genoa, Pisa, Bologna, and Rome, following in the footsteps of the earlier pilgrims, they studied in Florence. There they met by chance Archbishop Ireland who immediately became interested in their progress as a guide for the Sisters of his archdiocese. The Sinsinawa Sisters later went to Munich where they studied in the Royal Conservatory on the palace grounds. They attended Mass in the royal chapel and heard some of the world's greatest voices lifted in the singing of the Mass.

"Mother Emily was right," Sister Chrysostom said later. "I didn't want to go for I felt I had learned under Listemann at the Chicago Conservatory all I needed to know for teaching. But Florence and Munich gave us more than prestige. They gave us a wider world."

The Sisters, returning, shared the wider world with their companions. In a convent nothing is "mine." Everything is "ours." Thus greater enjoyment of art and music came to everyone at the Mound. It was an exercise in Christian social living, although no one as yet identified it by that name.

The work of pedagogy for the grade school teachers continued. In 1900 Dr. Shields, the perennial guide, philosopher, and friend of the Sinsinawa Dominicans, conducted an institute where L. D. Harvey, Wisconsin state superintendent of schools, lectured upon Fundamentals in Education and Character Building in Education. Miss Gertrude Schwartz of the Oshkosh public schools led a discussion on Methods of Teaching. Although not so named then, the Sinsinawa Dominican Education Conference of forty years later, was already progressing. Dr. Shields was building the steel skeleton of that structure which Sister Mary Joan was ultimately to use in the New York Corpus Christi School curriculum, and to combine with the Shields philosophy, expressed by Monsignor George Johnson and Bishop Francis J. Haas, to make *Guiding Growth in Christian Social Living*, the curriculum of the Commission on American Citizenship. It took long years for the Shields philosophy and methods to take hold in American Catholic education. Through those years the Sinsinawa Sisters tended the sturdy but not yet wide-flowering plant.

Public education was beginning to demand more from its educators. In 1903 Mother Emily, following the trend, sent a letter to all Superiors of grade schools. "Every teacher in the

Community is to take examinations in arithmetic, grammar and physiology if she has not already passed. Next year the examinations will be in United States history and in geography. All those working for secondary school certificates will take an examination in algebra." A little later she wrote, "I am told that, throughout the country certificates will be required by diocesan boards of examiners. It is necessary to prepare well that we may be ready. Vacations are to be spent in quietness and study. The day is not far distant when every inefficient and indifferent teacher will be shut out from school work. Let none of these be found among us."

In a letter soon afterward she wrote, "At the almost universal request of the Missions I am deferring Sisters' examinations until the last of July. I realize the heavy demands of the schools everywhere. Far be it from me to overburden you with work; yet we must all see the need of perfecting our methods and personal equipment in order to keep pace with the march of progress. I have fullest confidence that you will profit by this delay and reach a high standing." She urged them to speed the closing of schools, getting permission from the pastors, and to enter the summer schools open to them.

In 1904, with the consent of the council, she appointed a board of examiners, with Mother Bonaventure, Sister Constantia, Sister Walburga, and Sister Samuel as members. This board took up the work of examining, during the summer session at the Mound, the grade school teachers. If the Sisters were unable to come to the mother house, they were given the examinations in their temporary residences by their Superiors. Most of them, however, came to Sinsinawa for the Shields institutes and the following examinations.

The Sinsinawa system had progressed so far by 1904 that Bishop J. P. Carroll of Helena, Montana, could say of its founders: "A school does not consist in its walls, its pieces of brick and stone. The teachers make the school, the teachers are the school, and it was in them and with them that Mother Emily hoped to build the real St. Clara's. No expense, therefore, seemed too great, no risk too hazardous, if only she could provide her beloved institution with a body of teachers fully abreast of the times — instructed in every art, versed in every science. She gave the teachers all the advantages the best normal schools, colleges, and universities in the country could afford, and even sent them over the seas to study special branches at the feet of the masters of the old world. Is it any wonder that St. Clara developed from the school into the academy, from the academy into the college? Is it any wonder that the attendance increased steadily from 1867 until it counts nearly 300 in 1904? Mother Emily had the instinct of the true teacher, but she joined to it the administrative ability and the sympathy for all knowledge which are the characteristics of the educational leader. 'The wise teacher buildeth her house.' "

Mother Emily's program of social education advanced through the teacher training which went on in the Sinsinawa convent simultaneously with the educational training of girls in the school.

Forty years after the issuance of *Rerum Novarum* Pope Pius XI was to deplore the failure of many Catholics, even some of the clergy, to understand and apply the social doctrines of his great predecessor. There were, however, at the turn of the century, men and women in the Middle West who were studying the mighty words of Leo XIII and relating them to the conditions around them.

In St. Paul, young Father John Augustine Ryan read the encyclical and began to project that series of reforms which became political action thirty years afterward.

In Rockford, Bishop Peter Muldoon studied the burning phrases and started the building of that course which would become the Bishops' Program of 1919.

In Racine, the boy Francis Haas pored over the Pope's ideals of justice and thought of what they would mean if applied to the lives of his neighbors: a living wage that would provide the worker with security for himself and his family.

In Madison, the Wisconsin Progressive, Owen John O'Neill, who styled himself a working man with three trades — tinsmith, stonemason, and bricklayer — told his family as he set down his copy of *The Catholic Citizen,* "Pope Leo sounds like Bob La Follette."

In Sinsinawa Mother Emily pondered the text and said to her

Sisters, "This is what Father Samuel saw. This is what he taught us. This is what we must teach others."

For fifty years her clear eyes had been seeing the conditions under which men and women worked. She had seen the beginning in the Middle West of the practices of the Machine Age which had come so much earlier to England and then to the American eastern seaboard. She had seen how the machines had become more valuable to their owners than were the men who operated them. She saw the rich growing richer, the poor, poorer. She saw, as Father Mazzuchelli had foreseen, the widening of the gap between capital and labor. She saw how intolerable were many working conditions: long hours, miserable shops and mills, poor pay. The America she loved, the land of freedom, was changing. Great masses of men were no longer the free agents she had met on the Mississippi steamboat, had worked with in Benton, had come to know in dozens of towns and cities.

To her the remedy lay in Pope Leo's declarations. Plainly the Pope set down the rights of the poor, the rights of the rich, the rights of capital, the rights of labor. He defined the duties of the Church and of the State. The government, he said, had the right to interfere with capital when capital oppressed the poor, especially the workers who helped to augment it. He said that capital and labor must work together, not against each other. Capital had the right to fair return on investment. Workingmen had the right to unite, to organize into union by which they might the better seek to obtain justice for themselves.

The right to organize.

That was the crux of the labor situation in the years when *Rerum Novarum* was startling the world, even the Catholic world, by its daring. Many Catholics denied the right, despite the Pope's encyclical. Even some of the Sisters at the Mound protested. "But, Mother," they said, "surely men have not the right to strike!"

"Why not?" Mother Emily asked them, "if this is the only way they have to get justice?"

Justice, always the motivation of her actions, determined her stand on the issue. She knew practically nothing of the politics of the labor movement. Except for a slight acquaintance with John Mitchell in the time of the Spring Valley mine lockout, she knew no labor leaders. The great clerical exponents of the *Rerum Novarum* had not yet arisen, although it is possible, some of the old Sisters think, that she talked on the issue with Bishop Muldoon, who often came to Sinsinawa from neighboring Rockford. Certainly she made no public announcement of her acceptance of the encyclical; but there can be no doubt that St. Clara taught, with renewed power, the principles which Father Mazzuchelli had voiced to a little company of Sisters in a small Wisconsin lead-mining town and which Leo XIII had proclaimed to the world. It was Mother Emily's task to see that the old teaching was reinforced by the new pronouncement.

She brought to Sinsinawa, when it was feasible, speakers who were voicing the true Catholic position in social affairs. Bishop Muldoon and Dr. William Kerby of the Catholic University spoke, in 1908, on the Christian principles motivating Pope Leo's great letter. In the same year Professor J. C. Monaghan of the University of Wisconsin described the French crisis in terms of Christian doctrine. The Reverend H. C. Hengell, chaplain to the Catholic students of the University of Wisconsin, lectured upon the rights of labor, stating that society must enforce respect for the dignity of man.

At Edgewood, during the same period, the Sisters had the opportunity of hearing many lectures on the social question to which the Catholic Students Association of the university invited them and their students. Among these lectures were the Race Problem, by the Reverend John Daly of Milwaukee, Evolution and Catholicism, by the Reverend Joseph Berg of St. Francis Seminary, the French Situation, by the Reverend J. E. Copus, S.J., and the Church and Civilization, by the Honorable J. L. O'Conner of Milwaukee. They also heard, more often, Professor Monaghan, who was a frequent and fiery defender of Leo XIII.

Generally, Mother Emily's method was Socratic rather than formal. She established no classes for the study of the *Rerum*

Novarum but she found other methods of indoctrination. She used the Congregation custom of oral reading in the refectory to submit sections and interpretations of the Pope's letter. She gave copies to those whom she thought best fitted to become its apostles. She mentioned to individuals, as they told her some particularly flagrant social condition, that Pope Leo had seen and sought to cure these evils.

A big convent is, to no small extent, a switchboard of regional conditions. Father Mazzuchelli had sought to make the Sisterhood representative of the general area of the upper Mississippi Valley. Mother Emily had carried out his intention. After thirty years of her direction, the convent was definitely a microcosm of the area. There were now approximately 600 Sisters in the community. Most of them had similar backgrounds, homes on farms or in towns and cities that were solid enough but not so secure that they could not be affected by poor crops, strikes, lockouts, or general unemployment. Factory troubles in Peoria or Kewanee, stockyard difficulties in Chicago or Omaha, too heavy rains in Wisconsin, blizzards in Nebraska, wrecked cornfields in Iowa, blighted wheatfields in Minnesota, all these clamored, in time, on the Sinsinawa hill. Sometimes a postulant, hopefully and prayerfully waiting for the white veil of the novice, would regretfully realize that she must give up her dream and go home to become the principal support of her family. Always there was consciousness in the convent of troubled conditions in the world they were hoping to serve. It was the strength of the Dominican Rule, this human awareness; but it was no obstacle to the meditative life. Pope Leo had done much in showing that consideration of such conditions was a duty of religion. Mother Emily sought to drive home the lesson.

The tremendous job of fomenting a social consciousness in the minds of young women, whose idea of teaching was a matter of methods rather than of trends, was made somewhat easier by the mental atmosphere of the Wisconsin of that era. Father Mazzuchelli's vital interest in civic affairs had always kept the Sisters conscious of their obligation to the local community in which they lived. Because of the missions and of the residence of students in many other States the area of the community had enlarged, but Wisconsin still remained the homeland of the Sinsinawa Dominicans; and, in the early 1900's Wisconsin was, in social thought, the progressive lodestar of the nation.

Owen O'Neill had been right when he said that the *Rerum Novarum* sounded like Bob La Follette. It also sounded like Ely, the economist, and Ross, the sociologist, who were beginning to influence thoughtful college educators, including Woodrow Wilson. It sounded like the battle cry of those progressives, not yet a political party, who were violently protesting against the thefts of publicly owned forests by the lumber barons of the north. Because La Follette, as governor of Wisconsin, was able to integrate all this thinking, to dramatize it and to vitalize it by force of his personality, he was the natural leader of the social revolt.

There was more than a merely formal acquaintanceship between La Follette and Mother Emily. A letter, sent to her in 1905, and one of several, indicates the regard in which he held her.

EXECUTIVE CHAMBER
Madison, Wis.

May 31, 1905

Sister Mary Emily,
Saint Clara College,
Sinsinawa, Wisconsin.

Reverend Mother:
I wish to acknowledge receipt of your very kind letter of May 25, and to thank you sincerely for it.

It is with real regret that I decline the invitation to visit your college at the time mentioned in your letter, and I had thought and hoped that my official work would be in such condition as to permit of my visiting St. Clara College in June. As you are aware, however, our legislature is still in session, and, in all probability, will not adjourn until the middle of the month, and while that body is here, it is incumbent upon the executive of the state to remain constantly at the capital city, especially during the closing days when many important questions arise which must be promptly met.

Immediately upon the close of the session, I must prepare for a summer's work on the lecture platform, having contracted with the Slayton Bureau of Chicago to deliver a large number of lectures throughout the country. All of my time from June 20 until September 1 has been placed at their disposal.

I expected to obtain a few days rest before beginning my lecture work, but know now that, although I am greatly in need of it, it will not be possible. I assure you, could I have found a day's time, I should have given it to your college, for I am appreciative of the consideration you have shown me, and should have enjoyed a visit to Sinsinawa and the school. With the beauties of the former, I am familiar, and also know the high degree of excellence as an institution of learning your college has attained.

Had circumstances permitted my acceptance of your invitation, Mrs. La Follette would have been pleased to have accompanied me, and she joins me in sending cordial greetings to the teachers and pupils of St. Clara College.

Sincerely yours,

Robert M. La Follette

The progressive movement in Wisconsin had for platform a wide program of human betterment; an eight-hour law for employees in public work; a reasonable child labor law, and one which provided a certain amount of educational instruction for working minors; a workmen's compensation law; laws limiting the time and conditions of women workers; laws for better health and sanitation conditions; laws providing conservation of natural resources; laws authorizing co-operative societies; laws regulating the issuance and sale of corporate stock; a corrupt practices act; laws against legislation which sought to prohibit the destruction of competition in trade.

It was a program which has become almost commonplace in the fifty years which have passed since it was formulated. In its time it was almost revolutionary. Many Catholics, naturally conservative, shied away from it. Mother Emily, like Owen O'Neill, recognized in it the political application of the principles of the *Rerum Novarum*. Knowing, however, the dangers of political associations, she sedulously kept away from any direct association with the movement; but she emphasized the principles themselves.

Some social issues which have become important in later years

did not find emphasis in her era. The question of interracial relationships did not arise. As if to prepare the community for it Archbishop Ireland sent to Mother Emily in 1903 the copy of a speech
he had made at a Lincoln Day celebration 1891. The occasion of
the sending is not a matter of record but it was probably immediately after Senator Ben Tillman, of South Carolina, had told a
Madison audience that Wisconsin did not know how to handle the
Negro problem because it had never met it. In the speech the
Archbishop had declared: "I would break down all barriers. Let
the Negro be our equal before the law. . . . Let the Negro be
our equal in the enjoyment of all the political rights of the citizen.
. . . I would open to the Negro all industrial and professional
avenues — the test for his advance being his ability, but never
his color."

Mother Emily had other mentors. John Cunningham of the
Department of Commerce and Labor wrote her from Washington
in September of 1903 his regret that he would be unable to come
to Sinsinawa to lecture upon industrial education. "I hope," he
said, "that the Sisters will be able to devote a great deal of time
and money to the development of a system that will secure to
the masses, the millions who must toil, an education that will not
only better fit them for this life but for the life that is to come."

He could not have presented the idea to anyone more deeply
interested. She knew the need of an educational program to better
the lot of the great masses of the people. She also knew the need,
both for life and eternity, of the teaching of religion. Her feet were
on the earth, but her eyes, as always, were on heaven.

If the summer schools held at St. Clara mother house were the
factories of Christian social teaching, the Sinsinawa Dominican
mission schools were their proving ground.

There were, in 1900, twenty-four of these schools: the Immaculate Conception of Portage, the Immaculate Conception of Chicago, St. Michael's of Galena, the Immaculate Conception of Waukegan, St. Raphael's of Madison, St. Jarlath's of Chicago, St. Mary's
of Freeport, St. Mary's of Evanston, St. Joseph's of Bloomington,
St. Peter's of Oshkosh, Holy Rosary of Minneapolis, St. James of

Kenosha, St. Dominic's of Washington, St. James of Rockford, St. Thomas the Apostle of Chicago, St. Patrick's of Lemont, St. Mary's of Appleton, St. Dominic's of Denver, Holy Rosary of Kansas City, Visitation of Chicago, St. Rose's of Milwaukee, Visitation of Kewanee, St. John's of Milwaukee, and St. Mary's of Dixon.

Some of the very early schools had been closed. New Diggings, Shullsburg, Mineral Point, all pioneers, no longer existed. A school in Whitewater and one in Milwaukee had also been closed. Schools in Plattesmouth, Nebraska, and in Austin, Minnesota, were no longer open. The Spring Valley school which had been so closely associated with the disastrous lockout against the coal miners had passed with the coal mines of the region.

The general picture was more heartening, however, than the list showed. Nearly all the closed schools had been small. Some of the changes had been made necessary by parish rearrangements. Even then, the demand for mission Sisters was greater than the supply at St. Clara. Pastors of parishes kept coming to the Mound, pleading or demanding, according to their temperaments, for Sisters to staff their grade schools. Bishops reinforced the priests. Bishop Spalding even used displomacy in a request.

"If there is anything worthy of attention in me," he wrote in answer to an article about him in the *Young Eagle*, "it is my desire to know, appreciate and encourage all those who are striving to love God and serve mankind. And first among these I count the Sisters of Sinsinawa. Their work is a blessing to the thousands, and I am desirous that it should increase. Father Duffy is asking you to take charge of a new school."

There is no record that Father Duffy won assent to his well-routed request, but the diocese of Peoria got Sisters for St. Patrick in Bloomington in 1902, and for St. Bernard in Peoria in 1904.

Almost invariably the new missions were in struggling parishes. The church was poor, the pastor was poor, the people were poor. The Sisters were poorest of all, but they somehow managed to support the local convent and to send a little money back to the mother house, money that was desperately needed, for expenses of building and maintenance had grown great. Mother Emily insisted, though, that the Mission Sisters must keep for their own convents something more than the minimum of necessity. "I hope that the Sisters who have charge of the cooking will provide good food," she wrote to all the mission convents. "There is much toward making good health in good, palatable food." In another letter she counseled them to provide immediate medical care for any who needed it.

Her two constant preoccupations in these letters to the missions were with mental improvement and spiritual perfection. They must make their home life as happy as possible, but their main concerns were the betterment of their minds and the salvation of their souls.

Most of her letters from 1900 to 1909 set forth details of the educational program, telling the Sisters how to continue their studies, how to arrange their annual retreats. Every letter has some spiritual advice. Some letters are entirely concerned with the religious life.

A Lenten letter in 1905 to Superiors of mission convents reads, "We are beginning another Lent, and, oh, that it may be truly a redeeming time for all of us! Let every moment of these weeks be a spiritual gain to you and your dear Sisters. Your duties are such that you will not be allowed to fast, but in thousands of ways, more can be gained as you can readily and affectionately explain to your Sisters. Our dear Lord is a model of self-abnegation, obedience, obedience to death. Since we cannot fast, as we would wish, we can do other things which will please God as much if not more — have universal charity, have perfectly pure intention in our every thought, word, and deed, conquer excessive likes and dislikes, have more fervor in assisting at Mass and Holy Communion, exercise more zeal for the needs of those around us, and, in a word, live in the Presence of God, thus increasing each day the love of Him in our hearts so that He may find us ready to utter, when the call comes, 'Nunc dimittis.'

"That Heaven's choicest blessings may be yours, I am

Affectionately,

Sister M. Emily."

Sometimes she added "Mother General" to her signature, but always she signed her letters "Sister Emily." She shared both joys and sorrows with the mission Sisters as well as with those in the St. Clara Convent. She wrote them of Sister Gertrude's death and her one regret that she, with the others around her, had not realized the seriousness of her sister's illness. She wrote, thanking them for their sympathy at the time of Father Louis Power's death, and she had Sister Samuel, who had traveled to Newark with her, send a letter describing the funeral. Again she had Sister Samuel write of the deaths of Sister Eusebia Kelly, and of Sister Raymond Cochrane, who had been among the first postulants when St. Clara came back to Sinsinawa.

In her letter thanking the Sisters for their condolences upon the death of her brother, she advised, "The passing of holy souls should be an incentive to us who are yet in the weary struggle. What they have worked for and obtained, so can we. Let us try each day to live in such a way as we would wish to be when we meet God. . . . Let us try to have more faith and love and bring our Lord more directly into our lives and deeds. Never become discouraged, no matter how hard things are. Bear in mind for Whom you labor, and the reward, the victory, the rest, the Eternal Rest, will come. Do all the good you can, to the children, to those with whom you come in contact, and your own Sisters. Thank you again, my dearest Sisters, my best beloved and true friends."

Her last letter to the Mission Sisters, written in June, 1909, was concerned with the use of that year's vacations. Owing, she wrote, to the rebuilding of the powerhouse and the rearrangement of steam and water pipes, there would be a shortage of water that summer at Sinsinawa. The Sisters would therefore remain at their mission convents. There they should prepare for the community examinations which would take place at the end of the period. Novices should return to St. Clara. Others would make their retreats wherever they were stationed. "Make the vacation one full of charity in every house," she counseled.

Besides the two Peoria diocesan schools she opened eleven schools in the years between 1900 and 1909. Two of them were in

Chicago, St. Brendan's and St. Basil's, in the general South Side neighborhood of the Visitation School. St. Basil's did not open until 1905 but the other two schools were in operation during the nation-shaking Stockyards Strike of 1904. Visitation had just completed a new school of 15 rooms to take care of its more than 800 pupils. St. Brendan's under the direction of Sister de Ricci Fitzgerald, a great educator in a galaxy of great educators, had by 1904 about 700 pupils. Nearly every child in both schools was affected by the long and bitter strike. They needed no lessons in simplified sociology to inform them of the conditions of strikers' families.

"Some of them come to school hungry," Sister de Ricci told Mother Emily when she came to the school in the course of the difficulties. "More than half the school has not yet paid its tuition. What are we going to do?"

"We are going to carry them on the books until the strike is over," the Mother General said, "and we're going to find a way to feed them." Through use of the union fund and with the help of charitable citizens, the Sisters saw that no child went hungry. In both schools they did something just as important for the time and far more important for the future. Without statement of any dogma but by sympathetic attitude they showed the children of the strikers that the Catholic Church did not outlaw just strikes. The Church was with the worker. He, in his turn, must obey the laws of Church and State. While violence flared in other sections of the around-the-Yards district, the two parishes, hit though they were, remained entirely law-abiding while the workers stood firm for their rights.

"Anything could have happened," Sister de Ricci said long afterward. "There was poverty, want, misery before the men. They were desperate. They saw their children in need of everything. The police sympathized with them so that the packers had to call in outside forces for fear the Chicago authorities would not try to hold down any outbreak. But in that neighborhood, stricken though it was, there was no outbreak. Through their children the men had come to know that the great power of the Catholic

Church was on their side. They saw the dawn of hope in that, and they were willing to wait for the sun."

The strike cost had not yet been counted when another disaster struck the neighborhood. Just before Christmas there broke out the most terrible fire the Chicago Stock Yards has ever suffered. More than a score of firemen lost their lives in the blaze. Nearly all of them were Catholics, and nearly all of them lived in either the Visitation or St. Brendan's parish. Nearly all of them were fathers of children who went to these schools. With the smoke pall of the fire hung low over it, the neighborhood became a place of mourning.

Under their rule the Dominican Sisters can visit the stricken families of the dead or dying. The mission Sisters of the two schools set aside all their Christmas preparations and went, two by two, to the sad homes. From house to house, through the bitter days of a Chicago December, they moved, bearing messages of consolation by their coming. "They brought us God's own consolation," women said. They brought, too, hope in the form of the probability of scholarships for boys and girls that would let children go on through higher schools. "God bless and keep them," said the stricken people.

With the exception of the Sacred Heart School in Washington, established in a residential area of the nation's capital, a city of little industrial employment, most of the schools opened in this period were set in industrial centers: the Peoria and Bloomington schools, St. Thomas Aquinas in Milwaukee, Sacred Heart in Omaha. To a less degree than the South Side Chicago schools but to a noticeable extent they brought into their classrooms those life problems which arose from the injustices of machine production. "All I have to do to remember the Encyclical," one Sister said on her return to the Mound, "is to remember how my class looks and know the homes they come from."

Understanding like this wove a bond that was almost unbreakable. A mother, beset by worries, would confide in the Sister teaching her child when she would not go to the pastor. These confidential relationships gave to the Sisters deep knowledge of conditions in a parish. They knew the cost of milk and meat and bread, of shoes for growing feet, of first Communion and Confirmation outfits far better than did most pastors. They knew, too, what the payment for tuition and textbooks meant to a family that was barely subsisting. They were, therefore, the first to crusade for parish-paid tuition and textbooks, a consummation not yet achieved but much further on its way than at the beginning of the century.

Out of life rather than out of books the mission Sisters came into knowledge of the need of social betterment as distinguished from social service. It was right, they knew, it was necessary to perform the corporal acts of mercy; but there was something else to be done. Men must have justice. "Here is its gospel," they said of *Rerum Novarum*. It was little wonder that in later years their Sister Thomas Aquinas O'Neill and Sister Vincent Ferrer Bradford could sway great audiences in exposition of the social message of the Church of Christ, and that classes in Rosary College should become outstanding exponents of the social encyclicals. The Sinsinawa Dominicans had learned social justice the hard way.

The last mission school to be authorized by Mother Emily was, dramatically, St. Peter in Anaconda, Montana. Anaconda was, and still largely is, a copper smelting town. In 1907 it was practically a "company" town, with working destinies entirely controlled by company management. It was, however, a growing town, but with some local Catholic school difficulties. Bishop Carroll of Helena, knowing the Sinsinawa Dominicans, came to the Mound to request Mother Emily to take St. Peter's School.

Mother Emily granted the request, probably out of her high regard for Bishop Carroll since the distance was generally prohibitive. Had she known all the conditions existing and threatening in Anaconda, it is most improbable that she would have acceded.

In August, 1907, eleven Sisters under the guidance of Sister Albert Krantz, went to Anaconda. They arrived to find a situation which distressed although it did not altogether daunt them. On the debit side, they found that there was no school building. On the credit side, they found Father J. B. Pirnat, the pastor, and the majority of the congregation of St. Peter's,

St. Peter's church had been started in 1897 by Father Pirnat who then transferred to Livingston. His successor continued the work, and brought in the Ursuline Sisters to conduct a parochial school. This school was held in two buildings which Father Pirnat, returned to Anaconda, called "shacks." The congregation had grown so greatly, however, that he felt obliged to put up an addition to the church before he started the building of the school. The Ursulines, probably discouraged by the delays, gave up the elementary school and diverted their efforts to the building of a new academy in another parish. Bishop Carroll's predecessor, Bishop Blóndel, had refused permission for the Ursuline enterprise; but between the time of his death and Bishop Carroll's coming to Montana the building progressed. Bishop Carroll upheld Bishop Blóndel's ruling and sent for the Sinsinawa Dominicans who knew nothing of the situation until their Sisters arrived in Anaconda.

The newcomers found the Ursuline Sisters friendly, and the Sisters of Charity of Leavenworth, who conducted St. Ann's Hospital, were more than generous; but a large group of Catholics in the town misunderstood the situation and made it an issue. Father Pirnat, however, rallied to the Dominicans.

For the Sisters the priest bought a boardinghouse across the street from the church, and had it altered for a convent. The Sisters were unusually lonely, for "with few exceptions," as Sister Albert wrote, "the parishioners held aloof." The friendship of the Sisters at St. Ann's helped to break down the barrier, and the desire of most of the congregation to have their children attend a Catholic school brought six hundred children to the opening of the school (still in the shacks) in the first week in September.

Father Pirnat had already drawn up the plans for a new school building to cost $75,000. The excavation had been dug. The school would not be ready for use, however, until the following spring. In spite of past troubles all looked hopeful for St. Peter's. Then, without warning to the workers of Anaconda, came the financial debacle that was called the Heinze Panic.

The economic life of Anaconda rested squarely upon its mines and its great smelter, at that time the largest in the West. The town

had taken its direction as well as its name from the Anaconda
Mine, that vast copper bonanza located by Michael Hickey and
developed by four giants of the industry: Marcus Daly, James B.
Haggin, George R. Hearst, and Lloyd Tevis. There were mines
other than the Anaconda, some of them controlled by the Amalgamated Copper Company, which controlled the Anaconda, others
under independent ownership.

A young surveyor, F. Augustus Heinze, began a spectacular pro-
motional project by purchase of three independent mines, the
Rarus, the Belmont, and the Glengarry. As he took copper from
the Rarus the Amalgamated claimed that Heinze was raiding their
lode. Heinze tried to settle the case with the company, but the
Amalgamated insisted on taking it into court. There followed the
biggest lawsuit Montana ever saw. An auxiliary judge had to be
appointed to handle part of the litigation. Amalgamated threatened
to close all its mines and other operations unless the Montana
legislature passed new laws for its better protection.

The litigation shook the economic structure of the town, and
started a financial panic based on fear rather than on real danger.
Mines and smelter were closed. The effect on employment was
that of a lockout.

The panic struck the town as the Montana blizzard of 1886 had
struck the cattle ranges. Everything went down before it. Anaconda
was a one-industry town, and the one industry, the copper smelters,
was closed. Men and women had no money to buy, and the store-
keepers suffered with their customers. From September until the
following April, Anaconda was as Spring Valley had been, a stricken
community.

Father Pirnat could not raise the loans to continue the school
building, and work on it stopped. But, in spite of panic, in spite
of continued resentment, the people of St. Peter's parish sent their
children to school. "It was the charge of the Light Brigade," Sister
Placidia Concannon, one of the eleven Sisters there, remembers.
"Six hundred of them volleyed and thundered around us as we tried
to find places for them."

They solved the problem by using the church as study hall and classrooms. Every morning Father Pirnat removed the Blessed Sacrament to the priests' sacristy. The classes then took their allotted places in the body of the church, the boys' vestry, the gallery, the nave, and a large room in the basement. The setting might have either overwhelmed the youngsters or made them restless. Instead, they made model classes.

The class in penmanship had a necessary but unique method of work. The pupils sat, backs to the altar, on the kneeling benches and used the pew seats as desks. Bent over their tasks, they could not be seen from the front of the church. One priestly visitor stared in amazement when, in answer to a signal from a teacher, the students rose and the apparently empty church was suddenly transformed into a scene of children singing "O Virgin Queen, Our Lady of Good Counsel." In a little while Father Pirnat managed to get two residences to be used as classrooms; but the memory of the weeks in the church school are still treasured by native sons and daughters of Anaconda.

Adversity must have brought together the St. Peter parents and the St. Peter Sisters. Long before the year was out friendly relations had been established which have continued for more than forty years. Public school officials were friendly, too. The school superintendent gave good advice, and Miss Mabel Skelton, who taught music in the public schools of the town, also held classes in St. Peter's.

The panic was over before Mother Emily found it possible to visit Anaconda but throughout the time of strain and anxiety Sister Albert received from her letters of advice and comfort. "The people will come to know you," she wrote. "Do not worry about that now. Do what you can for them and their children." Mother Emily might be academic at the College. She was definitely practical on the Missions.

Public school relations were not always as pleasant as they were in the Montana town. The Immaculate Conception School, the first foundation of the Dominicans in Chicago, stood in a neighborhood which had grown tough and turbulent. The school had many truancies and no way of coping with them. The Reverend Thomas Pope Hodnett, pastor of the parish, asked the Chicago Board of Education for the services of a truant officer to check the absentees. Louis Larson, secretary of the board, replied that the city had not enough officers to care for the public schools, and refused the request.

Mrs. W. C. H. Keogh, a member of the Board of Education, came to the Sisters. A woman lawyer of ability and spirit, she marshaled the facts. Truant officers, she insisted, were paid from the public funds which were raised by the payment of taxes; Catholics, as well as non-Catholics, paid taxes. The Catholic schools were therefore entitled to the services of the truant officers. It was the old basic claim in the issue of Catholic education and public money. Usually, put to a test, it was defeated. In this case Mrs. Keogh at least won compromise. The Board of Education instructed the truant officer department that its officers must investigate any cases of truancy from the Immaculate Conception school which were reported to them by letter. The Sisters thereupon started a correspondence course with the truant department of the board, while at the same time they were striving to cut the truancies by moral suasion.

Moral suasion was the core of the mission teaching curriculum. The Sinsinawa Dominicans were not drillmasters, even in the boys' schools. St. John's, in Milwaukee, when it was for boys only, had for principals Sister Leo Tierney, Sister Seraphica Smith, and Sister Richard Barden, each one an army in herself but lovingly remembered by their pupils. Sister Richard always seemed to attain her results by a quick and kindly wit but hundreds of men in the city where she taught longest testify to her work in character building. St. Jarlath's in Chicago set a standard of service to the community that was shown at one time by an incident that brought out the fact that a judge, a newspaper editor, and the city censor who reviewed films for the Legion of Decency, all working for civic betterment, were all graduates of that school.

Mother Emily kept in touch not only with the Sisters of the

missions but with the pastors of the parishes, Father Cashman, Father Hodnett, Father McGuire, of Chicago were her devoted allies, as quick to aid her if she needed aid as they were to ask for her best teachers for their schools. Father Smyth of Evanston, Father Weldon of Bloomington, Father Cleary of Kenosha, recognized and approved her ultimate objectives. With other and younger pastors they formed a network of friendliness and good counsel.

As she had been in the Faribault school case, she was sometimes again caught between opposing forces. Father Cashman and Father Hodnett had been in the group of Chicago pastors who protested the appointment of Father Muldoon as Auxiliary Bishop of the Archdiocese of Chicago. As Bishop of Rockford, Muldoon had close relations with Sinsinawa. Mother Emily came to know and admire him greatly, although her newer friendship with him in no way affected her older friendships.

Through the missions she came into associations with many of the bishops of the period. Ireland, of course, remained her strongest and closest friend among them. Next stood Gibbons and Spalding, and Muldoon of Rockford during her last year of life. She did not know Archbishop Keane well until he came to Dubuque.

Other bishops also had confidence in her. The list of those who came to the Mound — O'Gorman of Sioux Falls, Cotter of Winona, Messmer of Milwaukee, Shanley of North Dakota, Glennon of St. Louis among them — reads like a roster of the hierarchy of the Middle West. These were the thought leaders of their time in the region as well as in the Church. Mother Emily could meet them on high intellectual terms as well as with an almost childlike simplicity of manner. With them she could plan a course of action for the schools; and both Church and State proved the better for that planning.

Work for the mission, as well as for college, academy, and convent, began to take toll from her. She had to travel oftener and farther every year on her official visitation. In one year alone she went to Minneapolis, Faribault, Omaha, Denver, Bloomington,

Kewanee, Freeport, Peoria, Chicago, and Washington. These visits were not made in a circle tour. A trip was occasioned by some crisis in a mission school. The house used by the Sisters might be falling down, and the pastor forgetful of ordering it fixed. Sisters might be taken seriously ill. Arrangements for new schools might have to be made. Meetings must be held, conferences arranged.

Sometimes misunderstandings arose in the mission convents. To a Sister who had doubted her own ability to carry on her work, she wrote, "I know the work is hard and heavy. Every kind of work that is successful must be hard. The stress is great, the effort mighty, but it must be a success if we want our credit kept up. It would be a dreadful thing to fail. I am sure that every bit of Dominican pride in you will rise up to defend the honor of the Order."

To another Sister who complained of difficulties in her work she wrote, "Sister Richard is trying hard and doing all she can to equalize the work and make you happy. Be cheerful and do as you have always done. Be helpful to those around you. God bless you." She signed the letter, "Your affectionate Sister Emily."

"Be cheerful," she told another. "You are needed there. I know conditions are hard but God will help and bless you." She wrote another work-weary teacher, "You don't know when to stop. Do not overwork. Be contented in your work. There is a purer joy in contentment."

Once in a while a letter gleamed with her innate humor. She had been called to Washington by an emergency in one of the schools and had a long conference with Cardinal Gibbons. Everything had gone well, although some of the questions considered were of serious import. But all she wrote back to the Sisters at Sinsinawa was, "Nothing new in Washington, only that John (a semijanitor at St. Dominic's convent) beat his mother nearly to death." Better than any one else she must have known what an anticlimax to their expectations her report would prove to the waiting group at the Mound. She must have known, too, how it would reassure them about herself.

There was no doubt that the Mother General was paying a high price for the extended range of community influence. In 1905 she was ill, and taken to a hospital. That was when she turned over some of her mission correspondence to Sister Samuel. She would not entirely give up, however, when she found that some of the Sisters were anxious about her when they did not hear from her directly. Occasionally she returned to the letter writing. With the old, steely determination she kept on her course, supervising the schools, leading the convent, inspiring the missions; but those who knew her longest began to see that Mother Emily was tired.

CHAPTER ELEVEN

Sinsinawa: Memorial
1909

FOR more than fifty years "the Little Ellen Power," as Father
Mazzuchelli had called her, had lived in the Upper Mississippi
River Valley. For more than fifty years she had looked out on the
wide scene of farmlands and river and hills, apparently unchanging
except as the seasons moved over them. For more than fifty years
she had witnessed, as if in panorama against its set backdrop, the
vast pageant of movement that was America.

She had seen the passing of the Mining Country. The miners
had gone and the farmers had come. She had seen the last stagecoach from Galena to Fairplay drive past the foot of the Mound.
She had seen the first smoke of railroad trains rising beside the
river. She had seen the first flashes of electric lights in the valley,
the first long lines of telephone poles, the spinning wheels of
motorcars.

She had watched the coming and going of wars: blue-uniformed
soldiers in the Benton street while Father Mazzuchelli prayed for
peace in the little chapel; khaki-clad soldiers entraining for Cuba
and the Philippines. She had glimpsed the long parade of presidents from Franklin Pierce to William Howard Taft, the long procession of prelates from Loras to Keane, from Kenrick to Gibbons.

She had known the passing of that slavery which had always
meant to her the auction block she had seen in New Orleans. She
had witnessed the industrial growth of America, the rise of factories, the building of mills, the spreading of cities, the pouring in
of peoples of many lands, the changing of a civilization, with its
sordid evils, its rising hopes.

She had seen the building of the Church in the nation. She could contrast the little churches of Father Mazzuchelli's founding with the cathedrals that now stood in the valley, the little school of New Diggings with the big schools of Chicago and Minneapolis. She could picture the vast extent of hospitals and orphanages, of convents and monasteries, of churches great and small across the land.

She had seen the nation grow great and the Church grow with it. She had seen Father Mazzuchelli's dream of harmony between the two great powers — a dream shared by Ireland, and Spalding, and Keane, and Gibbons — become a vital force in the nation.

She had done her part in this building, she knew, without pride. She had been but the instrument of God. This Mound of the great valley had been a height from which she had been shown a vision of service. God had set the task for her, and He had helped her to do whatever she had done. "Not I, but my Sisters, did it all," she said when someone spoke of her achievements. "It has succeeded because it was work for God."

Now she was a little tired. By the autumn of 1909 she was leaning on the Sisters nearest to her in administration, Mother Samuel, Mother Bonaventure, Mother Reginald, Sister Constantia, and Sister Peter. Just after Rosary Sunday Mother Bonaventure was in Bloomington, Mother Samuel in Appleton, and Sister Constantia in Rockwell, making visitation for her. Late in the week Father Schweitzer, former pastor of St. Joseph's, the prairie church near the Mound, came to visit. The community room was chilly, and some of the Sisters advised Mother Emily not to leave her room. "I couldn't do that to Father Schweitzer," she replied.

On Sunday she had a cold. On Monday she kept at work. Even on Tuesday, when she stayed in bed, she continued that work. Sister Hyacintha acted as her secretary, writing letters, taking messages. One of these is illuminating. Sister Benedicta was preparing an entertainment for Founder's day, the fourth of November. A sketch of Father Mazzuchelli was an established part of the program. Sister Benedicta was, as usual, setting down material from which the sketch would be written by one of the college students.

For years Sister Benedicta, evidently more impressed by the fact than her Superior, had been stressing the elements of the missionary's background. "Tell her *not* to say that his father was a banker," Mother Emily advised.

"Tell the Sisters this is nothing but a cold," she said on Wednesday to Sister Adrian when her sister told her of the concern of the community.

On Friday morning, October 15, she was noticeably worse but she insisted on seeing Dr. James J. Walsh of Fordham, who had come to the Mound to give a lecture upon his special subject, *The Thirteenth, Greatest of Centuries*. Dr. Walsh, who was physician as well as doctor of philosophy, saw her condition and became alarmed. "Call your doctor and a priest," he told Sister Adrian. "This is pneumonia. Mother Emily is dying."

Sister Genevieve, the subprioress placed in authority by the absence of the higher officers of the congregation, asked Mother Emily if she did not want the chaplain to come to her. "After I sleep," Mother Emily said. Dr. Walsh shook his head. "You'll sleep better if you have him come now," said Sister Genevieve.

The Dominican chaplain, Father Edward S. McGinnis, brought her the Last Sacraments. She lapsed, almost immediately, into a coma, and did not wake again.

The Sisters summoned Dr. Brownson from Dubuque. He came, and sent for other physicians. Word of her condition flashed through the long buildings. Sisters in the convent, in the infirmary, in the classrooms, in the kitchens moved in strained silence. The chapel was filled with Sisters and girls, praying for Mother Emily's recovery. Those beside her bed prayed for the last boon of a happy death.

Through Friday night and Saturday morning she lay in coma. The prayers for a soul departing, those mighty, mounting petitions of the Church, rose from murmur in the room to resonance in the corridors.

> *Lord, have mercy on us.*
> *Christ, have mercy on us.*

The long roll of the saints began. Peter, Paul, Andrew. . . . Gregory,

Ambrose, Augustine. . . . Dominic, Hyacinth, Raymund, Louis. . . . Mary Magdalen, Martha, Lucy. . . . Ursula, Catherine, Rose. The prayers for deliverance arose. *Deliver, O Lord, the soul of Thy handmaid as Thou didst deliver Job. . . . Deliver, O Lord, the soul of Thy handmaid as Thou didst deliver Peter and Paul.* There lifted the majestic convoying, May the heavens be opened unto her, and the angels rejoice her. . . . May all the holy apostles, to whom was given by the Lord the power of loosing and binding, pray for her. . . . May all the saints and elect of God, who have suffered torments in the world *for the sake of Christ, receive her.*

Suddenly the prayers ceased. The *Salve, Regina* began. *Hail, holy Queen, Mother of mercy,* old voices and young voices chanted. Then, as suddenly, the chant ended.

Mother Emily was dead.

Not at first did her Sisters realize what her death would mean to them. Too stunned to appraise the extent of their loss, they could only continue to pray for her soul, even though they were sure that her soul was triumphantly winging its way to its Creator. Gradually, the sense of sorrow bore upon them. They stood in little groups in community room and halls, commiserating one another. "What shall we do without her?" they asked one another, not realizing that her wise prevision would carry them down the coming years. Strong herself, she had built up strength in other women; and to them she left her burden.

Some of them had to assume this burden at once. There were telegrams to be sent, preparations made, rites to be observed, provision made for students. With an efficiency Mother Emily would have approved, the arrangements were made. There was a sadness such as the community had not known since Father Mazzuchelli's death. There were tears, but no loud demonstrations of grief. There was sorrow, but not hopeless sorrow. A Christian had gone to God. Other Christians must pray even while mourning for her.

For two days, at Sister Veronica's request, Mother Emily's body remained in her room so that it might be nearer to the Sisters of the community. Within the room and in the halls outside Sisters and novices prayed constantly, day and night. They continued their vigil after the body had been taken into the chapel.

There the girls of the schools came to look on her for the last time. Every one of them, from the youngest minim, to the oldest college senior had known her as a friend. "We were never afraid of Mother Emily," one child said. "Even when we were in trouble in school and she knew it, she talked to us so like our own mothers that we were sorry, and knew we would try to do better. Will we never see her any more?"

"She laughed with us, and joked with us," the older girls remembered, "and all the time she was doing something to help us."

Tearfully, kneeling in the pews she had so often passed, they prayed for her.

Telegrams poured into the convent, messages from men and women of high distinction. Priests began to come, and bishops, sadly arriving to do her honor. Saddest of all came the mission Sisters. Stricken, they spent long hours in the chapel. All of them who could, stayed there through the night while the vigil candles burned around the bier.

At dawn, before four altars, the Masses started, following each other as priest after priest came. At ten o'clock the Solemn Requiem Mass began. Bishop Muldoon was its celebrant. Father M. Weldon of Bloomington was archpriest. Father McGuire of the Visitation in Chicago and Father Knox of Madison were the deacons, with Father J. J. Flaherty and Father Edward Kelly of Chicago deacons of honor. Father C. J. Quille, head of the Chicago Newsboys Home, and Father Philip L. Kennedy, curate at St. Jarlath's were acolytes. Father M. Barry of Dubuque was master of ceremonies. Dominican priests constituted the choir.

More than twenty priests, all of them long-time tried and true friends of Mother Emily, were in the sanctuary, while more than fifty others occupied pews. Seldom, except for some solemn rite of the hierarchy, had there ever been such an assemblage of clergy in the upper valley.

In the sanctuary, with his lion's head of white hair bowed, knelt Archbishop Ireland, attended by Father Thomas F. Cashman and Father Thomas Pope Hodnett. The three men were her oldest friends, Father Cashman the oldest, for he had known her in the Benton days. To the three of them her death must have brought stirring memories of issues they had met together, difficulties they had overcome, plans they had made and carried out. The archbishop was to voice for them as well as for thousands more, the significance of her life.

Nearest the bier were her sisters, Sister Veronica, Sister Adrian, and little Alice Power. Beside them knelt the oldest members of the community: Sister Benedicta, Sister Philomena, Sister Pius, Sister Benvenuta, Sister Peter, Sister Lucina, Sister Constantia, Sister Augustine, Sister Alexius, and Sister Borromeo, the gay little Clara Stevens of the Benton days who had so loved "dear, sweet Sister Emily." After them were placed the religious of other communities who had come to do her honor: Sisters of Charity of the Blessed Virgin Mary from their mother house in Dubuque; Sisters of Mercy from Dubuque; Sisters of St. Dominic from Racine and Corliss; Sisters of the Holy Cross from Notre Dame; Sisters of St. Joseph from St. Paul; Sisters of St. Francis from Alverno in Milwaukee. Scores of alumnae knelt in farewell. Home Sisters and Mission Sisters crowded the chapel and the adjacent corridors.

There was a long silence as Mass ended and the Archbishop of St. Paul faced the congregation. It was, he said afterward, a most difficult moment. For one of the few times in his life John Ireland, master of oratory, felt unequal to the occasion. "Mother Emily was a great woman," he wrote later to Mother Samuel, "one of God's noblest creatures. What she did for God and His Church was a marvel. Since I have had time to review in more leisurely way her greatness, the proportions of her figure, as history should show her, has so grown upon me that I wish it were now that I were to make discourse about her."

No one else could have known his sense of inadequacy: for John Ireland, Archbishop of St. Paul, preached a funeral sermon that no one who heard him ever forgot. With deep emotion and with high purpose he limned the portrait of the woman he had known for forty years.

In the manner of his age, the archbishop painted at times in flowery words. "Away with sorrow of heart and tear-drop of eye!" he began. "A saint goes up to heaven: we celebate her birth into glory and never-ending happiness. A saint dies when dies Mother Emily Power: she enters heaven: shall we mourn while she rejoices in the blessedness of eternity?"

For moments the prelate spoke in panegyric impressiveness. His own deep emotion, voiced in the vibrant tones that gave no sign of age, bore his words high above any suggestion by hyperbole. Gradually, however, he swung into statements of Mother Emily's attainments and character, her keenness of mind, her genuine scholarship, her affectionate kindliness to those around her, both Sisters and students, her humility, her faith in God, her devotion to the Church. He came to the heart of his discourse.

"She was prepared," he said, "by nature and by grace to do the great work assigned to her by divine providence — to build into efficiency and power the Sisterhood of the Most Holy Rosary.

"Humanly speaking, what was the Church to do, especially in these modern days, without its Sisterhoods? Two of its strongest arms of combat are education and charity: both are wielded most powerfully by its Sisterhoods. They instruct childhood and youth, the hundreds of thousands who otherwise would pass into manhood and womanhood without religious formation, or with its merest veneering. They take charge of the charities of the Church, proving it to be the society of Him who 'passed by doing good,' and winning to it the good will of multitudes that otherwise should give no heed to its teachings. And, then, our Sisterhoods are the active exemplars, the quiet but efficient preachers of the supernatural life, they themselves conspicuously living of it, and thereby reminding others that they, too, should live of it, at least in some inferior degree. The good done by the Catholic Sisterhoods is incalculable. The woman that builds up within the Church a great Sisterhood is a benefactor of religion, to whom children and soldiers of the Church owe a boundless debt of gratitude.

"The Congregation to which Mother Emily devoted her talents and energies, was called into existence by one of the most remarkable priests in the American Church, Father Samuel Mazzuchelli. An honor and an encouragement for the Congregation it ever will be, that this great and far-seeing apostle breathed life into it, and laid down the rules which were to guide its activities. In his wide vision of things he recognized the needs of modern times: he fashioned his Congregation to meet those needs. But death took him from it while it was yet in its beginnings, while yet struggling to overcome difficulties always encountered by newly-born institutes, esecially when working amid a sparse Catholic population, in the poverty of recently settled regions. A master hand was wanted to continue the task of Father Mazzuchelli, to enlarge the scope of his institute according as it grew in needs and opportunities, to place it on solid foundations from which naught thenceforth could unsettle or move it. The master hand was that of Mother Emily.

"When Mother Emily entered religion, the Sisterhood numbered a score of Sisters: ten or twelve others had been added by the time she took to herself the reins of government. Its one home was the humble village of Benton in Wisconsin; elsewhere it was unknown. It had no strong friend, no wise counsellor. Mother Emily and her Sisters were cast upon their own resources — all the better in a way, as full room was allowed to show what intelligent, devoted womanhood may accomplish, what self-sacrificing daughters of the Church may do, when they work for the Lord and He works with them.

"Mother Emily's monument in history is the Congregation of the Most Holy Rosary of Sinsinawa. Some twenty members made up its membership when she entered religion; some thirty when she was made Superioress. Today the Congregation numbers over six hundred members; instead of the one small home in Benton it counts, outside the Mother House of Saint Clara, forty-eight other foundations, dispersed between the Atlantic and the Pacific, harboring within their walls over fifteen thousand pupils, and taking highest ranks among the educational institutions of the country —

a remarkable development, even amid the fresh and vigorous life of the Church of America. And so much of all this is due to Mother Emily, to her watchfulness over the Congregation in every stage of its growth, her ceaseless care to infuse into it the plenitude of the spirit of religion, her intelligent formation of its members for the functions to which its mission assigned them! The best she could do, the best a Sister, a Superioress could do, Mother Emily did for the Congregation: the good Lord did His part: her Sisters, catching up the fire of her soul, did their part: the Congregation waxed strong and prospered.

"She labored incessantly and intelligently to increase the membership of the Congregation — ever casting out for vocations, and encouraging her Sisters to follow her example. One of the holiest of works it is to foster vocations. Vocations, indeed, come primarily from Heaven: but it is left to us to second the designs of Heaven. How many the spiritual flowers never opening their petals to the dews of the skies, because no hand is extended to guard them from weeds and thorns, because no word is spoken to urge them into bloom. Yet how much is lost in this way to the glory of God and the welfare of the Church! Be it yours, dear Sisters, to encourage vocations, wherever they peer through the souls of the youth over whom Providence gives you influence, thus enlarging the armies of the Lord and dividing with others the joys of your own blessed calling.

"As the Congregation grew, Mother Emily sought through prudent legislation to strengthen its bonds, and to fit it thoroughly to the requirements of its ever-widening sphere, most attentive, however, always to preserve to it the original features of life and work, as delineated by its founder, Father Mazzuchelli. When its constitutions had been fully formulated and proven in the crucible of practical application, she carried them with her, in 1877, to the feet of the Supreme Pontiff and petitioned for them the solemn approval of Holy Church, a favor which in due course of time was graciously accorded.

"No means did she spare to develop the efficiency of the Congregation, as an agency of Christian education; and here it is that we see at its best her power of intellect — her broadness of view, her insight into the needs of time and of place and her readiness to meet those needs. The mission of the Congregation is the education of youth. Well did Mother Emily understand that schools, necessarily and deservedly, are doomed to fail unless the most skilled of teachers preside over their classes; and that it were nothing short of a crime against religion to drape school-rooms with its banners, unless within those school-rooms there is given, together with a deep and intelligent knowledge of religion the most ample instruction in branches of secular learning.

"The building up of her schools to the highest standard of religious and, no less, of secular instruction, was Mother Emily's life-long ambition. To this end she labored tirelessly and incessantly, fearing no criticism, stopping short of no necessary expenditure of money. Her Sisters were sternly bidden to conceal no talent, to put into their studies the full energy of their souls. Educational conferences were held at the Mother-house to bring to the attention of the Sisters the latest and the best methods of school work: instructors of high proficiency were called thither from outside schools and colleges, when such were not forthcoming from the inner ranks of the Congregation: the more capable of the Sisters were sent to famed seats of learning, even in cities of distant Europe.

"Through Mother Emily's aspirations and practical good sense, within the years of her life-time, the Congregation of the Holy Rosary rose to be one of the great teaching Sisterhoods of the Catholic Church in America, a Sisterhood that no educational agency of the country dares pass by without offering to it a well-merited tribute of deference and honor. The Church, the country, owe to Mother Emily abiding gratitude and praise most sincere for her noble achievements in behalf of education and religion.

"And now," he ended, "let us pray. Let us pray for Mother Emily: so pure is the light of Heaven, Holy Church teaches, that even saints for a time may not be pure enough to behold it, the smallest speck of dust from the winds of earth holding it back for further cleansing. Eternal rest, O Lord, grant to her soul: may the radiance of Thy countenance shed upon her its most effulgent rays. Let us pray for ourselves. Some day, we, too, shall die: some day, sooner or later, while the dirge of Holy Church echoes around our mortal remains, our spirits will have arisen to the throne of eternal justice. Departed saint, pray as we pray, that with something of thy purity of soul, with something of thy faith and confidence we may appear before the Master, and from Him receive something of the welcome which is thine: 'Well done, good and faithful servant; enter into the joy of the Lord.' "

The archbishop, with Bishop Muldoon assisting, said the last rites. No one knew it then, but the great past and the great future of the Catholic Church in the United States were meeting over Mother Emily's coffin. As surely as Ireland had waged the valiant battle of the Church for political betterment, Muldoon was to lead the brave battle for social betterment. They gave their last blessing to the woman who had worked with them both, the little Irish girl who had given mighty service to the nation she had come to love so dearly. Their *Requiescat in pace* was more than formal benediction. It was farewell to a great soul.

Down the wide stairway and into the October sunlight the cortege went. "Direct our feet into the way of peace," sang the priests. At the west gate stood the students in open ranks. For the last time Mother Emily passed among them.

They buried her at the foot of the great cross which stands on the Sinsinawa hillside. Slowly priests and people, Sisters and students turned away, going back to waiting tasks, to a life that had been made better for them by the dreams and the work of the woman they had laid to rest. She had lived and died in the Lord. Now she slept on the hill she had reclaimed for Him.

Between Father Cashman and Father Hodnett the Archbishop of St. Paul walked back to the convent. No one of them spoke until they came to its door. Then John Ireland sighed. "A great woman has gone from us," he said. "We shall not look upon her like again."

Source Materials

THE sources of material used for this book are almost entirely original: annals, records, contemporaneous newspapers, historical collections, recollections, interviews, unpublished memoirs. Among these have been:

For CONDITIONS IN IRELAND, 1844–1852:

John Mitchel's Jail Journal, Jameson, Ferguson; Glasgow
State of Ireland in the 19th Century, Lacker, Lampson, Constakle; London
Irish Immigration to the United States, Stephen Byrne; Catholic Publications Society, New York
History of Ireland, Stephen Gwynn; Talbot Press, Dublin

For THE DESCRIPTION OF THE IMMIGRANT SHIP, 1852:

The Report to Parliament of the Royal Commission on Conditions in Immigrant Ships: London, 1854

For BACKGROUND OF NEW ORLEANS, 1852–1853:

Daily Orleanian
Daily Picayune
Weekly Tropics
Commercial Bulletin

For BACKGROUND OF ST. LOUIS, 1853:

Daily New Era
Daily Evening News
Evening Pilot
Republic

For BACKGROUND OF GALENA, 1853:

Miner's Free Press (Mineral Point)
Galenian
Galena Weekly Gazette

272 Source Materials

For Background of Wisconsin, 1853-1866:
Belmont Gazette
Burlington Gazette
Madison Weekly Argus

For Background of Wisconsin in Both These and in Succeeding Years to 1909:
Collections of the Wisconsin State Historical Society

For Description of Benton, 1850-1866:
Sinsinawa Records
Mazzuchelli Journals
Golden Bells in Convent Towers, Sister Charles Borromeo, Sinsinawa

For Iowa Associations, 1853-1866:
Dubuque Democrat
Dubuque Herald
Miner's Express
Dubuque Telegraph-Herald
Dubuque Express and Herald

For Montana Situation, 1907-1908:
Anaconda Standard
Butte Miner
Annals of Anaconda Convent

For Spring Valley, Illinois, Situation, 1888:
Miner's Journal, 1888
History of Coal Mining in the United States, Andrew Roy
John Mitchell, Elsie Gluck, John Day
Annals of Spring Valley Convent
Interviews with Sister Theodosius, who was at Spring Valley in 1888

For Faribault Situation, 1892-1893:
Interviews with Mother Samuel, Sister de Ricci, Sister Eligius, who were in Faribault in 1892-1893
Annals of the Faribault Academy
The School Controversy, Daniel Reilly, O.P.; Catholic University Press

Throughout the work constant references have been founded upon materials in the Sinsinawa Archives: The *Annals of St. Clara,* the *Annals of the Missions,* Annual Catalogues, Year Books, Catholic Directories, *Wisconsin Historical Collections,* Letters to and from Mother Emily and files of the *Young Eagle,* School Courses of Study and Programs. This work in the Archives could not have been done without the able and kindly aid of Sister Paschala, director of the Sinsinawa Archives. Personal remembrances of Mother Emily came from Mother Samuel, Sister Thomas Aquinas, Sister Hyacintha, Sister Eligius, Sister Richard, and Sister Chrysostom. Sister Eva generously gave not only recollections but inspiring interpretations of them.

Many incidents associated with Mother Emily and the Sisters who worked with her have come from the author's personal recollections.

Index

Adamson, Sister George, 183
Allemany, Bishop, 126
Allen, Huldah (Fairplay), 42
Anaconda (Montana) Lockout, 9, 251–254
Apple River, 37
Asia (Atlantic Ship), conditions on, 15 f

Barden, Sister Richard, 255
Barrettstown (Ireland), birthplace of Mother Emily, 11
Benton (Wisconsin), 27; political situation, 70 f
Berg, Rev. Joseph, 241
Bethlehem Academy (Faribault), 2, 121–124
Bishops' Program, publication of, 8
Black Hawk War, 45
Borstadt, Sister Chrysostom, 236 f
Bouquillon, Dr. Thomas J., 200
Boutanne, Mary, 55
Bowman, Sister Evangelist, 112
Bradford, Sister Vincent Ferrer, 251
Brother Louis (Thomas Power), 34
Brownson, Dr. Charles, 160, 261; Orestes, 108
Burlington, 27, 32
Butler, Dr. Thaddeus J., 124; Rev. Patrick, 128
Byrne, Sister Dominica, 125

Cahill, Sister Josephine, 123
Callan, Josephine McGarry, 222
Carroll, Bishop J. P., 238; Katherine L., 219
Cashman, Rev. Thomas F., 128–132, 256, 264, 269
Catholic Education, problems of (1880's), 156–159
Catholic University of America, 8, 78–81, 161, 183, 200, 222, 236

Caulcannon, 44
Chicago Fire, 125 f
Chicago Stock Yards, fire, 250; labor troubles, 9; strike, 249
Chief Whirling Thunder, 30
Christian Social Doctrine, 7 f
Cicognani, Marcolino (Procurator-General of Dominicans), 153
Clark, Mother Joanna, 73
Cochrane, Sister Raymond, 111
College of Notre Dame in Maryland, 212
Columbian Catholic Summer School, 180 ff
Commission on American Citizenship, 183, 237; foundation of, 9
Community, expansion of, 175 f
Congregation Annals (December, 1860), 7
Congregation of the Most Holy Rosary, 1, 2
Constitution, difficulties in changes, 151; readjustments, 187, revision of, 146 f
Constitutions of Community, 114; revisions, 134 f
Constitution of Stone, 151 f; approved, 153
Copus, Rev. J. E., S.J., 241
Corpus Christi School (New York), 183, 237
Coughlin, Mother Samuel, 123, 235, 238, 258, 264
Course of Studies (Benton), 62
Cousin Jacks (Cornish Miners), 37
Cunningham, John, 245

Daly, Rev. John, 241
Davenport, 27, 32
Delaney, Sister Fidelia, 112
Desmond, Humphrey J., 180
Devlin, Charles J., 208